PENAL ISSUES IN CANON LAW

Penal Issues in Canon Law

Msgr. Brendan Daly

Paulist Press
New York / Mahwah, NJ

Nihil Obstat and Imprimatur:
✠ Richard Laurenson, JCL
Bishop of Hamilton, NZ

October 11, 2024

Cover design by Sharyn Banks
Book design by Lynn Else

Library of Congress Cataloging-in-Publication Data
Names: Daly, Brendan, 1952–, author.
Title: Penal issues in canon law / Msgr. Brendan Daly.
Description: Paperback. | New York / Mahwah: Paulist Press, 2025. | Includes bibliographical references and index. | Summary: "This book addresses the changes to the penal code over the past century with particular interest in the sex abuse crisis"—Provided by publisher.
Identifiers: LCCN 2024051583 (print) | LCCN 2024051584 (ebook) | ISBN 9780809157600 (paperback) | ISBN 9780809189274 (ebook)
Subjects: LCSH: Sex crimes (Canon law) | Child sexual abuse by clergy (Canon law) | Criminal procedure (Canon law) | Catholic Church—Clergy—Sexual behavior.
Classification: LCC KBR3751 .D35 2025 (print) | LCC KBR3751 (ebook) | DDC 262.9/46—dc23/eng/20250102
LC record available at https://lccn.loc.gov/2024051583
LC ebook record available at https://lccn.loc.gov/2024051584

ISBN 978-0-8091-5760-0 (paperback)
ISBN 978-0-8091-8927-4 (ebook)

Published by Paulist Press
997 Macarthur Boulevard
Mahwah, NJ 07430
www.paulistpress.com

Printed and bound in the
United States of America

CONTENTS

Foreword ... vii

Acknowledgements ... xi

1. Preliminary Investigations ... 1
2. Extrajudicial Processes ... 15
3. Obligations and Responsibilities of the Promoter of Justice ... 26
4. Rights of Alleged Victims ... 46
5. Authority and Obligations of a Bishop and a Religious Institute ... 57
6. Mandatory Reporting of Sexual Abuse ... 76
7. Requirement to Report Sexual Abuse ... 90
8. Reporting to Civil Authorities ... 95
9. Scandal in Canon Law ... 103
10. Spiritual Abuse as a Delict ... 119
11. The Crime of Solicitation and Canon Law ... 131
12. Making the Abuse of Minors an Irregularity ... 146

Appendix: Sample Diocesan Letters ... 159

Notes ... 165

Glossary ... 209

Selected Bibliography ... 215

Index ... 223

FOREWORD

When discussing the sexual abuse crisis in the Church, we are not referring to a new phenomenon. Sexual abuse by clergy and religious is not limited to the twentieth or twenty-first centuries, and ecclesial laws against sexual abuse are not new. The *Didache*, the oldest catechism in history from the second century, instructs clerics "not to seduce young people." In the fourth century, the Council of Elvira legislated against sexual abuse, although it was defined as a sin, and the victims were not specifically mentioned.[1] In 1049, Peter Damian wrote to Pope Leo IX about the growing issue of sexual abuse spreading within the Church, noting that children and adolescents were being forced and seduced into sexual acts by priests and bishops.[2] In his decree *Crimene Falsi*, Pope Innocent III mandated the degradation of clergy who committed sexual abuse against minors and their handover to secular authorities.[3] At the Fifth Lateran Council (1512–1517), Pope Leo X insisted that clerics who abused children be removed from their positions and handed over to ecclesiastical or secular justice.[4]

The phenomenon of sexual abuse by clergy and religious toward children, young people, and women has always existed. What has led to the worldwide crisis is that victims began to report their abuse within the Church. A reality that had long been concealed is now being confronted and acknowledged.

An important legal distinction is that previously, abuse was viewed primarily as a sin committed by the perpetrator and was not classified as a crime. When civil society began to categorize it as a crime, the Church did not enforce any civil laws internally. It wasn't until 1983, with the promulgation of the new canon law, that Canon 1395 §2 established sexual abuse of minors as a crime.

In the last decades, various international independent reports, including the Royal Commission in Australia, the Sauvé Report in France, and investigations in Germany and Ireland,[5] have revealed the extent of abuse within the Church and the inadequacy of oversight and sanctions. These findings have prompted the Church to revise its internal policies for the protection of minors and vulnerable adults.

In response to these reports, Canon Law has been reformed to ensure that those responsible for abuse, as well as those who cover up these crimes, face clearer and more severe consequences. The changes also aim to address and sanction any form of cover-up.

This book provides a step-by-step guide to these new norms, laws, and procedures, making it an essential reading. Daly navigates the complex intersections of ecclesiastical law, moral responsibility, and pastoral care.

Daly's exploration begins with a thorough examination of preliminary investigations, highlighting their crucial role in addressing allegations within the Church. He discusses how the norms previously applied to clerics have now been extended in *Vos Estis Lux Mundi* 2023 to include Institutes of Consecrated Life, societies of Apostolic Life, and moderators of international Associations of the Faithful recognized or established by the Apostolic See. Additionally, Daly insists on the imperative of mandatory reporting of sexual abuse to civil authorities. He highlights the importance of reporting sexual abuse not only by clerics but also by members of religious congregations and by laypeople.

In this book, the rights of victims are highlighted as a crucial area for a real change within the Church. Daly emphasizes that penal law must not only focus on the crime committed but also center on the needs, expectations, and rights of the victims. He invites all the faithful to put their efforts into ensuring that victims' rights are upheld and protected, necessitating a widespread understanding of penal processes. *Vos Estis Lux Mundi* emphasizes the necessity of providing support services, including therapeutic and psychological assistance tailored to the specific needs of victims. Daly goes beyond these recommendations and proposes an important way to support victims: the establishment of an assistance coordinator or an advocate to advise them about their rights throughout the process. Daly also highlights the importance of tribunal officials having trauma-informed training to better support victims as they navigate the legal system. Victims should have the right to access information about their cases, including the documents related to the decree of adjudication or sentence. The author is aware that often the victims are not aware of this right, underscoring the need for clearer communication and guidance.

Overall, the author's insights advocate for a more supportive and informed approach to victim care within the Church's penal processes, ensuring that victims are empowered and aware of their rights throughout the proceedings.

Daly is a renowned international canon lawyer, and his voice within the universal Church has contributed to the development of these penal laws. In this book, he himself points out the omissions or gaps that canon law still needs to address and dedicates an entire chapter to spiritual abuse. He states that many cases of spiritual abuse are being reported around the world and consideration needs to be given to spiritual abuse as a delict or crime in canon law. As there is no specific canon regarding spiritual abuse, Daly proposes the existing delict of abuse of power or office defined by c. 1378 §1. This canon considers the so-called abuse of power as an autonomous delict and punishable.

Another gap Daly identifies is the lack of specific laws to protect women from sexual and spiritual abuse. *Vos Estis Lux Mundi* mentions minors and vulnerable adults, but the term "vulnerable adult" is ambiguous. A woman who is not typically considered vulnerable can still become a victim of abuse depending on pastoral settings that render her vulnerable. For example, Daly addresses complaints about intrusive questioning of women on sexual matters during the sacrament of penance.

By equipping readers with this knowledge, Daly's work contributes to a stronger, more transparent Church where protection is prioritized and those responsible for harm are held accountable. This book is not merely a legal analysis; it is a heartfelt appeal for reform, justice, and pastoral care within the Church. Daly invites readers—whether canon lawyers, clergy, or laypersons—to engage with these critical issues, challenging us all to foster a culture of integrity, empathy, and justice. In doing so, he provides a path forward, one that honors the dignity of every individual and upholds the moral mission of the Church.

As we embark on this journey through the intricacies of canon law, may we be inspired by the author's commitment to truth and justice, striving together for a safer and more just and compassionate ecclesial community.

—Dr. Rocio Figueroa

ACKNOWLEDGEMENTS

Just before printing, I have the happy task of thanking those who have helped with the writing of this book. I thank Dr. Rocio Figueroa, who wrote the preface. I especially wish to thank Barbara Brown, who spent a great deal of time checking the manuscript and making very helpful suggestions. I also wish to thank Dr. Rodger Austin, Mark Hangartner, and Elizabeth Ong for their help doing research. I thank Catholic Theological College Te Hepara Pai for the opportunity to do research for this book.

I am thankful to the Canon Law Society of Australia and New Zealand and the American Canon Law Society for the use of material that I had included in previous articles that have now been updated and revised because of recent legislation. There is a little repetition in several places, but this is necessary because of the original source documents.

1

PRELIMINARY INVESTIGATIONS

When information is received about the possible commission of a delict or offense, it is very important that the Ordinary ascertains if it is "knowledge, which at least seems true."[1] The Dicastery for the Doctrine of the Faith explained that "a *notitia de delicto* (cf. canon 1717 §1 CIC; canon 1468 §1 CCEO; art. 10 SST; art. 3 VELM), occasionally called a *notitia criminis*, consists of any information about a possible delict that in any way comes to the attention of the Ordinary or Hierarch. It need not be a formal complaint."[2] It could come from the media, the police, or an anonymous source. The *Vademecum* states:

> When a *notitia de delicto* (information) is received, a preliminary investigation ought to ensue, provided that the report is "*saltem verisimilis*." If that plausibility proves unfounded, there is no need to pursue the *notitia de delicto*, although care should be taken to keep the documentation, together with a written explanation regarding the reasons for the decision. (no. 16)

The preliminary investigation is outlined in canons 1717ff. of the 1983 Code (CIC) or canons 1468ff. of the Code of Canon Law for the Eastern Churches (CCEO):

> Whenever an ordinary has knowledge, which at least seems true, of a delict, he is carefully to inquire personally or through another suitable person about the facts, circumstances, and imputability, unless such an inquiry seems entirely superfluous. (Can. 1717 §1)

If a cleric admits his guilt, or has been found guilty in a secular court, a preliminary investigation is not necessary.[3]

VOS ESTIS LUX MUNDI (2023)

Pope Francis promulgated the original *Vos Estis Lux Mundi* (VELM, You are the Light of the World) on May 7, 2019[4] as experimental law for three years.[5] There were conflicts in the text between *Vos Estis* and the revised Book VI of the

Code, and after consultation, revised norms were promulgated in Italian on March 25, 2023 and came into effect on April 30, 2023 (VELM).[6] These changes can impact preliminary investigations.

Article 1 of VELM addresses the scope of the application. The norms now also apply to *moderators of international associations of the faithful.*[7] Delicts against the sixth commandment of the Decalogue now apply to three categories of persons: *minors*, *vulnerable adults*, and *persons who habitually have imperfect use of reason*. The scope of the provisions concerning pornography has been extended to include recruiting or inducing a minor or vulnerable adult or a person who habitually has imperfect use of reason "to pose in a pornographic manner or to participate in real or simulated photographic exhibitions."[8]

The provisions concerning reporting have been refined. Clerics previously were not required to report information learned through their sacred ministry. The revised VELM clarifies this as learning of "*information during the exercise of ministry in the internal forum*,"[9] including the seal of confession and spiritual direction.

Laypersons, particularly those holding offices or ministries in the Church, are *encouraged to report sexual abuse*.[10]

Any cover-up, by clerical leaders such as bishops, major superiors of religious institutes, and lay faithful who are or have been *moderators of international associations of the faithful*, is defined as a crime.[11]

The 2019 VELM noted that investigations were to be completed within ninety days or as specified by the Dicastery. The 2023 VELM states the "*investigation is to be completed in short order* and in accordance with the instructions listed in art. 11 §2."[12]

Some of the changes simply involved changing the original norms according to the revised Book VI of the Code of Canon Law in December 2021.[13] The revised canon 1398 includes "commits an offence against the sixth commandment of the Decalogue with a minor or with a person who habitually has an imperfect use of reason."

The wording of canon 1398 is now used in the revised *Vos Estis Lux Mundi*. Instead of "engaging in sexual acts," VELM now uses the words "*a crime against the sixth commandment of the Decalogue*." This is the traditional phrase used by the Church in its law and other documents such as the *Catechism of the Catholic Church*. The traditional phrase encompasses all sexual sins and means that the Church's definitions of crimes do not have to be continually updated.

A significant change in the text of VELM is the inclusion of *lay leaders of international associations* who have either committed abuse themselves or who have failed to investigate complaints of abuse or dealt with allegations in their communities. There have been several lay leaders of international associations who have been abusers of vulnerable people and minors, and these include Luis Figari[14] and Jean Vanier, the founder of L'Arche.[15]

VELM 2023 uses the phrase "vulnerable adult" instead of "vulnerable person." The change to "adult" does make the law more precise. All persons are adults or minors. All minors are considered vulnerable in law and the Dicastery for the Doctrine of the Faith is exclusively competent to deal with these cases.[16] However, the crime of abusing vulnerable adults is not reserved to the Apostolic See. The bishop of the diocese where the crime took place must deal with these cases.[17] The abuse is not defined as sexual misconduct but rather as a canonical delict or crime.

VELM 2019 said "no constraint of silence may be imposed on the person making an alert as to its content." Article 4 §3 of VELM 2023 states that "no constraint of silence may be imposed on the person making a report, on the persons claiming to have been wronged and on *witnesses* as to the content of the report, subject to article 5 §2." The changed revision makes it clear that a person making a report, alleged victims, and witnesses cannot be prevented from taking the case to secular authorities for action and prosecution.

COMPETENCE

One of the most significant changes in VELM concerns the competence to conduct the preliminary investigation. When a complaint is received, the primary responsibility and right to carry out the preliminary investigation lies with the Ordinary of the place where the alleged delict took place:

> Except as provided for by art. 3 §3, the Ordinary who received the report shall transmit it without delay to the Ordinary of the place where the events are said to have occurred, as well as to the Ordinary of the person reported. Unless otherwise agreed upon by the two Ordinaries, it is the responsibility of the Ordinary of the place where the events are said to have occurred to proceed according to the law provided for the specific case. (VELM 2 §3)

It is possible for the local Ordinary of the alleged events to agree that another Ordinary investigates. Previous law was not clear as to who had the right to investigate.[18] There must be good communication and transparency among all the Ordinaries involved in a case, including Religious Ordinaries.

DECREE OPENING THE PRELIMINARY INVESTIGATION

First, the Ordinary or Hierarch decrees the opening of the preliminary investigation.

Then the Ordinary usually appoints a "suitable person"[19] to conduct the investigation.[20] The decree should also state that the person carrying out the investigation has the powers of an auditor:

> The person who conducts the investigation has the same powers and obligations as an auditor in the process; the same person cannot act as a judge in the matter if a judicial process is initiated later. (Can. 1717 §3)

The investigation involves collecting proofs that sometimes may also involve deciding what proofs are to be collected and the manner of collecting them.[21] There may be affidavits, interviews, and so on. The person conducting the investigation cannot take part later as judge in a trial. The Dicastery for Legislative Texts states:

> In choosing the person in charge of the investigation, the Authority must evaluate, among other things, the type of relationship that he could have with the person under investigation, the necessary conditions of age, prudence, discretion, training. In this phase, if the Authority deems it appropriate or necessary, he can assume the task of carrying out the investigation by himself without delegating it to anyone else. Be that as it may, the appointee should be an expert in canon law or, at least, possess a certain expertise to direct his investigations in a practical way in order to obtain the necessary elements to shed light on the information received.[22]

It is wise for the Ordinary to appoint another suitable person to carry out the investigation. The local Ordinary, usually the diocesan bishop, has the responsibility to care for all the faithful, including victims and complainants,[23] as well as accused clergy[24] and religious. There are obvious conflicts of interest for someone with these responsibilities who attempted to investigate information and then had to make decisions about the adequacy of the evidence and any ensuing penal process.

The Ordinary also appoints a notary who should be a priest in cases where the person under investigation is a priest.[25] The *Vademecum* advises:

> Although not expressly provided for by law, it is advisable that a priest notary be appointed (cf. canon 483 §2 CIC and canon 253 §2 CCEO, where other criteria are indicated for the choice), who assists the person conducting the preliminary investigation, for the purpose of ensuring the authenticity of the acts which have been drawn up (cf. canons 1437 §2 CIC and 1101 §2 CCEO). (no. 41)

QUALIFICATIONS OF THE PERSON CARRYING OUT THE INVESTIGATION

The person must have the appropriate knowledge to carry out the investigation. It is vital, when the victim is a child, that the person has the required training and experience to interview child victims. The Pontifical Commission for the Protection of Minors, in its *Universal Guidelines Framework,* requires:

> The Church Authority must ensure the availability of trained and qualified personnel who are skilled in listening to allegations, performing canonical preliminary investigations, and managing associated risks.[26]

It is critical that the person be competent in canon law and understand the alleged crimes they are investigating, especially when they concern the sacrament of Penance and the seal of confession. The person carrying out the investigation can be a "cleric or lay person outstanding for their good character, prudence, and doctrine."[27] It is most important that the investigation be seen to be credible, professional, and independent.[28] Usually the people carrying out the investigation are laypersons, which is encouraged in most Western countries.[29]

The person conducting the investigation must be careful to respect the right to privacy of the alleged victim. Furthermore, the good name of the accused must also be protected: "Care must be taken so that the good name of anyone is not endangered from this investigation."[30] For example, when information about a cleric's withdrawal from ministry is placed on the internet, the information usually cannot be completely removed, which affects his good reputation if he is found to be innocent.

The *Vademecum* of the Dicastery for the Doctrine of the Faith explains that the preliminary investigation of an alleged delict or crime seeks to establish whether there is "the sufficient basis both in law and in fact so as to consider the accusation as having the semblance of truth."[31] The allegation may be indisputable or notorious because of information available to the public, or it may be impossible to have taken place for some reason. Then the preliminary investigation would be superfluous. However, the *Vademecum* states:

> Given the sensitive nature of the matter (for example, the fact that sins against the sixth commandment of the Decalogue rarely occur in the presence of witnesses), a determination that the *notitia* lacks the semblance of truth (which can lead to omitting the preliminary investigation) will be made only in the case of the manifest impossibility of the commission of a delict according to the norms of canon law. (no. 18)

The preliminary investigation should be "a true procedure, albeit brief and administrative in nature,"[32] so "the Ordinary can draw the conclusion that knowledge of a delict has been received which seems to be true."[33] The purpose of having a preliminary foundation is to establish whether there is a solid basis for conducting a penal process. A libellus can only be rejected if the petition lacks any basis and it does not seem possible that a basis will result from carrying out a process.[34]

In secular justice systems police might conduct a criminal investigation[35] for the prosecutor to determine whether there is enough evidence to proceed or what charges could be laid. In American courts, there is often a preliminary hearing by a judge to determine whether a person charged with a crime should be held for trial. A hearing is held in felony cases prior to indictment, during which the state is required to produce sufficient evidence to establish that there is probable cause to believe that a crime has been committed and that the defendant committed it.[36]

Most legal systems have preliminary procedures prior to a trial. In New Zealand, they are outlined in a Justice Department flowchart.[37]

SUFFICIENT EVIDENCE

The person carrying out the investigation inquires carefully about "the facts, circumstances, and imputability"[38] of the accused. The Ordinary decides when it seems that sufficient evidence has been collected:

> When it seems that sufficient evidence has been collected, the ordinary is to decide: 1/ whether a process to inflict or declare a penalty can be initiated; 2/ whether, attentive to can. 1341, this is expedient; 3/ whether a judicial process must be used or, unless the law forbids it, whether the matter must proceed by way of extrajudicial decree.[39]

However, if the Ordinary decrees that there is insufficient evidence to proceed with a penal process, this may be changed by a new decree:

> §2. The ordinary is to revoke or change the decree mentioned in §1 whenever new evidence indicates to him that another decision is necessary. §3. In issuing the decrees mentioned in §§1 and 2, the ordinary is to hear two judges or other experts of the law if he considers it prudent. §4. Before he makes a decision according to the norm of §1 and in order to avoid useless trials, the ordinary is to examine carefully whether it is expedient for him or the investigator, with the consent of the parties, to resolve equitably the question of damage.[40]

The preliminary investigation should establish the following:

- The facts on which the investigation is based
- The number of criminal acts
- When they took place
- The circumstances in which they took place
- The general details of the alleged victims.[41]

The person carrying out the investigation needs to verify the external acts that occurred which would constitute a delict. The investigation is not supposed to try to prove the allegation with moral certainty. Sometimes preliminary investigations include hundreds of pages of evidence, but this should not happen because it means that a preliminary investigation is more like an administrative penal process. The procedures of a trial or penal process safeguarding rights are nonexistent. A preliminary investigation only needs to establish that the "knowledge of the delict" (*notitia de delicto*) seems to be true. It is most important that the accuser or a witness gives their testimony under oath, signs at the end of a typed-up transcript, and initials each page of the transcript. This may prevent the person from being required to be reinterviewed.[42] Often the complainant will refuse to be interviewed again. Therefore, it is very important that the first interview is comprehensive and obtains as much relevant information as possible.

SACRAMENT OF PENANCE

When an accusation or a case involves the sacrament of Penance, it is vital that the confidentiality of the seal of the sacrament is upheld. The DDF *Vademecum* states:

> Care should also be taken care to determine any possible relation to the sacramental internal forum (in this regard, however, account must be taken of the prescriptions of art. 4 §2 SST). At this point, any other delicts attributed to the accused (cf. art. 9 §2 SST) can be added, as well as any indication of problematic facts emerging from his biographical profile.[43]

The person carrying out the investigation must not reveal the identity of the alleged victim to the accused priest. *Sacramentorum Sanctitatis Tutela* (SST) is explicit about this protection for the sacrament of Penance and the accuser.[44]

SCOPE OF THE INVESTIGATION

The person carrying out the investigation should focus on the specific allegation against the accused. For example, if the bishop is accused of not dealing with the allegation of abuse against a priest, the person carrying out the investigation should focus on that priest and not trawl through all the files of the priests in the diocese. The person carrying out the investigation should only look at the file of another priest if a particular failure to act is revealed. This will also help to avoid delays in dealing with a particular allegation.[45]

The person carrying out the investigation is not carrying out a general inquiry into how the accused performed his ministry, but if other unlawful or criminal behavior is revealed, this should be investigated. The person carrying out the investigation may need to request the Ordinary to amend the opening decree of the preliminary investigation if other delicts or misconduct come to light.

PROHIBITION TO EXERCISE SACRED MINISTRY

The Ordinary or Hierarch has the right to impose precautionary measures[46] from the beginning of the investigation.[47] He should prohibit the accused from the exercise of sacred ministry if a more grave crime is alleged or if the allegation is about a recent serious incident:

> To prevent scandals, to protect the freedom of witnesses, and to guard the course of justice, the ordinary, after having heard the promoter of justice and cited the accused, at any stage of the process can exclude the accused from the sacred ministry or from some office and ecclesiastical function, can impose or forbid residence in some place or territory, or even can prohibit public participation in the Most Holy Eucharist. Once the cause ceases, all these measures must be revoked; they also end by the law itself when the penal process ceases.[48]

The accused cannot normally exercise any ministry or function including public concelebration of the Eucharist until the investigation and any process has concluded. Usually, the accused must reside at a specified residence and is forbidden to have any contact with the accuser, or their relatives and friends. The *Vademecum* explains:

> The precautionary measures referred to in no. 58 are imposed by a singular precept, legitimately made known (cf. canons 49ff. and 1319 CIC and 1406 and 1510ff. CCEO).
>
> It should be noted that whenever a decision is made to modify or revoke precautionary measures, this must be done by a corresponding decree, legitimately made known. This will not be necessary, however, at the conclusion of the possible process, since at that moment those measures cease to have legal effect. (nos. 64–65)

The Ordinary should impose the precautionary measures in a precept. It is very important that the Ordinary require the accused to keep the name of the accuser and other details confidential to respect the privacy of the accuser. There have been instances of the accused telling other people who then verbally or even physically attack the alleged victim.

IMPUTABILITY

There is the maxim "the accused is innocent until proven guilty" in "The Declaration of Human Rights" from the time of the French Revolution.[49] However, according to canon 1321, if it is proven that the accused committed the action, the presumption of the law is that the accused is culpable for the offense.

The person carrying out the investigation is to assess the imputability of the accused.[50] "Imputability is a person's moral responsibility for an act they have performed."[51] This depends on how freely, deliberately, and intentionally the person violated the law, without compulsion or limits on their freedom of action. The imputability of a person is presumed when it is shown that the person performed the action.[52] However, some factors such as reoffending may increase imputability,[53] while other factors such as ignorance may decrease imputability.[54]

PROTECTING GOOD REPUTATIONS

When someone is convicted of a crime, they lose their good reputation. This has happened legitimately because of a legal process and their own action. However, canon 220 states: "No one is permitted to harm illegitimately the good reputation which a person possesses nor to injure the right of any person to protect his or her own privacy." "Illegitimately" includes careless use of information, lack of concern for privacy, or libel. If it is proven with moral certainty in a penal process that a person has committed an offense, that person will lose his good reputation, but this has come about legitimately.

Any investigation must take care that the reputation of anyone involved is not endangered. This includes the accused, the accuser, and witnesses. All these people have a right to privacy and protection against prejudice, retaliation, or discrimination.[55]

PROTECTION OF WHISTLEBLOWERS

Significant measures in recent law provide for accusers and whistleblowers to be protected from retribution.[56] *Vos Estis Lux Mundi* provides protection for them:

> Article 4 – Protection of the person submitting the report. §1. Making a report pursuant to article 3 shall not constitute a violation of office confidentiality. §2. Except as provided for by canons 1390 CIC and 1452 and 1454 CCEO, prejudice, retaliation, or discrimination as a consequence of having submitted a report is prohibited and may constitute the conduct referred to in article 1 §1, letter b). §3. An obligation to keep silent may not be imposed on any person with regard to the contents of his or her report.[57]

The person making the report is protected from prejudice, retaliation, or discrimination because of submission of the report. This brings the Church legislation into line with most civil jurisdictions.

Obviously, persons making a report could easily be members of a religious institute or diocesan clergy. Paragraph 3 makes it clear that no obligation to silence or secrecy can be imposed on a person about their report or its contents. This eliminates nondisclosure agreements and makes it clear that the person making the report is free to report to any police or civil authority concerning the abuse.

RIGHTS OF THE ACCUSED

The accused does not have any procedural rights during the preliminary investigation apart from their rights in natural justice. At some stage of the process, the accused would normally be informed unless it might compromise the integrity of the investigation or the evidence. When the accused is informed, he should be encouraged to get civil and canonical advice and be invited to respond to the accusation against him.[58]

At any stage of the process, a cleric may admit his guilt and his unsuitability to be a minister. Then he can apply to be dispensed from the obligations of celibacy, but he can never present himself again as a minister of the Church (no. 157).

PASTORAL CARE

The complainant, the one(s) harmed, the one under investigation, and the community involved may need pastoral care including spiritual, medical, and psychological help.[59] The diocesan bishop would be the first person responsible for offering it.[60]

The accused should not be driving him/herself to the meeting with the Ordinary to ensure the safety of all involved.

This means the Ordinary arranges for a friend/support person to drive the accused to the meeting.

CONCLUSION OF THE INVESTIGATION

Investigations vary in length. Some investigations may only involve several photos or some text messages. The person carrying out the investigation and the Ordinary need to continually evaluate whether "it seems that sufficient evidence has been collected."[61] At a certain point a decision can be made that it is unlikely that evidence will be found that significantly contradicts what seems to be the truth of the case and whether it seems to be true that an ecclesiastical delict was committed.

The person carrying out the investigation, that is, the delegate, should make a report and give it and the evidence collected to the Ordinary. The report should give an overview of the investigation, reporting who was interviewed and the key outcomes from each interview. The investigator needs to be aware of the potential to modify or fake data. Evidence that has been found on social media, including text messages, documents, and photographs, needs to be analyzed. If a person refused to be interviewed, this needs to be explained. The delegate should assess what has been found in the evidence and suggest anything else that could be done to collect further evidence.

DECREE CLOSING THE PRELIMINARY INVESTIGATION

The Ordinary or Hierarch must decree the conclusion of the preliminary investigation.[62]

Then he must decide whether the allegation has a sufficient basis in law and in fact to have a semblance of truth.[63] A decision must also be made whether prescription has precluded a penal process.

The Ordinary needs to consider whether it concerns a delict reserved to the Holy See. If the investigation concerns a *graviora delicta*, the Ordinary or Hierarch must, according to the *Vademecum*, do the following:

> In accordance with art. 16 SST, once the preliminary investigation has concluded, whatever its outcome, the Ordinary or Hierarch is obliged to send, without delay, an authentic copy of the relative acts to the DDF. (no. 69)

Even if the Ordinary concludes that the accusation is unfounded or unproven, the Dicastery for the Doctrine of the Faith (DDF) *Vademecum* states that he must forward the acts of the case with his votum to the DDF:

> Whenever the Ordinary who carried out the preliminary investigation is not the Ordinary of the place where the alleged delict was committed, he is to communicate to the latter the results of the investigation.

The acts are to be sent in a single copy; it is helpful if they are authenticated by a notary who is a member of the curia, unless a specific notary had been appointed for the preliminary investigation.

Canons 1719 CIC and 1470 CCEO state that the original of all the acts is to be kept in the secret archive of the curia.

Again, according to art. 10 SST, once the acts of the preliminary investigation have been sent to the DDF, the Ordinary or Hierarch is to await communications or instructions in this regard from the DDF.

Clearly, if other elements related to the preliminary investigation or new accusations should emerge in the meantime, these are to be forwarded to the DDF as quickly as possible, in order to be added to what is already in its possession. If it appears useful to reopen the preliminary investigation on the basis of those elements, the DDF is to be informed immediately. (nos. 71–75)

The revised Book VI of the Code (2021) includes the crime of neglecting to report an offense, whether it be to an Ordinary or the Apostolic See:

> A person who neglects to report an offence, when required to do so by a canonical law, is to be punished according to the provision of can. 1336 §§2–4, with the addition of other penalties according to the gravity of the offence. (Can. 1371 §6)

INFORMING CIVIL AUTHORITIES

The Ordinary or Hierarch is to inform the civil authorities of the receipt of the allegation according to the following principles:

> Two principles apply: a/ respect for the laws of the state (cf. art. 19 VELM); and b/ respect for the desire of the alleged victim, provided that this is not contrary to civil legislation. Alleged victims should be encouraged—as will be stated below (no. 56)—to exercise their duties and rights vis-à-vis the state authorities, taking care to document that this encouragement took place and to avoid any form of dissuasion with regard to the alleged victim. (no. 48)

If the law requires the Ordinary or Hierarch to report, they must do so. When civil authorities issue subpoenas, the Ordinary or Hierarch must obey them.[64]

THE COMPLAINTS ADVISORY COMMITTEE/ REVIEW BOARD

These committees may be created by a particular law. They advise about the credibility of the report and what to recommend to the Ordinary and the Holy See. A committee cannot carry out an investigation. There must be an individual person carrying out the investigation.[65]

Non-reserved Delict

Many sexual abuse allegations against clergy and religious concern crimes of abuse of authority.[66] Canon 1718 §1 states that the Ordinary must discern and decide about initiating a penal process:

> When it seems that sufficient evidence has been collected, the ordinary is to decide: 1/ whether a process to inflict or declare a penalty can be initiated.

The Ordinary may decide that the matter can be resolved with other measures:

> 2/ whether, attentive to canon 1341, this is expedient.

It must be remembered that the penal process has the objects of repairing scandal, restoring justice, and reforming the offender.[67] Canon 1345 notes that the offender "must be punished if there is no other way to provide for the restoration of justice and the repair of any scandal that may have been caused."

If a penal process is to be used, he must decide which process:

> 3/ whether a judicial process must be used or, unless the law forbids it, whether the matter must proceed by way of extrajudicial decree.

Sometimes other complaints or information are received many years later. If new evidence comes to light:

> The ordinary is to revoke or change the decree mentioned in §1 whenever new evidence indicates to him that another decision is necessary. (Can. 1718 §2)

The Ordinary is required to consult two judges or experts in canon law if he considers it prudent:

> In issuing the decrees mentioned in §§1 and 2, the ordinary is to hear two judges or other experts of the law if he considers it prudent. (Can. 1718 §3)

The Ordinary might resolve the matter between the parties if it involves libel:

> Before he makes a decision according to the norm of §1 and in order to avoid useless trials, the ordinary is to examine carefully whether it is expedient for him or the delegate, with the consent of the parties, to resolve equitably the question of damages. (Can. 1718 §4)

Anonymous Complaints

The *Vademecum* states that anonymous complaints must be accepted, although they are harder to verify:

> At times, a *notitia de delicto* can derive from an anonymous source, namely, from unidentified or unidentifiable persons. The anonymity of the source should not automatically lead to considering the report as false, especially when it is accompanied by documentation that attests to the likelihood of a delict. Nonetheless, for easily understandable reasons, great caution should be exercised in considering this type of *notitia*, and anonymous reports certainly should not be encouraged. (no. 11)

The anonymous complaint may give clear knowledge of a delict, especially if it alleges the exact time, date, and place of the delict. Of course, when someone makes an anonymous complaint, the person's motive and hiding of their identity may be suspect. However, the anonymity of the complainant may be understandable if there is a danger of retribution in their culture or political situation.

Credibility

The accuser is presumed to be telling the truth until the contrary is demonstrated. However, the person carrying out the investigation should validate the plausibility of the complaint. This is particularly important if the case involves the sacrament of Penance because the accused priest cannot reveal any conversation within the sacrament but can only admit or deny the offense.

Evidence from other processes, such as a declaration of marriage nullity, may be included in the file by the person carrying out the investigation:

> It can be useful to assemble testimonies and documents, of any kind or provenance (including the results of investigations or trials carried out by civil authorities), which may in fact prove helpful for substantiating and validating the plausibility of the accusation. It is likewise possible at this point to indicate eventual exempting, mitigating or aggravating factors, as provided for by law. It could also prove helpful to collect at this time testimonials of credibility with regard to the complainants and the alleged victims. An Appendix to the present *Vademecum* contains a schematic outline of useful data that those carrying out the preliminary investigation will want to compile and have at hand (cf. no. 69). (no. 34)

Other useful data could include evidence from any civil investigation. Although there may be no witnesses, the credibility of the persons involved, the consistency of the facts and the accounts of what happened, other accusations against the accused, previous patterns of offending, documents, and so on, all help to establish the truth of the accusations.

Accused Deceased

If the accused is deceased, it is not possible to have procedures such as a preliminary investigation, a trial, or an extrajudicial process.

The Ordinary where the alleged events occurred will have to investigate the allegation(s) to ascertain what happened, who is the alleged perpetrator, and the likelihood that the alleged events happened. This may reach the standard of probability that the abuse happened, and then there will need to be redress for the victim.

CONCLUSION

Kevin McKenna wrote an article about due process and referred to an American survey that showed that 82 percent of priests fear being falsely accused.[68] The preliminary investigation is a crucial part of the procedures before a penal process. If the investigation is performed correctly, it serves to ensure a just outcome for all those involved.

A fundamental act for any investigation is to fill in as much as possible the "Tabular Summary for Cases of *Delicta Reservata*" (fact sheet)[69] issued by the Dicastery for the Doctrine of the Faith at the beginning of any preliminary investigation. Then, if new information is received and the case changes to a more grave crime, for example because of absolution of an accomplice in a sin against the sixth commandment, the correct tabular summary is already in use. All tribunal marriage cases have detailed fact sheets and contact details of the parties that save so much time and effort as evidence in the case is gathered.[70]

2

EXTRAJUDICIAL PROCESSES

Extrajudicial processes take place frequently because the Dicasteries of the Apostolic See recognize the shortage of qualified personnel in the local churches and authorize extrajudicial or administrative processes on a regular basis. The Dicastery for the Doctrine of the Faith explains:

> The extrajudicial penal process, sometimes called an *administrative process*, is a type of penal process that abbreviates the formalities called for in the judicial process, for the sake of expediting the course of justice without eliminating the procedural guarantees demanded by a fair trial (cf. canons 221 CIC and 24 CCEO).[1]

Canon law has traditionally favored a trial as the judicial process to be used for imposing penalties, rather than the extrajudicial process.[2] Canon 1342 also implies that a judicial procedure is the preferred procedure for imposing a penalty:

> §1. Whenever there are just reasons against the use of a judicial procedure, a penalty can be imposed or declared by means of an extrajudicial decree, observing canon 1720, especially in what concerns the right of defence and the moral certainty in the mind of the one issuing the decree, in accordance with the provision of can. 1608. Penal remedies and penances may in any case whatever be applied by a decree. §2. Perpetual penalties cannot be imposed or declared by means of a decree; nor can penalties which the law or precept establishing them forbids to be applied by decree. §3. What the law or decree says of a judge in regard to the imposition or declaration of a penalty in a trial is to be applied also to a Superior who imposes or declares a penalty by an extrajudicial decree, unless it is otherwise clear, or unless there is question of provisions which concern only procedural matters.

The canon acknowledges that just reasons exist for an Ordinary not to use a judicial procedure and instead to use an extrajudicial process. Some special laws promulgated since 2000 have provisions enabling the Dicasteries for the Doctrine of the Faith, Clergy, and Evangelization to dismiss or approve guilty clerics receiving perpetual penalties including dismissal from the clerical state.

Juan Arietta explains:

> The judicial trial is the ordinary means for imposing penalties, since it is the one that best fulfils the requirements of justice. It is, however, possible—and sometimes necessary—to have recourse to the administrative procedures where there are "just reasons," that is, when the just and efficient administration of justice recommends it.[3]

Article 19 of *Sacramentorum Sanctitatis Tutela* allows the Dicastery for the Doctrine of the Faith to authorize an extrajudicial process and to impose a perpetual penal remedy such as dismissal from the clerical state:

> §1. Whenever the Congregation for the Doctrine of the Faith has decided that an extrajudicial process should be initiated, can. 1720 CIC or can. 1486 CCEO is to be applied. §2 With the prior mandate of the Congregation for the Doctrine of the Faith, perpetual expiatory penalties may be imposed.[4]

The stipulation requiring a penal trial in canon 1342 §2 is derogated for crimes reserved to the Dicastery for the Doctrine of the Faith. The decision must be made with moral certainty[5] and the prior mandate of the Dicastery is required to impose a perpetual penalty.

COMPETENCE

When information (*notitia de delicto*) is received by an Ordinary, it must first be decided who is the local Ordinary competent to deal with the information.[6] Pope Francis legislated in *Vos Estis Lux Mundi* (2023):

> Article 3—Reporting. §1. Except for when a cleric learns of information during the exercise of ministry in the internal forum, whenever a cleric or a member of an Institute of Consecrated Life or of a Society of Apostolic Life learns, or has well-founded motives to believe, that one of the acts referred to in art. 1 has been committed, that person is obliged to report it promptly to the local Ordinary where the events are said to have occurred or to another Ordinary among those referred to in canons 134 CIC and 984 CCEO, except for what is established by §3 of the present article.

The revised *Vos Estis Lux Mundi* makes it the norm that unless the Ordinaries agree otherwise, the Ordinary of the place where the facts are alleged to have occurred is to proceed with the investigation:

> Article 2. §3. Except as provided in article 3 §3, the Ordinary who has received the report transmits it without delay to the Ordinary of the place where the events allegedly took place, as well as to the Ordinary proper to the person reported. Unless otherwise agreed between the two Ordinaries, it is the task of the Ordinary of the place

> where the facts would have taken place to proceed according to the norm of law according to what is provided for the specific case.[7]

The Ordinary would usually be the diocesan bishop, but it could be the apostolic or diocesan administrator. Usually, there must be a preliminary investigation when information about an alleged delict is received. There must be decrees opening and closing the preliminary investigation, as well as a decree appointing the notary and the delegate to carry out the investigation. The Ordinary must take account of the fact that the appointed delegate cannot act as a judge in an ensuing trial, nor can he be a delegate or an assessor for an ensuing extrajudicial process according to canon 1717 §3 CIC and 1468 §3 CCEO. The Dicastery for the Doctrine of the Faith advises:

> In appointing the person who carries out the investigation, and taking into account the cooperation that can be offered by lay persons in accordance with canons 228 CIC and 408 CCEO (cf. art. 13 VELM), the Ordinary or Hierarch should keep in mind that, according to canons 1717 §3 CIC and 1468 §3 CCEO, if a penal judicial process is then initiated, that same person cannot act as a judge in the matter. Sound practice suggests that the same criterion be used in appointing the delegate and the assessors in the case of an extrajudicial process. (*Vademecum* 39)

Unless a preliminary investigation is entirely superfluous because the accused has been arrested and charged by the police, the local Ordinary must ensure there is a preliminary investigation carried out either by himself or another Ordinary, or someone he delegates to carry out this task. Most Ordinaries will delegate someone to carry out this task because there are usually many conflicts of interest with accused priests[8] and alleged victims.[9]

During the preliminary investigation, the alleged victim will usually be interviewed. It is extremely important that there be a good, comprehensive interview of the alleged victim. Frequently, alleged victims will only be interviewed once and will refuse to be interviewed again during the extrajudicial process. Therefore, it is crucial that as much relevant information as is possible is obtained in any interview with the alleged victim.

The accused will usually have been interviewed as part of the preliminary investigation. The accused must be informed of the right to remain silent,[10] and if a cleric he has a right to present a petition to be dispensed from all the obligations associated with the clerical state:

> From the time of the *notitia de delicto*, the accused has the right to present a petition to be dispensed from all the obligations connected with the clerical state, including celibacy, and, concurrently, from any religious vows. The Ordinary or Hierarch must clearly inform him of this right. Should the cleric decide to make use of this possibility, he must write a suitable petition, addressed to the Holy Father, introducing himself and briefly indicating the reasons for which he is seeking the dispensation.

> The petition must be clearly dated and signed by the petitioner. It is to be transmitted to the DDF, together with the *votum* of the Ordinary or Hierarch. In turn, the DDF will forward it and—if the Holy Father accepts the petition—will transmit the rescript of dispensation to the Ordinary or Hierarch, asking him to provide for legitimate notification to the petitioner. (no. 157)

PROHIBITION TO EXERCISE SACRED MINISTRY (ADMINISTRATIVE LEAVE)

Crimes Reserved to the Dicastery for the Doctrine of the Faith

The Code of Canon Law and article 10 of *Sacramentorum Sanctitatis Tutela* provide for the accused at any stage of the process to be prohibited from the exercise of sacred ministry:

> To prevent scandals, to protect the freedom of witnesses, and to guard the course of justice, the ordinary, after having heard the promoter of justice and cited the accused, at any stage of the process can exclude the accused from the sacred ministry or from some office and ecclesiastical function, can impose or forbid residence in some place or territory, or even can prohibit public participation in the Most Holy Eucharist. Once the cause ceases, all these measures must be revoked; they also end by the law itself when the penal process ceases. (Can. 1722)

The Dicastery for the Doctrine of the Faith explain this in their *Vademecum*:

> To defend the good name of the persons involved and to protect the public good, as well as to avoid other factors (for example, the rise of scandal, the risk of concealment of future evidence, the presence of threats or other conduct meant to dissuade the alleged victim from exercising his or her rights, the protection of other possible victims), in accordance with art. 10 §2 SST, the Ordinary or Hierarch has the right, from the outset of the preliminary investigation, to impose the precautionary measures listed in canons 1722 CIC and 1473 CCEO. (no. 58)

These precautionary measures constitute a taxative list, so only one of these reasons may be chosen for prohibiting an accused from the exercise of sacred ministry, which is often referred to as "administrative leave" (no. 59). Depending on the circumstances, the accusation, and the accused, an Ordinary may impose other disciplinary measures such as requiring residence in a particular place.[11]

Precautionary measures are not penalties but administrative acts for the purposes of defending the good name of the persons involved, protecting the public good, and avoiding the rise of scandal. The imposition of precautionary measures will help prevent issues that might dissuade the alleged victim from exercising his or her rights, as well as ensure the protection of other possible victims. The purpose of these precautionary measures must be carefully explained to the accused.

Crimes Not Reserved to the Dicastery for the Doctrine of the Faith

According to the DDF *Vademecum*, there are three possible penal procedures: "a judicial penal process; an extrajudicial penal process; or the procedure introduced by article 26 SST."[12] The procedure in article 26 is explained in the 2021 norms:

> It is the right of the Congregation for the Doctrine of the Faith, in whatever stage and grade of the unfolding of the proceedings, to present directly the most grave cases mentioned above in articles 2–6 to the decision of the Supreme Pontiff with regard to dismissal or deposition from the clerical state, together with dispensation from the law of celibacy, when it is manifestly evident that the delict has been committed, after having given the guilty party the possibility of defending himself. (SST 26)

INITIATING A PENAL PROCESS

After the preliminary investigation, if the alleged crime is not reserved to a Dicastery of the Apostolic See, the Ordinary must decide whether there is to be a penal process:

> When it seems that sufficient evidence has been collected, the ordinary is to decide: 1/ whether a process to inflict or declare a penalty can be initiated; 2/ whether, attentive to can. 1341, this is expedient; 3/ whether a judicial process must be used or, unless the law forbids it, whether the matter must proceed by way of extrajudicial decree. (1718 §1)

In 2021, Pope Francis changed canon 1341[13] so that, if other remedies are perceived to be insufficient, there is an obligation on the Ordinary to initiate a judicial or administrative penal process for "justice [to] be sufficiently restored, the offender reformed, and the scandal repaired":

> The Ordinary must start a judicial or an administrative procedure for the imposition or the declaration of penalties when he perceives that neither by the methods of pastoral care, especially fraternal correction, nor by a warning or correction, can justice be sufficiently restored, the offender reformed, and the scandal repaired. (Can. 1341)[14]

As a result of the changes in 2021, a discretionary penalty must be imposed if the offender abused his ecclesiastical office or position of authority.[15] Juan Arrieta explains the significant change in canon 1341:

> The text of this canon substantially modifies the corresponding canon promulgated in 1983. Whereas at that time provision was made for following the punitive route only when it was perceived by the authority that other remedies dictated by pastoral concern were not sufficient, the text now imposes on the Ordinary the duty

> to initiate disciplinary sanctions if from the information received in the preliminary investigation (cf. c. 1717) he considers that the other remedies are not enough to achieve the purposes of the penalty. The entire discipline now contained in book VI is governed by this same criterion and by that set out in c. 1311, §2.[16]

This means "penalties are always to be applied with canonical equity and having in mind the restoration of justice, the reform of the offender, and the repair of scandal."[17]

DELEGATE IN AN EXTRAJUDICIAL PROCESS

The Ordinary must decide whether to preside over an extrajudicial process personally or to name a delegate with expertise in canon law.

The Ordinary may delegate the entire process to a delegate or reserve the final decision to himself. The Ordinary must also appoint two assessors to assist him or the delegate in the evaluative stage of the process.[18] In choosing them, the Ordinary should consider the criteria set forth in canons 1424 and 1448 §1 CIC.[19]

All these officials must be appointed by a decree of the Ordinary, and they are to take an oath to faithfully fulfill the task to which they have been appointed.[20]

The accused must be summoned by a decree from the Ordinary or the delegate, clearly indicating why he is being summoned, the accusation, and the proofs gathered so far. The accused must be reminded that he is not obliged to admit the offense and does not have to take an oath, although he may decide to do either or both of these things.[21]

The *Norms* promulgated in 2021 (cf. art. 20 §7 SST) require, for the case of an extrajudicial process in matters reserved to the DDF, that the accused, in accordance with the prescriptions of canons 1723 and 1481 §§1–2 CIC, be assisted by an advocate and/or procurator, either of his own choice or, otherwise, appointed *ex officio*:

> The Ordinary (or his delegate) must be informed of the appointment of the advocate and/or procurator by means of a suitable and authentic procuratorial mandate in accordance with canon 1484 §1[22] CIC, prior to the session in which the accusations and proofs are made known, in order to verify that the requirements of canon 1483 CIC have been met. (no. 98)

If the accused neglects to appoint an advocate, the Ordinary must appoint an advocate for him and inform him who it is. If the accused does not respond to the summons, he should be summoned again. His response is to be noted in the acts of the case, and the process continues to its conclusion.

The acts of the case are to be shown to the accused and his advocate. If the accusation involves the sacrament of Penance, the accused can only be told the name of the accuser if the alleged victim explicitly consents to their name being made known to the accused.[23]

The assessors are not required to be

involved in collecting proofs such as interviewing the parties or witnesses, but of course they may. Proofs include:

> all those materials collected during the preliminary investigation and any other materials acquired: first, the record of the accusations made by the alleged victims; then pertinent documents (e.g., medical records; correspondence, even by electronic means; photographs; proofs of purchase; bank records); statements made by eventual witnesses; and finally any expert opinions (medical, including psychiatric; psychological; graphological) that the person who conducted the investigation may have deemed appropriate to accept or have carried out. Any rules of confidentiality imposed by civil law should be observed. (no. 96)

Often, the Ordinary or his delegate may decide that further proofs may need to be collected. The proofs need to be shown to the advocate and the accused, and they should also be made available to the alleged victim and an advocate.

The accused and his advocate/procurator may present a written defense or be given a reasonable time limit to present a defense to the Ordinary or his delegate. The defense may include a request for further witnesses to be interviewed. The Ordinary or his delegate has the authority to decide whether to admit or not admit new evidence according to the criteria of universal law on contentious trials.

The Ordinary or his delegate must decide on the credibility of all those taking part in the process. Testimonials to the credibility of the accuser could be obtained and inconsistencies in the accuser's evidence could be pointed out. It is most important to ascertain whether the accused has any ulterior motive in accusing the cleric.

The accuser may have given evidence during the preliminary investigation and may decide not to be interviewed again. In this scenario, the process continues. Similarly, the accused may simply say "prove the allegation" and refuse to be interviewed or to provide a statement.

The extrajudicial process concludes when the Ordinary or his delegate has decided that sufficient evidence has been collected and the right of defense has been provided for. The Ordinary or his delegate invites the two assessors to provide their evaluation of the proofs and arguments of the defense in accord with canon 1720 within a reasonable period. He can invite them to come to a joint session to facilitate discussion, debate, and analysis of the case. The written opinions of the assessors should be included in the acts of the case, but the *Vademecum* 117–18 makes it clear that the *vota* should not be shared with the accused or his advocate/procurator. Minutes of the meeting should be included in the acts.

Afterward, the Ordinary or his delegate decides whether or not the case is proven and writes a decree of adjudication. Although it looks like a sentence, it is not one, because this process is not a trial. The Ordinary or his delegate should cite the principal elements of the accusation, the development of the process, the reasons for the decision in law and in fact, as well as any mitigating or aggravating circumstances.[24] If the delict is proven with moral certainty (cf. c. 1720, 3° CIC), the Ordinary or his delegate must issue a decree concluding the process, imposing and/or declaring the penalty, or imposing a penal remedy or penance that he considers most suitable for the reparation of scandal, the reestablishment of justice, and the amendment of the guilty party.

The accused and the accuser must be notified about the outcome and the accused may appeal the decision. The accused must sign acknowledging the receipt of the decree. If he refuses to sign acknowledging receipt of the decree, others present, such as the notary, must sign a written document testifying that the accused was given the decree. The accused must also be advised how to appeal, the time limits, and to whom the appeal is to be addressed.[25]

EXTRAJUDICIAL PROCESS

Alleged Crimes Reserved to the Doctrine of the Faith

Following the preliminary investigation, the Ordinary must decide whether or not the alleged crime is reserved to a Dicastery of the Apostolic See.

If the alleged crime is reserved to a dicastery, the local Ordinary must send all the acts of the preliminary investigation to the competent dicastery. In this scenario, the competent dicastery will give the case a protocol number and will instruct the local Ordinary about the conduct of an extrajudicial process or trial. For example, an alleged crime involving the sexual abuse of a minor or the sacrament of Penance is reserved to the Dicastery for the Doctrine of the Faith. If the alleged crime does not involve a more grave crime but has been committed by a bishop, the competent dicastery mission territories, such as New Zealand, is the Dicastery for Evangelization.

When the Dicastery for the Doctrine of the Faith authorizes or decides there is to be an extrajudicial process, the Ordinary and/or his delegate must carefully follow their instructions as outlined in the previous section: "Delegate in an Extrajudicial Process." However, in this case, there is no need to appoint a promoter of justice, because that person at the DDF will participate in the process.

There are some differences in procedure with extrajudicial processes according to the CCEO. Some priests are bi-ritual and function in churches of different rites. If a priest who is bi-ritual is accused of a crime, it may be necessary to seek the guidance of the Dicastery for the Doctrine of the Faith.[26]

PROCEDURAL DIFFERENCES FOR AN EXTRAJUDICIAL PENAL PROCESS

There are several key differences from CIC[27] in the extrajudicial penal process as described in the CCEO.[28]

a) Prescription. The prescription of canon 1486[29] CCEO must be strictly followed, under pain of invalidity of the penal decree. (no. 131)

b) Assessors. The CCEO does not mention assessors.
c) Promoter of Justice. The involvement of the promoter of justice is obligatory and the notification of the accusation and proofs must take place with the obligatory presence of the promoter of justice and the notary.
d) Penalties. The Dicastery for Legislative Texts advises that particular attention should be given to the question whether, on the basis of the gravity of the delict, the penalties listed in canon 1426 §1 CCEO are indeed adequate for achieving the provisions of canon 1401 CCEO. Canons 1429 and 1430 CCEO should be observed in imposing any penalty.[30]
e) Mandate for Perpetual Penalty. Hierarchs and their delegates must remember that, according to article 19 §2 SST, the prohibitions of canon 1402 §2 CCEO are not applicable. Perpetual expiatory penalty by decree can only be imposed with the prior mandate of the DDF as required by the same article 19 §2 SST. The concession of this prior mandate from the DDF must be explicitly mentioned in the decree.[31]
f) Penal Decree. The decree must meet the criteria in numbers 119–26 of the Dicastery for Legislative Texts's *User Guide*.[32]
g) Notification of the Decree. The accused is notified of the decree according to the terms of canon 1520[33] CCEO and in proper form.[34]

POSSIBLE DECISIONS

The Dicastery for the Doctrine of the Faith explains that three types of decisions are possible:

> The decision that concludes the penal process, whether judicial or extrajudicial, can be of three types:
>
> - *conviction* (“*constat*”), if with moral certainty the guilt of the accused is established with regard to the delict ascribed to him. In this case, the decision must indicate specifically the type of canonical sanction imposed or declared.
> - *acquittal* (“*constat de non*”), if with moral certainty the innocence of the accused is established, inasmuch as no offense was committed, the accused did not commit the offense, the offense is not deemed a delict by the law or was committed by a person who is not imputable.
> - *dismissal* (“*non constat*”), whenever it has not been possible to attain moral certainty with regard to the guilt of the accused, due to lack of evidence or to insufficient or conflicting evidence that the offense was in fact committed, that the accused committed the offense, or that the delict was committed by a person who is not imputable.
>
> It is possible to provide for the public good or for the welfare of the person accused through appropriate warnings, penal remedies, and other means of pastoral solicitude (cf. can. 1348 CIC).

> The decision (issued by sentence or by decree) must refer to one of these three types, so that it is clear whether it is "*constat*," "*constat de non*," or "*non constat*." (no. 84)

THE END OF THE PENAL PROCEDURE

If the pope made the decision, there is no possibility of appeal against his decision.[35] Apart from that circumstance, there are different possibilities available for those who were parties in the process.

If it was a penal judicial process, a legal challenge is possible, namely, a complaint of nullity, *restitutio in integrum*,[36] or appeal.[37] Article 16 §3 SST states that the only tribunal for appeals is the Supreme Tribunal of the Dicastery for the Doctrine of the Faith. For appeals, the prescriptions of law must be followed, noting carefully that article 16 §2 SST modified the time limits for the presentation of an appeal, imposing a peremptory time limit of sixty useful days, to be calculated according to what is laid down in canons 202 §1 CIC and 1545 §1 CCEO.[38] If it were an extrajudicial penal process, recourse can be made against the concluding decree within the terms provided by canons 1734ff. CIC and 1487 CCEO (cf. Section VIII).[39]

When an appeal or recourse is made according to canons 1353 CIC and 1319 and 1487 §2 CCEO, appeals and recourses have a suspensive effect on the penalty.[40] However, this also means that any precautionary measures remain in force with the same caveats and procedures mentioned in nn. 58–65.[41]

In taking recourse against a penal decree, the accused and/or his advocate/procurator, according to canon 1734 CIC, must first seek its emendation or revocation from the author (the Ordinary or his delegate) within the peremptory time limit of ten canonical days from the legitimate notification of the decree.[42]

The author of the decree, according to canon 1735, within thirty days after receiving the petition, can respond by emending his own decree or by rejecting the petition. He can also not respond, and his response is presumed to be negative after thirty days.[43]

If the author rejects the petition to amend the decree or does not reply for thirty days, then the accused can apply to the *Congresso* of the DDF directly or through the author of the decree (cf. c. 1737 §1 CIC) or through a procurator, within the peremptory time limit of fifteen useful days provided for by canon 1737 §2 CIC.[44] If the accused presents the hierarchical recourse to the author of the decree, he must immediately transmit it to the DDF (cf. canon 1737 §1 CIC). Thereafter, the author of the decree awaits possible instructions or requests from the Dicastery for the Doctrine of the Faith. The Dicastery will inform him about the result of the examination of the recourse.

CONCLUSION

Canon law recognizes that a penal trial is the best process for achieving justice for alleged victims and the accused. However, the realities of delays, shortages of qualified personnel, and the number of cases mean that, out of necessity, many cases are dealt with by an extrajudicial process. The Ordinary and/or his delegate and assessors must be careful to uphold the rights of both the accused and the alleged victim.

3

OBLIGATIONS AND RESPONSIBILITIES OF THE PROMOTER OF JUSTICE

Before 2000, the promoter of justice used to be a sinecure position in tribunals. The person who held this office had little to do, and most clergy in the diocese had no idea who this person was, let alone their role and responsibilities. Usually, an older priest held the position, and it was something akin to a retired common law lawyer being appointed as a consultant to a firm.

Black's Law Dictionary defines the promoter as "one who promotes, urges on, encourages, incites, advances, etc."[1] The promoter of justice speaks for the public and watches out for the public good of the Church:[2]

> A promoter of justice is to be appointed in a diocese for contentious cases which can endanger the public good and for penal cases; the promoter of justice is bound by office to provide for the public good. (Can. 1430)

Bill Woestman describes the promoter of justice as:

> the court official with the obligation of seeing that the law, both substantial and procedural, is observed and intervening whenever the common good is at stake. In a penal trial, his role is that of prosecutor, i.e. state's attorney or according to the Canadian law, crown attorney or counsel, or simply the crown.[3]

So, the promoter of justice is much more than a prosecutor in canon law and does not try to get the accused convicted at any cost. Rather, the promoter focuses on getting to the truth concerning the commission of the alleged crime. Therefore, the promoter of justice has the right and duty to intervene when, in the name of law, a gross injustice is being committed. Peter Akpoghiran notes that "the public good entails protecting the rights of the accuser and of the accused as well as the good of the Church."[4] The promoter of justice advises the Ordinary and others involved in processing a case. Thomas Brundage points out that the promoter of justice is to act as a conscience for other officials in achieving true justice in a case.[5] Urru teaches that "the promoter of justice is to ensure, to the best of his or her abilities, that everything is done *ad normam iuris* and *secundum veritatem*, not *in fraudem iuris*."[6] The promoter of justice is needed to help ensure true justice in every case and safeguards against procedural irregularities, thereby ensuring the integrity of the ecclesiastical, judicial process.

The role of the promoter of justice in the tribunal, especially in penal and marriage cases, was spelled out in the 1917 and 1983 Codes of Canon law. Regarding solicitation, the promoter's role was developed in the Instruction of the Holy Office on March 16, 1962.[7] The role of the promoter of justice is significant in the canonization process and is explained very well in Jason Gray's thesis.[8]

ORIGINS OF THE OFFICE

Roman law is the source of most procedural law and legal institutions in canon law; however, no offices in Roman law had any resemblance to the office of promoter of justice.

This office as it exists today was instituted almost exclusively for the prosecution of crimes. In Roman law, the prosecution of crime was in the hands of individual citizens. When an individual citizen accused someone of a crime, the burden of proof and prosecution lay with that citizen. This system was used for the prosecution of crime in canon law for many centuries and false accusations were common. To remedy this, the First Council of Constantinople (381) instituted the penalty of retaliation (*poena talionis*). An accuser then had to prove his or her accusation or receive the same penalty or punishment that was sought for the accused.[9] This reduced the number of false accusations.

From about the ninth century, there was the development of the concept of the denunciation of a crime instead of an accusation against someone. The Church began allowing crimes to be prosecuted and investigated without an accuser when many thought that someone had committed a crime. Consequently, an accused person was prosecuted by a judge but there still had to be an accuser. Gratian had taught: "No accusation is brought against anyone unless there is a legitimate and qualified accuser," and "no one is judged without an accuser."[10] Judges had to be impartial, so Gratian stated: "In one and the same cause, no one can be simultaneously accused and judge."[11]

Many problems existed over false accusations of abuses and crimes committed by orthodox bishops.[12] Heretics sometimes accused bishops of crimes to take the pressure off themselves. Someone could claim to a judge that a crime had been committed without having the obligation to prove it since judges often did nothing about the accusation.

Pope Innocent III (1198–1216) aimed to eradicate clerical abuses. Faced with notorious crimes involving simony and heresy, Pope Innocent III ordered investigations without an accuser and then justified his actions to teachers of canon law in a letter of December 2, 1199. Consequently, the Fourth Lateran Council (1215) introduced an inquisitorial procedure to replace the accusatory procedure. A legitimate judge was to investigate the facts of an alleged crime or accusation when the superior learned of it from honest people.[13] A case could proceed by way of accusation, denunciation, or inquisition: "Yet, nevertheless, diligent caution is to be employed in all things, lest per chance grave harm come for only a slight gain: in the same way, legitimate inscription must precede the accusation."[14]

Care had to be taken to protect the reputation of the accused, who was to be summoned to defend himself. From the thirteenth century, this inquisitorial system was predominately used. Doubts about whether a judge could be impartial and whether he had a conflict of interest resulted in the use of a procurator to promote action against the accused person.

In the Digest (about 533) and the Code of Justinian, personnel had titles closely resembling the title "Promoter of Justice," but they did not have the role of that position. In the law of Justinian, there were titles such as De Procuratoribus et Defensoribus, De Officio Caesaris seu Rationalis, and De Defensoribus Civitatum.[15] None of these officials acted officially to prosecute criminal offenses.

Scholars believe that the office of promoter of justice owes its origins to canon law or the civil courts of France. Procurators of the King existed in 1274.[16] The Church, in the Diocese of Paris, had an official called the "*promoter fiscalis Episcopi Parisiensis*" from 1274. Many French dioceses in the fourteenth century had these officials.[17] The Council of Magdeburg (1370) decreed that promoters of justice were to prosecute criminals and protect the poor such as orphans, widows, and abandoned persons. This made the promoter an agent of equity and justice.[18] Cardinal Lega held that the origins of the office of the promoter of justice were hidden in ancient obscurity, but that it certainly had its beginnings in canon law.[19] Vidal and Wernz think that the office of promoter owes much of its development to the civil courts of France.[20] John Glynn[21] in his thesis argues that there is more support for Lega's opinion. Probably both legal systems contributed to the development of the office, and because of the limited evidence, it is hard to be too definite about how much each system contributed.

Pope Innocent IV made further developments and instituted the "minister inquisitionis" or the "minister of the inquisition." This office was later developed in the French civil courts in the fourteenth century as the "Procurateurs de Roi," or "procurators of the King." These were the first official prosecutors in any legal system.

Pope Benedict XIV wrote a treatise about the canonization of saints, stating that the "*Promoter Fidei*" from that process had its origin in the Procurator Fiscalis. The writings of Pope Benedict XIV show that the office was established in the fourteenth century to cite and prosecute criminal offenses, as well as to act occasionally as Promoter of Faith in the canonization process.[22] However, many dioceses were slow to adopt the new office.

The Sacred Congregation of Bishops and Regulars issued an instruction on June 11, 1880, which established a summary procedure for dealing with cases.[23] Chapter XIII of the instruction provided for a promoter in every diocesan curia. By the decree *Cum Magnopere* of 1884, the Sacred Congregation for the Propagation of the Faith extended the requirement of the 1880 instruction to include all mission territories.[24] In the latter part of the nineteenth century, the office of the promoter of justice was given the right and duty to act as plaintiff in various cases to do with marriage, including when the impediment was public.

The proper law for the Roman Rota and the Apostolic Signatura on June 29, 1908 provided for the office and its nature and duties in the curia in Rome.[25] These laws, as well as custom, decrees, and instructions, clearly spelled out the obligations, rights, and duties of the promoter of justice prior to the 1917 Code.

THE 1917 CODE

Appointment

The 1917 Code required each diocese to have a promoter of justice.[26] The promoter of justice acted in criminal cases and in contentious cases when, in the judgment of the Ordinary, the public good could have been called into question. When the involvement of the promoter of justice was required, the acts were invalid if he was not cited and yet participated.[27] The same person could have held the office of the promoter of justice and defender of the bond unless there were too many cases for him to deal with.[28]

Qualifications

The Ordinary selected the promoter of justice, who was required to be a priest, have a doctorate in canon law or be otherwise expert, and have both proven prudence and zeal for justice.[29] In the tribunal of a religious institute, the promoter of justice had to be a member of that religious institute.[30] When there was a case of possible dismissal from the religious or monastic congregation, the promoter of justice was appointed by the supreme moderator and council according to the norms of canon 1589 §2.[31] The promoter of justice in this role was required to defend the professions of religious.

Term

When the promoter of justice was appointed for all cases, his responsibility did not cease when the see became vacant. He could not be removed by the Vicar Capitulary but needed confirmation from the new diocesan bishop. A diocesan bishop, when he was appointed or at any other time, could remove the promoter of justice for a just cause.[32]

Conflict of Interest

The promoter of justice had to abstain from exercising his office in any case in which he was involved because of consanguinity or affinity by marriage, in any degree of the direct line and first degree of the collateral line. He also had to abstain from functioning in cases of a relationship with a party because of guardianship, care of a person, any involvement in their life, great animosity, conflict of interest, or if he had acted as an advocate or procurator for a party previously.[33]

Role in Marriage Cases

Anyone could act in processing a declaration of nullity of marriage case, unless prohibited by law.[34] The promoter of justice could introduce a petition for nullity in those cases in which impediments to the marriage were of a public nature.[35] When a spouse was the guilty cause of the nullity of the marriage or the invalidating impediment, the promoter of justice had to introduce the petition for nullity unless:

a) the impediment had become public and was certain from the evidence;
b) the removal of scandal demanded that the party petition for nullity;
c) even after the impediment had ceased it was impossible that the marriage be contracted. The law did not define what a public impediment was, but commentators such as Wernz-Vidal said that if the impediment could be proved by public record, public ceremonies, or qualified witnesses, then it was public.[36]

Criminal Action

Every criminal procedure involves three essential elements: the accusation, the trial, and the sentence. All three elements are necessary. The accusation is made by a victim/complainant. But only the promoter of justice could introduce the petitioner to begin the trial of the accused.

According to the 1917 Code, when a member of the faithful had accused another member of the faithful of a crime, an investigation had to be carried out according to canons 1939–1946. Following the investigation, when it was decided that judicial correction was insufficient to repair scandal and restore justice, or if the defendant denied the delict, or if judicial correction was applied without result, then the bishop or an official with a special mandate was required to hand over the acts of the investigation to the promoter of justice. In criminal cases, only the promoter of justice could introduce the criminal action or accusation, so once he had received the acts, the promoter of justice immediately had to present a petition to the judge.

Contentious Cases

A promoter of justice could pursue an action on his own as often as this seemed warranted by the public good.

Contentious trials, like all trials, aim to discover the truth of the matter so that justice can be achieved. Justice is achieved through knowledge of the truth of the matter in question and this justice is achieved through a contention or a legal dispute over a specified question or questions.

When a case was between two clerics concerning a benefice, and one of the clerics died or resigned while the case was in process, the promoter of justice prosecuted the case against the survivor on behalf of the liberty of the benefice or the Church. An exception to this was when the benefice was one freely conferred by the Ordinary and he preferred to award the benefice to the survivor as if he had won.

Provida Mater Ecclesiae

The role of the promoter of justice was clarified in 1936 by the Instruction, *Provida Mater Ecclesiae.*[37] It was always the role of the promoter of justice to petition for the nullity of marriages, and even the Ordinary, who received information concerning the nullity of the marriage, could not act. *Provida Mater* pointed out that the promoter of justice must be involved in the case in which he was attacking the marriage and whenever there was an issue of safeguarding procedural law. When procedural matters were at stake, the involvement of the promoter could come about by decree of the bishop; or the collegiate tribunal either *ex officio* or at the initiative of the promoter of justice himself; or at the request of the defender of the bond; or one of the parties.[38]

Article 35 §1 of *Provida Mater* stated that the parties to the marriage could not petition for the nullity of the marriage if they were the cause of the impediment.[39] Blood relatives of the parties to the marriage could only denounce the nullity of the marriage to the Ordinary or to the promoter of justice. A petition could not be introduced by blood relatives, nor by the parties if they were non-Catholics, baptized or unbaptized.[40] The 1917 Code held that non-Catholics lacked the capacity to act in a tribunal in the Catholic Church. For the public good, non-Catholics needed to be able to get justice within the Catholic Church when, for example, one of them was previously married and now wanted to marry a Catholic in a second marriage or wanted to become a Catholic. The promoter of justice provided the means for them to receive justice.

When there was a case of simulation or conditional consent, the first obligation of the promoter of justice was to advise the parties to come to a decision in conscience and, if possible, remove the cause of the impediment, for example, by making a new act of consent.[41] The parties to a marriage could not petition the nullity of the marriage on the grounds of simulation or condition if they were the ones responsible for the existence of these grounds.[42] In such cases, it was up to the promoter of justice to petition for the nullity of the marriage in question, provided that the guilty party or parties had shown signs of repentance and that there was sufficient supporting evidence for the ground concerned.[43]

When someone denounced a marriage as being invalid with probable evidence of this, the Ordinary or the promoter of justice was to investigate the denunciation cautiously and secretly to ascertain whether the case was a proper one for an *ex officio* accusation according to articles 38 and 39 or whether there should be a dispensation to revalidate the marriage. If, however, the promoter of justice learned that the claim of nullity could not be sustained in law or fact, he was to withdraw it.[44]

When the plaintiff or his or her procurator failed to appear for the joinder of issues after being summoned a second time, the promoter of justice could prosecute the action. The promoter of justice could also prosecute the action when the bishop judged that the public good, namely, the removal of scandal, required it.[45]

If the promoter of justice participated in a case, the presiding judge had to hear his or her submissions[46] before issuing a definitive judgment that settled the main issue in question, settled an incidental question in an interlocutory judgment,[47] summoned witnesses,[48] or removed an advocate by a decree.[49]

THE 1983 CODE

The 1983 Code renewed the requirement that a promoter of justice must be appointed in every diocese for penal cases, as well as for contentious cases in which the public good might be at stake:

> A Promoter of Justice is to be appointed in the diocese for penal cases, and for contentious cases in which the public good may be at stake. The promoter is bound by office to safeguard the public good. (Can. 1430)

Universal law "expressly requires the establishment in each diocese of the ecclesiastical office of promoter of justice."[50] The promoter is restricted to work within the canonical processes of the tribunal and cannot operate with a general mandate to promote justice in the Church.[51] The office of the promoter of justice fosters and safeguards the public good of the Church. The promoter needs to be in full communion according to canon 205, since the person is looking after the interests of the Church in judicial matters. The promoter of justice must take an oath of office, observe secrecy, and not accept gifts.[52] A large diocese could have more than one promoter of justice.

Qualifications

A layperson, either man or woman, can now be appointed as promoter of justice. The promoter of justice must have a doctorate or a licentiate in canon law and is to demonstrate prudence and a zeal for justice.[53] This is to ensure the promoter is competent and professional. For cases involving a priest, however, the promoter must be a priest.[54]

The promoter of justice is to have a reasonable reputation for pursuing matters of justice so that, in carrying out the duties of the office, he or she is considered neither imprudent nor overzealous in pursuing cases.

Term

There is no set term of office, such as five years for the Diocesan Finance Officer in canon 494 or the Episcopal Vicar 477 §1. Canons 187–89 stipulate that the promoter of justice can resign for a just cause or can be removed by the diocesan bishop for a just cause according to canons 192–95. The promoter of justice may be appointed indefinitely or until otherwise provided for.

Public Good

The promoter of justice is bound by office to safeguard the public good. The "public good" is not the same as the "private good" of an individual. Juan Arrieta describes the "public good" as "something closely related to the common good,"[55] which Vatican II described as "the sum total of the social conditions which allow people, either as groups or as individuals, to reach their fulfillment more fully and more easily."[56]

The office of promoter of justice is required to protect the public good and the rights of the Church. The law sometimes clarifies when the public good is involved, such as in marriage cases.[57] The public good is very much at stake in marriage cases that affect families and society. Judgments also affect the salvation of souls. So, a great deal is at stake with decisions about the validity of marriages. The church community is considered to be affected when: laws have been violated; judgments are made concerning juridical persons such as parishes and religious institutes; and in penal cases. In penal cases, the reputation of the Church is often at stake because cases are reported in the media, and so the promoter of justice must protect the good of the Church.

Private individuals whose rights have been violated can personally bring actions to vindicate their rights. A curator or promoter of justice must be involved to protect the rights of: minors; people unable to act for themselves because of diminished mental capacity; or people who cannot act in their own interests for some reason.

Contentious Cases

In contentious cases, which usually concern the private good of individuals, it is for the diocesan bishop to decide if the public good is also at stake.[58] The common good could be at stake when: there is a dispute between a parish priest and a religious institute; prominent people are involved; the event has notoriety; there is damage to third parties; or there could be scandal for the faithful. Great harm could be done to the public good of the Church, and the intervention of the promoter may be necessary to protect the faithful from scandal.[59] Once the promoter of justice has been involved in one instance, it is presumed that he will be involved in any further instances of the case.[60]

Regional Tribunal

When a regional tribunal[61] is established for all cases, as is the situation in New Zealand, provision is to be made for at least one promoter of justice for each diocese in the region. One person could act as a promoter of justice in several dioceses, but, if necessary, more than one promoter of justice could be appointed for the regional tribunal.

In a regional tribunal, the promoter of justice, like other key office holders, is appointed by an absolute majority of the votes cast in a common assembly of the bishops.[62] Once appointed, the Apostolic Signatura must be notified of the appointment. As a rule, the person appointed is to be a priest, a person of integrity, possessing judicial learning and experience, and having the time to properly discharge their duties.[63] A promoter of justice in a regional tribunal can be removed by a common assembly of the bishops, although in an emergency the bishop who acts as moderator of the tribunal could suspend the promoter of justice.[64]

Conflict of Interest

The promoter of justice in a regional tribunal cannot perform other functions in another tribunal, such as act as an advocate or procurator.[65] Just like a judge, the promoter of justice cannot act in a case where the promoter has a personal interest. Personal interest includes having relatives or friends involved in the case. It also includes the situation in which someone has a marked hostility to the promoter of justice, or where the promoter is a trustee or a guardian of a party, or when the promoter could lose money or make a profit because of a decision.[66] A party involved in a case could raise an objection against the promoter of justice so that the promoter is then disqualified from the case as provided for by canon 1449 §4.[67] It is not possible for a promoter of justice to function as such and also be a Defender of the Bond in the same case.[68] (Cf. canons 152; 1436 §1.)

Marriage Cases

Spouses rarely approach a tribunal in a case involving the separation of spouses prior to a divorce. In such a case, the separation of spouses would usually be dealt with using the oral contentious process.[69] This canon also allows for the promoter of justice or a party to seek the ordinary contentious process that would have the effect of slowing the separation process down. Since this ordinary contentious process might cause unnecessary delays, the oral contentious process is the norm.

A marriage may only be examined at the instigation of someone with a lawful right to initiate the process. Since the 1983 Code came into effect, simulators of consent and non-Catholics, whether baptized or not, can petition for a declaration of marriage nullity. As well, the 1983 Code allows for the promoter of justice to introduce a case for the nullity of a marriage when the nullity of the marriage has become public and it cannot be validated or it is not expedient to do so.[70] There may be a number of reasons that make it impossible to convalidate a marriage. The couple might be divorced. There could be extraordinary situations, such as when a mentally ill person will not petition on their own behalf, but a psychiatrist thinks that it would be good for the person that there is a declaration by the Church that this was not a marriage according to the criteria of the Catholic Church. In such a case the promoter of justice could petition for nullity. Another case could be when a Catholic is civilly married to a previously married non-Catholic, who refuses to seek a declaration of nullity despite public evidence that he was invalidly married; for example, because of ligamen, the promoter of justice could petition for a declaration of nullity. According to canon 1674 of the 1983 Code, the promoter of justice may intervene in a marriage case to petition the invalidity of a marriage:

> The following are qualified to challenge a marriage: 1/ the spouses; 2/ the promoter of justice when nullity has already become public, if the convalidation of the marriage is not possible or expedient.

Unlike a penal case, where the participation of the promoter of justice is obligatory,[71] in a marriage case the participation of the promoter is more often at the discretion of the judge.

Dignitas Connubii article 57 requires the promoter of justice to intervene when it is a matter of safeguarding procedural law:

> §1. The Promoter of Justice must take part when he challenges a marriage in accordance with art. 92, no. 2. §2. The Promoter of Justice, by virtue of a decree issued by the judge, whether ex officio or at the instance of the defender of the bond or a party, must take part when it is a matter of safeguarding a procedural law, especially when the question concerns the nullity of the acts or exceptions.[72]

The promoter of justice is to ensure that the procedural law of the Church is followed. His or her involvement can only be requested by the parties or an officer of the tribunal such as a defender of the bond.

The acts of a case are invalid if the promoter of justice was not cited as required:

> Article 60. If the defender of the bond or the Promoter of Justice, if his presence is required, have not been cited, the acts are invalid unless the same persons, even though not cited, actually took part, or at least, having examined the acts, were each able to perform their proper function before the sentence (cf. canon 1433).[73]

The law provides for the validity of the acts if the promoter of justice was present and could have acted, even though he had not taken part.

If the marriage is being challenged by the promoter of justice in accordance with article 92, both petitioner and respondent are to be cited:

> Article 126. If the marriage is being challenged by the Promoter of Justice in accordance with art. 92, no. 2, both parties are to be cited.[74]

The promoter of justice can be present at the examination of parties and witnesses.[75] The promoter can also inspect judicial acts, even if they are not yet published, and can also examine documents produced by the parties. The promoter of justice can have a more obvious presence in a case under the 1983 Code because of provisions giving the right to be present when parties or witnesses are interviewed.

Serial Marriage Cases

If an abuse of procedural law occurs in a tribunal, the promoter of justice must deal with the abuse. Tribunal officials should denounce abuses to the promoter of justice, who can then challenge procedures used and the decisions given. On June 18, 1987, the Apostolic Signatura wrote concerning abuses in declaring serial marriage null and said:

> If a tribunal has used another method of proceeding in declaring the nullity of several marriages successively entered, the Defender of the Bond of the tribunal which declared the nullity of the first marriage, and also any other person apprised of the matter, is bound to denounce the abuse to the competent Promoter of Justice who, by reason of the public good, will be held to attack the decisions respecting the successive marriages, and also of a new marriage ultimately entered.[76]

This is a practical example of the role of the promoter of justice when a tribunal has ceased to uphold the teaching of the Church on marriage.

The promoter of justice could also address the situation where the official witness of the Church did not properly investigate the freedom of the parties to marry. This could be the situation when a party concealed a previous marriage, or where a priest celebrant ignored the fact that a party was previously married, or thought that it was invalid, and still officiated at a new wedding. The promoter of justice could act as petitioner in such a case to protect the public good.[77] There could be pastoral considerations that make it important that the promoter of justice be the petitioner to regularize the situation.

Penal Cases

The good of the Church community is always at stake in penal cases. Therefore, the law provides for the involvement of the promoter of justice in all penal cases[78] and the promoter of justice is the petitioner.[79]

The Preliminary Investigation

When there is a claim that a crime has probably been committed by a cleric,[80] the Ordinary must arrange for a preliminary investigation to be carried out according to canons 1717–1719. Sometimes, the preliminary investigation cannot be fully carried out because the Ordinary is notified that a priest has been arrested by civil authorities. The Church must wait until the civil processes are finished. Carrying out a church investigation would often be impossible, or in conflict with, or counterproductive to the police investigation. However, the law does provide for more grave crime allegations, in canon 1722, that the Ordinary can, after consulting the promoter of justice and summoning the accused person to appear, prohibit the accused person from the exercise of sacred ministry, or from exercising an ecclesiastical office or position, or impose or forbid residence in a certain place or territory, or even prohibit public participation in the blessed Eucharist.[81]

> At any stage of the process, in order to prevent scandal, protect the freedom of the witnesses and safeguard the course of justice, the Ordinary can, after consulting the Promoter of Justice and summoning the accused person to appear, prohibit the accused from the exercise of the sacred ministry or of some ecclesiastical office and position, or impose or forbid residence in a certain place or territory, or even prohibit public participation in the blessed Eucharist. If, however, the reason ceases, all these restrictions are to be revoked; they cease by virtue of the law itself as soon as the penal process ceases. (Can. 1722)

Ordinaries often do not consult the promoter of justice, but for the validity of the process, they must follow this requirement of procedural law. The promoter of justice must "protect the rights of the accuser and the accused."[82] Victoria Vondenberger notes that "immediately removing a priest from ministry when an accusation is first received may do harm to the priest's reputation which cannot be adequately repaired if the preliminary investigation finds that there is no semblance of truth to the accusation."[83] Therefore, the Ordinary must consult with the promoter of justice before acting. The cleric must be "given an opportunity to be heard and to respond to the accusations which have been made against him."[84] However, a cleric cannot be told the name of his accuser in delicts concerning the sanctity of the sacrament of Penance unless the accuser expressly consents to this.[85] The rights of an accused cleric must be respected and he can only be punished in accord with the norm of law.[86] Ordinaries often explain that the accused cleric is on "administrative leave." This means that he cannot present himself as a priest or wear clerical dress and is prohibited from the exercise of public ministry. This enables Ordinaries to prevent scandal, demonstrate a concern for the integrity of the process, protect the freedom of witnesses, and expedite the course of justice.

When the allegations concern crimes that are not categorized as "more grave crimes," at any stage of the penal process, the Ordinary can invoke canon 392 and prohibit the exercise of sacred ministry and decide where the accused will live and under what terms. The Dicastery for Legislative Texts (no. 191) explains:

> *Disciplinary measures that may be necessary*
>
> When the circumstances require it, the ecclesiastical Authority can take certain disciplinary measures (other than the precautionary ones [cf. 206]) against the suspect. The reason why these measures are necessary (formally different from those allowed only once

> the process has started) is that they help protect the good reputation of the people involved, they help protect the public good, they help avoid scandal and they help prevent the recurrence of what was reported. Can. 1722 explicitly authorizes the adoption of precautionary measures "at any stage of the process." However, during the preliminary investigation, with just cause and on the basis of the ordinary attributions that are proper to it (cf. can. 392), the ecclesiastical Authority can adopt by Decree (cf. Appendix 3) adequate disciplinary measures, proportional, and reasonably limited in time: for example, by limiting the exercise of the pastoral ministry or ecclesiastical office of the subject under investigation, even in cases not reserved to the Dicastery for the Doctrine of the Faith.[87]

The United States Conference of Catholic Bishops decided in no. 5 of their *Charter for the Protection of Children and Young People* that "it is desirable that the Promoter of justice participate in the meetings of the review board."[88] The promoter of justice is not a member of the review board, but hearing the discussions of the board should give the promoter a good understanding of the various aspects of a particular case.

Penal Judicial Process

Following the preliminary investigation, if the delict is not reserved to the Dicastery for the Doctrine of the Faith, the Ordinary may initiate a penal trial. If the delict has a semblance of truth and is reserved to the Dicastery for the Doctrine of the Faith, the Ordinary must send the case to that Dicastery with his votum, reporting the delict and stating what actions he has taken. Article 19 of the norms for grave delicts allows for the extrajudicial process (administrative):

> Art. 19 §1 Whenever the Congregation for the Doctrine of the Faith has decided that an extrajudicial process should be initiated, can. 1720 *CIC* or can. 1486 *CCEO* is to be applied. §2 With the prior mandate of the Congregation for the Doctrine of the Faith, perpetual expiatory penalties may be imposed.
>
> Art. 20 §1 The extrajudicial process may be carried out by the Congregation for the Doctrine of the Faith or by an Ordinary or Hierarch or by their Delegate.[89]

The Dicastery for the Doctrine of the Faith has the right to present directly to the Supreme Pontiff the gravest cases for dismissal from the clerical state:

> Art. 26: It is the right of the Congregation for the Doctrine of the Faith, in whatever stage and grade of the unfolding of the proceedings, to present directly the most grave cases mentioned above in articles 2–6 to the decision of the Supreme Pontiff with regard to dismissal or deposition from the clerical state, together with dispensation from the law of celibacy, when it is manifestly evident that the delict has been committed, after having given the guilty party the possibility of defending himself.[90]

The Ordinary may request authorization for a penal trial or an administrative process for dismissal from the clerical state.

Penal Trial

A penal trial may be authorized by a diocesan bishop or a dicastery such as the Dicastery for the Doctrine of the Faith. If the Dicastery for the Doctrine of the Faith authorizes a penal trial, their promoter of justice is acting in the case. If the alleged crimes are not reserved to the Dicastery for the Doctrine of the Faith, the Ordinary decrees that there be a penal trial and gives the acts of the preliminary investigation to the promoter of justice, asking the promoter of justice to present a petition of accusation for the judges to accept the case:

> If the Ordinary decrees that a penal judicial process is to be initiated, he is to pass the acts of the investigation to the Promoter of justice, who is to present to the judge a petition of accusation in accordance with canons 1502 and 1504. (Can. 1721 §1)[91]

The petition in a penal trial must be addressed to the Judicial Vicar, signed by the promoter of justice, and state:

1. what is being sought and from whom;
2. the right upon which the petitioner bases the case and in general the facts and proofs;
3. the domicile or quasi-domicile of the respondent.[92]

Penal trials that can result in dismissal from the clerical state must be judged by a collegiate tribunal:

> §1. With every contrary custom reprobated, the following cases are reserved to a collegiate tribunal of three judges:...2/ penal cases: a) concerning delicts which can entail the penalty of dismissal from the clerical state; b) concerning the imposition or declaration of an excommunication. §2. The bishop can entrust more difficult cases or those of greater importance to the judgment of three or five judges. (Can. 1425)

The tribunal must be competent and would usually be the tribunal where the delict was committed.[93] If two or more tribunals were competent, the right of adjudicating belongs to the one that legitimately cited the respondent first.[94]

The promoter of justice is required to establish with moral certainty that the crime was committed[95] by the accused since canon 1526 §1 states: "The burden of proof rests upon the person who makes the allegation." The case should be concluded within one year.[96]

The promoter of justice can present the petition to any competent judge. Usually, there are two sources of competence (lawful jurisdiction and legal authority) in a penal trial. They are:

a) the forum of the respondent[97]
b) the forum where the alleged offense was perpetrated.[98]

The petition (libellus), dated and signed by the promoter of justice, requests the judge to begin a penal trial of the person accused of having committed a particular offense.[99] Like any petition, it should state in general terms the facts, the accused and his address, and the witnesses and proofs to support the allegation,[100] and should raise the issues for the judge of the tribunal to decide:

1. Did the accused commit the crime?
2. Is the imputability of the accused confirmed as it is presumed by canon 1321 §4?[101]
3. If the accused is guilty, what penalty is to be imposed?
4. If they have not yet been addressed, how are damages to be addressed?[102]

The petition must be accepted or rejected by the judge. The judge must be competent and the time limit for criminal prosecution must not have elapsed. When the judge has accepted the case, he must cite the promoter of justice and the accused to appear,[103] and invite them to respond in writing or to appear before him within twenty days. A copy of the petition is to be attached to the citation.

At the joinder of issues, it is important that the issues to be addressed are clear and specific. They must concretize the issues in the case, otherwise, the administration of justice will be more difficult.

The judge decrees the joinder of issue and notifies the promoter of justice and the accused person of this. Both the promoter of justice and the accused have ten days within which to object to the joinder of issue.[104] Once the joinder of issue has been decreed, the preliminary part of the trial is completed, and the evidence is then collected. The judge gives the promoter of justice and the accused a suitable period to present their proofs,[105] and it is the promoter of justice who must present the proofs on behalf of the accuser. It must be remembered that it takes a great deal of courage for an accuser, without an advocate, "to submit oneself to an unknown process run by a Church through whose minister one suffered abuse. The promoter of justice must be careful to see that the penal trial respects the accuser."[106] Vondenberger gives the example of a penal process in which the clerical judges did not wear clerical dress when the accuser was interviewed to make it easier for him.[107]

The judge or the auditor who is his delegate questions the witnesses. Both the accused person and the promoter of justice may submit questions to the judge that they would like the accused person and witnesses to be asked.[108] The judge may allow the promoter to be present at the questioning of any of these people.[109] The promoter's presence then also enables further questions to be posed according to canon 1561.[110]

The promoter of justice is responsible for organizing the evidence in the case (canon 1526) and for providing evidence on behalf of the accuser, who also has a right to a good reputation.[111] The necessary and relevant evidence would include information from a cleric's personnel file; secular court records if they exist; psychological and medical records.[112] The promoter of justice may request evidence from an expert witness or ask to have a psychological expert give an evaluation or an opinion based on the evidence in the acts.[113] The promoter of justice must work to ensure that the truth of the matter in question is manifested, and the promoter's role is not to seek a conviction at any cost.[114] The promoter of justice has the right to reply to the rejoinder of parties.[115] Furthermore, the judge could ask the promoter of justice to present observations if the parties fail to provide sufficient evidence.

The diocesan bishop would have appointed the delegate to carry out the preliminary investigation. The delegate should have accessed the personnel file of the priest as part of the preliminary investigation.[116] How much evidence was collected during the preliminary investigation will determine how much more evidence needs to be collected during the extrajudicial process and trial. Witnesses may need to be interviewed on oath to confirm the truth of their statements made during the preliminary investigation.

Evidence might include statements of the accused, reports of experts, visits to the presbytery/site of the alleged crime, other corroborating elements, and evidence of other accusations against the priest that might establish patterns in how assaults happened. If there is only one witness, the revised canon 1678 for marriage cases could be invoked; testimonials to the credibility of the accuser could be obtained and consistencies in the accuser's evidence could be pointed out.

The promoter of justice has a right to see all the evidence in the case[117] and to review documents before they are published.[118]

When all the acts of the case have been published, both the promoter of justice and the accused are to be given the opportunity to present further evidence.[119]

The promoter of justice has the right to respond to every written reply of the accused.[120] Replies of the accused would include his explanations about what happened. The accused person has the right to give the last evidence and submission.[121] Therefore, following the conclusion of the case, the promoter of justice presents his or her pleadings first. Then the advocate for the accused presents his/her pleadings.[122]

The promoter of justice may lodge a plaint of nullity by virtue of his or her public function to defend the good of the Church.[123] Grocholewski argues that the promoter has the obligation to argue in favor of the public good of the Church.[124]

The promoter of justice must argue why he believes it has been proven that the accused was guilty of the crime. The promoter could identify the absence of elements that might diminish or rule out imputability and finally propose an appropriate penalty.

In a penal trial it may become apparent that the accused is falsely accused or that the allegations cannot be proven. Under these circumstances, the promoter of justice can renounce the trial at the order of or with the consent of the Ordinary.[125] The promoter of justice cannot renounce the trial if the Ordinary is opposed to the renunciation.[126] However, for validity, the accused must accept the renunciation unless the judge has declared the accused absent from the trial.[127] If it has become widely known that the penal process is occurring, then the accused may want to seek a judicial acquittal, so that there is a definite judgment that he has not been proven guilty and is innocent.[128]

Administrative Process for Dismissal

If the Dicastery for the Doctrine of the Faith authorizes an administrative penal process, the Ordinary decrees accordingly and gives the acts of the preliminary investigation and the decree of the Dicastery for the Doctrine of the Faith to the promoter of justice. Canon 1721 §1 states that the promoter "is to present to the judge a petition of accusation in accordance with canons 1502 and 1504."

The Dicastery for Evangelization or the Dicastery for Clergy may authorize an extrajudicial process for dismissal from the clerical state using their special faculties. These special faculties require the involvement of the promoter of justice.[129]

The petition of the promoter of justice must state: the right upon which the petitioner bases the case and, in general, the facts and proofs; the decision of the relevant Dicastery; the law concerning the alleged crimes; what is being sought and from whom; the domicile or quasi-domicile of the respondent; and be signed by the promoter of justice.[130]

The evidence would be collected in a similar manner and from similar sources as they would be in a penal trial.

The promoter of justice has a right to see all evidence in an administrative case.[131] The promoter of justice can inspect the judicial acts and review all the evidence[132] and can respond to the replies of the accused and his explanations about what happened.

The promoter of justice[133] must argue why he believes it has been proven that the accused was guilty of the crime. The promoter could identify the absence of elements that might diminish or rule out imputability and finally propose an appropriate penalty. However, the accused has the right to give the last evidence in the case and his advocate makes the final submission.[134]

FAILURE TO ACT

In the unlikely event that a promoter of justice refuses to present the petition as the Ordinary decreed, the Ordinary could appoint another promoter of justice. However, this would not appear to be objective and would give the impression of an unjust process.

If the public good of the Church is at stake, the promoter cannot abstain from acting. Grocholewski argues that if a promoter fails to act as he should, this is grounds for removal from office or for the imposition of a penalty.[135] Examining the acts is absolutely necessary in his/her role.[136]

If the Ordinary refuses to act on a complaint concerning a delict of a cleric, the promoter of justice is powerless to act. The promoter of justice cannot obtain the acts of the case directly from the delegate and independently of the Ordinary.

Appeal by the Promoter of Justice

All the faithful have a right to a decision that is consistent with the truth.[137] If the evidence indicates that the accused has committed another crime, the promoter can bring it forward to the Dicastery for the Doctrine of the Faith.[138] It can then be judged by the Dicastery.

Apart from the issue of whether the sentence is consistent with the truth of the matter, the judge might have only imposed a very light penalty for an offense or might not have even imposed any penalty at all.[139] The promoter of justice might consider that the decision does not sufficiently provide for the reparation of scandal and the restitution of justice and is in fact unjust to the good of the Church or the victim.[140]

The promoter of justice has wide rights and could lodge a plaint of nullity against the sentence.[141] This right to lodge a plaint of nullity is based on the importance of protecting the public good, which is the purpose of the office. The resulting decree of nullity could be either of remediable or irremediable nullity.[142] The promoter could also seek a *restitutio in integrum*.[143]

Once the judge pronounces judgment, the promoter of justice could appeal a decision[144] that he believes does not restore justice, reform the offender, or repair the scandal. Canon 1628[145] enables the promoter of justice to appeal cases to a higher judge, except in those circumstances listed in 1629.[146]

The promoter of justice of the Appeal Tribunal can renounce an appeal.[147] This office holder is independent of the promoter of justice at first instance and may simply see the facts and/or the law differently from the first-instance promoter of justice.

If the promoter of justice has intervened at any instance, it is presumed that the promoter of justice is required at any further instance.[148] Therefore, if a promoter of justice was involved in a case at first instance, then the promoter of justice for the appeal tribunal must be involved in the case. The acts would be invalid if the promoter of justice was required and was not given the opportunity to fulfill the role properly.

Contentious Cases

The promoter of justice may present a petition in a contentious case to the diocesan bishop.[149] This provision is because of the public good that the promoter of justice by office aims to protect. In contentious cases, it is for the diocesan bishop to decide whether or not the public good is at stake.[150]

Nullity of Orders

There is no reference to the promoter of justice petitioning in an invalidity of orders case (c. 1708). The canon only mentions the cleric, the bishop of ordination, and the Ordinary to whom he is subject. The promoter of justice could always inform the Ordinary if there was public scandal about the invalidity of the ordination.

The promoter of justice may also initiate a case declaring the invalidity of an ordination. The Congregation of Divine Worship and the Discipline of the Sacraments issued a decree on October 16, 2001, concerning the regulations to be observed for the declaration of nullity of sacred ordination. Article 2, stated concerning the petition:

> §1. Apart from the cleric and the Ordinary competent according to Canon 1708, the validity of ordination may be impugned by the Promoter of justice of the diocese of incardination or of the residence of the cleric.[151]

Canonization

Under the 1917 Code, a promoter of justice had to participate and be cited in the canonization process for its validity.[152] The promoter of justice could be constituted for all causes or be appointed for a particular cause.[153]

The present law refers to the promoter of justice being involved at the diocesan level and being responsible for protecting the common good of the Church by furthering justice. He must see to it that the truth prevails concerning the life and actions of a person who is proposed for canonization. At the Dicastery for the Causes of the Saints, the promoter is referred to as the "promoter of faith."[154]

The diocesan bishop appoints the promoter of justice for the cause. He must be a priest, competent in theology and canonical matters. If the person proposed for canonization lived a long time ago, the historical skills possessed by a promoter of justice are very important as well. The promoter of justice is to receive all documents and reports and from these can prepare a list of questions to be asked of witnesses. This part of the diocesan inquiry concerns the virtues, martyrdom, or miracles of the candidate proposed for canonization. Jason Gray notes:

> Among the officials, however, the promoter of justice is singled out for his particular vigilance over the completeness of the inquiry: "Art. 56 §1. The Promoter of Justice must be vigilant so that everything prescribed by law is faithfully observed in instructing the cause. §2. He must also see to it that all the acts and documents relative to the object of the Inquiry have been gathered in a thorough manner."[155] The particular nature of these obligations distinguishes the promoter of justice from the other officials in the inquiry. These duties to see that the law is observed and that all the proofs have been gathered help to uniquely define his role and demonstrate the importance of his participation.[156]

Usually, the promoter of justice is present when witnesses are questioned. If the promoter of justice is absent, he must explain for the acts of the case why he was absent and then must examine the acts afterward. He may ask for further inquiry or questioning on particular points. Once the promoter of justice, the postulator, and the bishop or his delegate are satisfied that all the proofs have been collected, the diocesan inquiry concludes. Then the acts of the cause are forwarded to the Dicastery for the Causes of the Saints.

CONCLUSION

The role of the promoter of justice in marriage cases has declined since the law now allows non-Catholics and simulators to be petitioners before the tribunals.

However, the office of promoter of justice is growing in importance in other areas of tribunal activity. There have been hundreds of accusations of sexual abuse by clergy, and as the accusations have mounted, the credibility of the Church has been undermined. The most appropriate ways for bishops to handle these accusations are through penal trials and administrative processes. In such processes, the promoter of justice has an essential role and must be chosen wisely. In all cases and circumstances, the promoter of justice should facilitate reaching the truth of the matter in question.

4

RIGHTS OF ALLEGED VICTIMS

People everywhere are becoming more aware of human rights. There are now general expectations that nations and organizations do their best to prevent violations of human rights, properly investigate any violations that do happen, ensure there is full reparation for victims, and take all measures to ensure the violations do not happen again.[1]

In judicial systems in the past, the emphasis was on the prosecution of the crime. Now there has been a move from a focus on the one who allegedly committed the crime to more care for the alleged victim. Maria Ines Franck notes that "the emphasis, therefore, seems to have shifted from determining the guilt of the perpetrator and the sanction to be applied to that criminal conduct, to the rights, feelings and expectations of those who have suffered the crime."[2] However, as Kevin McKenna rightly indicates, the Church can provide both due process for accused clergy and religious and justice for sex abuse victims.[3]

The rights of victims have been advanced in civil law by the European Parliament and these have been implemented by European countries.[4] Within the framework of European Union law, Directive 2012/29/EU, on the rights and protection of crime victims, all member European States have to ensure that "in criminal investigations, all statements taken from child victims may be recorded by audiovisual means and these recorded statements may be used as evidence in criminal proceedings" (art. 24.1.a). Directive 2012/29/EU of October 25, 2012, also established minimum standards on the rights, support, and protection of victims of crime. Similarly, French law has also been changed so that victims have rights to information, to active participation in the criminal trial, and to reparation for damages. The preliminary article of the French code of criminal procedures states that "criminal procedure must be fair and adversarial and preserve the balance of the rights of the parties."[5] Most European countries provide counseling and other support for victims.

The federal statutes of the United States

recognize a list of ten minimum rights, presented here by Mary Graw Leary:

> To be reasonably protected from the accused; obtain a reasonable, accurate and timely notice of any public court proceeding or any parole proceeding involving the crime or of any release of or escape by the accused; not be excluded from any public court proceeding, unless the court, after receiving clear and convincing evidence, determines that testimony by the victim would be materially altered if the victim heard other testimony at that proceeding; be reasonably heard at any public proceeding in the district court involving release, plea, sentencing or any parole proceeding; confer with the attorney for the government in the case; full and timely restitution as provided in law; proceedings free from unreasonable delay; be treated with fairness and with respect for the victim's dignity and privacy.[6]

Within the Catholic Church, the issue of rights of victims in canon law is being discussed, and proposals are being made to ensure victims' rights are upheld. There was a seminar in 2019 on "Promoting and Protecting the Dignity of Persons in Allegations of Abuse of Minors and Vulnerable Adults: Balancing Confidentiality, Transparency and Accountability." One of the papers was presented by Archbishop Scicluna entitled "The Rights of Victims in Canonical Penal Processes."[7] This led to another seminar in December 2021 organized by the Pontifical Commission for the Protection of Minors on "The Rights of Alleged Victims in Penal Procedures." The status of victims' rights in canon law has been analyzed and recommendations were made for better procedures and standards.

RIGHTS OF VICTIMS TO ASSISTANCE AND SUPPORT

Canon lawyers working on marriage cases consider it routine for each of the parties to have an advocate. While the present code provides for advocates for both parties in a marriage case according to canon 1481, the same provision is not made in the Code of Canon Law for the alleged victim in a penal case. Only the accused must have an advocate as per canon 1723.

Pope Francis wrote a letter to the Chilean people on May 31, 2018, in which he admitted with shame that victims were not listened to and Church authorities did not react in time.[8] Pope Francis legislated for the rights of victims to assistance and support in the revised *Vos Estis Lux Mundi*:

> Art. 5. Care for persons. §1. The ecclesiastical Authorities shall commit themselves to ensuring that those who state that they have been harmed, together with their families, are to be treated with dignity and respect, and, in particular, are to be: a) welcomed, listened to and supported, including through provision of specific services; b) offered spiritual assistance; c) offered medical assistance, including therapeutic and psychological assistance, as required

> by the specific case. §2. The legitimate protection of the good name and the privacy of all persons involved, as well as the confidentiality of their personal data, must be ensured. To the aforementioned persons the presumption addressed in article 13 §7 shall apply, without prejudice to the provisions of article 20.

Article 5 gives alleged victims and their families the rights to be treated with dignity and respect; to be welcomed and listened to; and to be supported with medical, psychological, and spiritual help. This article states that victims and their families are to be "supported, including through provision of specific services," which would include advocates and canonical advisors.

The Dicastery for the Doctrine of the Faith states in its *Vademecum*:

> The ecclesiastical authorities must ensure that the alleged victim and his or her family are treated with dignity and respect, and must offer them welcome, attentive hearing and support, also through dedicated services, as well as spiritual, medical and psychological help, as required by the specific case (cf. art. 5 VELM). (*Vademecum* 55)

Alleged victims need a knowledge of the processes and what will happen in their specific case. For an alleged victim to be cared for, there needs to be someone such as a victim assistance coordinator[9] and, if necessary, an advocate to advise the alleged victim about processes and their rights. Yeshica Calderon notes that victims need to be aware of structures in dioceses so that they can present a complaint.[10] This requires an accessible system and possibly the help of a victim assistance coordinator. The United States Conference of Catholic Bishops explains to victims that they can:

> Contact a diocesan or eparchial victim assistance coordinator who is available to help victims/survivors make a formal complaint of abuse to the diocese or eparchy. The Victim Assistance Coordinator is also available to arrange a personal meeting with the bishop or his representative and to obtain support for the needs of the individual and families.[11]

Victims often suffer from post-traumatic stress disorder (PTSD). The alleged victim has suffered spiritually, emotionally, and psychologically. Mark Bartchak states that, in his experience, all those involved with dealing with alleged victims need to be trauma informed as well as knowledgeable about canon law.[12] Tribunal officials can easily retraumatize victims by making unnecessary, judgmental statements about alleged victims without any understanding of the trauma they have experienced.

Bartchak noted that crimes involving the sacrament of Penance, such as solicitation, can affect the victim physically, psychologically, emotionally, and spiritually.[13] The alleged victim is a key witness and often the only one who witnessed the crime. When the judge or delegate interviews the alleged victim,[14] the person must be treated properly, and their complaint must be taken seriously.

For this reason, Bartchak believes that it is very important for the judge or the delegate to interview the alleged victim personally.

RECEPTION OF INFORMATION CONCERNING A CRIME

When information is received about an offense, the Ordinary should initiate a preliminary investigation to establish the facts and circumstances of the allegation as well as the imputability of the offense unless this enquiry would be entirely superfluous. The Doctrine of the Faith *Vademecum* states:

> Art. 10 §1 SST (cf. also canons 1717 CIC and 1468 CCEO) states that, when a *notitia de delicto* is received, a preliminary investigation ought to ensue, provided that the report is "*saltem verisimilis*." If that plausibility proves unfounded, there is no need to pursue the *notitia de delicto*, although care should be taken to keep the documentation, together with a written explanation regarding the reasons for the decision. (no. 16)

The alleged victim will usually be interviewed as part of this preliminary investigation, so already at this stage, the alleged victim should have the help of a victim's assistance coordinator and an advocate. After the preliminary investigation is completed, the Ordinary will decide whether the accusation is credible and if a judicial or extrajudicial process is to be used.

RESOLVING DAMAGES AT THE END OF THE PRELIMINARY INVESTIGATION

Canon 1718 §4 allows for the process to resolve the question of damages at the end of the preliminary investigation:

> Before making a decree in accordance with §1, the Ordinary is to consider whether, to avoid useless trials, it would be expedient, with the parties' consent, for himself or the investigator to make a decision, according to what is good and equitable, about the question of damages. (Can. 1718 §4)

The alleged victim needs to have an advocate advising them of the options available to them during the process. The alleged victim cannot participate in the judicial or extrajudicial penal process that follows if they accept an award for damages at the end of the preliminary investigation.

PENAL PROCESS

The penal process has the aims of the restoration of justice, the reform of the offender, and the repair of scandal.[15] The penal process is initiated by the promoter of justice,[16] not the alleged victim, because the good of the church community is always at stake in penal cases. Therefore, the promoter of justice is the petitioner in a penal trial and is a party in the process.[17] Gianpaolo Montini explains that the public good and public order are protected by penal law and, correspondingly, by the penal process: "Public good and public order are proper to all members of the Church and are not exclusive to any particular individual member."[18]

RIGHTS OF THE VICTIM AND RIGHTS OF THE ACCUSED

The Dicastery for the Doctrine of the Faith in its *Vademecum* (no. 54) advises in the interests of justice that an accused has legal advice from when he is notified of the accusation during the preliminary investigation. It is not obligatory in law for the accused to have an advocate during the preliminary investigation, but the accused must have an advocate during a penal trial.[19] The Dicastery for the Doctrine of the Faith in its *Vademecum* insists that the accused has legal advice in an extrajudicial penal process:

> With the new *Norms* promulgated in 2021 (cf. art. 20 §7 SST), it is explicitly stipulated by the law for the case of an extrajudicial process in matters reserved to the DDF that the accused, in accordance with the prescriptions of canons 1723 and 1481 §§1–2 CIC, be assisted by an advocate and/or procurator, either of his own choice or, otherwise, appointed *ex officio*. The Ordinary (or his delegate) must be informed of the appointment of the advocate and/or procurator by means of a suitable and authentic procuratorial mandate in accordance with canon 1484 §1 CIC, prior to the session in which the accusations and proofs are made known, in order to verify that the requirements of canon 1483 CIC have been met. (no. 98)

If the alleged victim does not have canonical advice about their rights and the procedures being followed, the perception will be that the system is biased against them.

Justice System Needs an Alleged Victim

Victims have common needs, as explained by Mark Bartchak:

1. to feel safe;
2. to express their emotions;
3. to know what comes next after their victimization.[20]

These needs can only be met in a process in which the victims feel cared for. In canon law, the alleged victim cannot initiate and promote penal action and is not necessarily a party in the penal process. The accused must have an advocate/procurator and is advised to have a civil lawyer. Justice requires that the alleged victim also have representation and advice about procedures and their rights.

It is a fact that any justice system cannot exist without the active participation of the alleged victim. Gianpaolo Montini observes that in canon law the victim has a right to:

> know the accusations and evidence disputed in the summons of the accused (cf. can. 540 SN)[21]; 19. establish one or more defenders (lawyers) and a procu-

rator (cf. can. 553, §1 SN); 20. as well as request free legal aid;—propose exceptions and proof (cf. can. 553, §1 SN);—participate in the discussion of the case (cf. can. 569, §1 SN); 22. request an exemption from legal expenses (cf. can. 576 SN). 23. In a single word, the victim is a "party" in the penal process in all respects, "as a true party in the case," as underlined in can. 553, §1 SN.[22]

Protection from the Accused

The Dicastery for the Doctrine of the Faith is conscious of the need to ensure such things as the avoidance of contact between the accused and the alleged victim. Even an accidental meeting at a shopping center can cause grave upset for the alleged victim. The accused must be living far enough away from the alleged victim to avoid such accidental meetings:

> Here it should be mentioned that in cases of improper and imprudent conduct, even in the absence of a delict involving minors, should it prove necessary to protect the common good and to avoid scandal, the Ordinary or Hierarch is competent to take other administrative provisions with regard to the person accused (for example, restrictions on his ministry), or to impose the penal remedies mentioned in canon 1339 CIC for the purpose of preventing delicts (cf. canon 1312 §3 CIC) or to give the public reprimand referred to in canon 1427 CCEO. In the case of delicts that are *non graviora*, the Ordinary or Hierarch should employ the juridical means appropriate to the particular circumstances. (no. 20)

Knowledge and Understanding of the Process

In 1950, Pope Pius XII published an apostolic letter, *Sollicitudinem Nostram*.[23] It contained procedural canon law for the Eastern Churches in full communion with Rome and remained in force until 1991 when the Code of Canons of the Eastern Churches, hereafter CCEO, came into force. Gianpaolo Montini is of the opinion that:

> although the procedural rules of the aforementioned motu proprio [*Sollicitudinem Nostram*] are not formally in force today, they can still be considered binding due to the fact that they emerge as logical deductions from the setting of the current canons 1729–1731, canons that fully transpose, albeit in abbreviated form (as in the style of the current Code) the setting of the aforementioned motu proprio.[24]

Aidan McGrath notes:

> This position appears to find support in canon 1477 §1 CCEO: "The promoter of justice, the accused and the advocate for the accused, and the injured party mentioned in can. 1483 §1 and that person's advocate take part in the discussion." If the injured party and the advocate for that party can take part in the discussion of a case, this logically means the injured party has the rights highlighted by Monsignor Montini.[25]

Intervention in the Process

A victim must be informed of their right to intervene so that they can participate and exercise their right.[26] Gianpaolo Montini points out:

> 1) no right exists for the victim to intervene in an administrative penal process; 2) the Ordinary can—at his discretion—deny the victim who requests it the opportunity to intervene in the administrative penal process with the request for the reparation of damages; 3) the victim may request access to the final decision in the administrative penal process to then assess whether to request compensation for damages in front of the tribunal of the competent ordinary (request to be resolved as provided above [n. 4] in case n. 5).[27]

The intervention of the alleged victim is at the discretion of the Ordinary. The Apostolic Signatura has accepted that for a disciplinary process, the victim could be allowed to intervene in the extrajudicial process for the reparation of damages since canons 1729–31 apply by analogy.[28] This means that since the victim can request for reparation of damages,[29] the alleged victim must be fully informed about their rights as the case proceeds. The Church process can require a clerical abuser with assets to use them for reparation. Also, there could be a directive that a percentage of a cleric's remuneration be diverted to a victim. These measures also show the Church being proactive using its own processes as much as possible so that victims are not forced to go to civil courts.

The jurisprudence of the Apostolic Signatura allows for the redacted publication of the decree of adjudication or sentence.[30] The alleged victim has the right to see these documents but often the alleged victim is not made aware of this right.

This requires an official who informs them of their rights and tells them of procedural developments such as the accused being summoned. They then have an opportunity to participate and give their views in the citation hearing.[31] The victim could then inform the judge of one of these stances:

> 1) simple or qualified absence; 2) disinterest in the penal process; 3) request to be informed of the progress of the penal process; 4) request for admission to constitute a civil party; 5) request to accede to the definitive judicial decision in view of the possible proposal of an (autonomous) case for the reparation of damages.[32]

Montini notes that positions 3, 4, and 5 necessitate the victim having a lawyer or procurator whom they have chosen to assist them.

Montini identifies the right of the alleged victim to intervene in the penal process.[33] Canon 1729 states: "In the penal trial itself an injured party can bring a contentious action to repair damages incurred personally from the delict, according to the norm of can. 1596."

Canon 1730 allows the judge in a penal trial to defer but not to deny a judgment for damages until after a definitive sentence has been given or because of an appeal:

> §1. To avoid excessive delay in a penal trial, the judge can postpone the trial concerning damages until he has given a definitive judgement in the penal trial. §2. When the judge does this he must, after giving judgement in the penal trial, hear the case concerning damages, even though the penal trial is still pending because of a proposed challenge to it, or even though the accused has been acquitted, when the reason for the acquittal does not take away the obligation to make good the damages.

Active Participation throughout the Penal Process

Canon 1596 outlines how a third party who could be a victim, can intervene in the penal process:

> §1. A person who has an interest can be admitted to intervene in a case at any instance of the litigation, either as a party defending a right or in an accessory way to help a litigant. §2. To be admitted, the person must present a libellus to the judge before the conclusion of the case; in the libellus the person briefly is to demonstrate his or her right to intervene. §3. A person who intervenes in a case must be admitted at that stage which the case has reached, with a brief and peremptory period of time assigned to the person to present evidence if the case has reached the probatory period.

Montini notes that, by making an intervention, a victim becomes a party in the penal process. As a party, the victim can be involved in obtaining proofs, discussing the evidence, and the final phase preparing for a decision. Montini says that the victim can exercise their right to intervene in the penal process once the accused has been summoned. The alleged victim cannot be involved in the discussion of the case, but provided the alleged victim was involved in the first instance case, the victim can be involved in an appeal (see c. 1729 §2). The victim can seek reparation of damages if the penal process ended for any reason.[34] Furthermore, the victim has a right to appeal (see c. 1729 §3).[35] Canons 1596–97 provide for the intervention of a third party in a case.

This same right applies to victims. Montini quotes the Congregation for the Doctrine of the Faith concerning a case:

> The document should express more clearly the right of a victim to intervene in canonical procedures as an injured party and, therefore, his or her right to bring a contentious action to repair damages incurred personally from the delict, within the same canonical process.[36]

This means victims do have a right to participate in extrajudicial process.

Being Interviewed

Since a victim is a witness to a crime, the judge or delegate should interview the person as the injured party. The interview needs to be carried out carefully in a supportive environment with an advocate or support person present.

The Victim's Family

Grace Millane, an English tourist to New Zealand, was murdered in 2018. All the details of her personal life were in the newspapers, but everything concerning her killer was suppressed. Her family could do little about this.[37] No one would ever have known her name or anything about her sexual explorations if she had not been a victim.

In one case, a victim who was a minor experienced details about the actions of the cleric against him being published in the newspaper and on the radio. He found it very difficult going to public places, such as McDonald's, and hearing people talking about him. His family were also impacted by this publicity. While these examples are issues for New Zealand civil law, the cases highlight how the families of victims are greatly impacted by abuse. In Church processes, they need to be properly cared for and given all the support and help they need, including legal help.[38] Publishing personal details about a victim's personal life has a huge impact on people close to them. Legal systems, especially canon law, need to ensure that the alleged victim's family are cared for, their privacy is respected, and their mental health and other needs are provided for.

Reparation of Damages

The Church faces enormous legal challenges as victims sue for damages in civil courts. In the past, the canonical legal processes have not always been implemented and victims have not been offered the opportunity to participate fully in penal cases enshrined in canon law. It is not surprising that the victims have resorted to civil court action for damages.

The victim has a clear right in canon law to initiate a litigation case for damages suffered from the crime and for damages suffered within the penal process.[39] The victim may make the application before, during, or after a penal process. The application can even be made if the victim did not wish to participate as a party to the trial.[40] If the application for damages is made before or during the penal process, the judge will usually suspend the application for damages until after the penal process has ended.

Right to Legal Aid

A victim has the right to ask the judge for the perpetrator who caused damages to be brought to trial:

> SN c. 554. "§1. A party who, according to the norm of ecclesiastical law or civil law legitimately received in canon law, must respond concerning the civil damage perpetrated by the offender, has the right to intervene for safeguarding his right in a criminal trial."[41]

Canon 1479 provides for the judge to appoint a guardian or a curator for a victim if it is considered to be needed or required in the circumstances:

> Canon 1479. A guardian or curator appointed by a civil authority can be admitted by an ecclesiastical judge, after he has consulted, if possible, the diocesan Bishop of the person to whom the guardian or curator has been given. If there is no such guardian or curator, or it is not seen fit to admit the one appointed, the judge is to appoint a guardian or curator for the case.

Sometimes, it is necessary for a guardian or curator to be appointed if there are health issues. Carlo Gullo outlines the appropriate qualities of such a guardian or curator to make them competent for this role, including their qualifications and relationship with the victim.[42]

BETTER PROVISION OF VICTIMS' RIGHTS

Victim advocates or procurators, with the required personality and skills, need to be properly trained and qualified. These advocate/procurators need to be educated in trauma and its impact on victims, including PTSD. Ideally, canon law qualifications mean a doctorate or licentiate degree in canon law. Obtaining these qualifications can take significant time and expense. It is easier and cheaper to train clergy and religious who do not have family commitments. However, victims often do not want to deal with clergy and/or religious if they have been abused by one of them. Training lay people with families as advocates requires real commitment and investment of money from church leaders. Some might already have training and work experience working on declaration of marriage nullity cases. This means that they are already familiar with some church judicial processes.

Once a few procurator/advocates are trained, alleged victims can then be offered such a service from the time the "Ordinary receives information, which has at least the semblance of truth" (c. 1717). The alleged victims can then choose who represents them.

VICTIM IMPACT STATEMENTS AND UPDATING INFORMATION

Many civil jurisdictions ensure that victims can make a victim impact statement giving information to the court about how the offense has affected them. They can express their views about the experience and make the offender aware of how they have been affected. The judge will consider this information when sentencing the offender.[43]

After sentencing in civil courts, victims in many countries are informed about: where the abuser is living; when the abuser is released from prison; and any application the offender makes to return to a previous job or position. Victims and their families can report how the abuse is still affecting them when these decisions are made.

The Church should be providing ongoing care and support for victims, including keeping them informed about when an abuser is being returned to ministry. Victim(s) should be consulted/informed about this and the vigilance[44] or safety plan that is in place. Victims should be advised when their abuser dies,[45] as they consider this to be very important. Archbishop Scicluna told a meeting convened by Pope Francis in February 2019 that victims feel they are not respected when they are not updated about the status of the case and significant events.[46]

CONCLUSION

There needs to be a concerted effort in all areas of the Church to ensure the provision and upholding of victims' rights. This requires a widespread knowledge and understanding of penal processes. Archbishop Scicluna is conscious of the need to have an instruction on the procedures for penal processes, akin to the instruction *Dignitas Connubii*[47] for the processing of marriage cases. Penal law aims to achieve three ends: the restoration of justice, the reform of the offender, and the reparation of the scandal. For justice to be achieved for victims and for justice to be seen to be done, victims must be cared for, represented, and enabled to exercise their rights fully in all preliminary investigations, penal trials, and extrajudicial processes.

5

AUTHORITY AND OBLIGATIONS OF A BISHOP AND A RELIGIOUS INSTITUTE

The Royal Commission of Inquiry into Abuse in Care in New Zealand[1] and the Australian Royal Commission into Institutional Responses to Child Sexual Abuse[2] seriously questioned the relationship between diocesan bishops and religious institutes. Commissioners in both commissions sometimes struggled to understand complex governance relationships in the Catholic Church. Religious institutes, societies of apostolic life, secular institutes, and personal prelatures often seem the same. The following descriptions should help to distinguish between them.

RELIGIOUS INSTITUTES AND OTHER SIMILAR CHURCH BODIES

Societies of Apostolic Life resemble religious institutes in several ways. Members are not required to live in a community and do not make public vows as defined by canon 1192 §1.[3] Societies of apostolic life, such as the Columbans, are distinct from religious institutes, but like religious clerics, clerical members of societies must obtain faculties from the local Ordinary.

"A *secular institute* is an institute of consecrated life in which Christ's faithful, living in the world, strive for the perfection of charity and endeavor to contribute to the sanctification of the world, especially from within."[4] Secular institutes are a form of consecrated life whose members are not required to live in a community like religious brothers and sisters.[5]

Personal prelatures, such as Opus Dei, may be established by the Apostolic See after consultation with the bishops' conferences concerned. They are composed of deacons and priests of the secular clergy (often referred to as diocesan clergy). Their purpose is "to promote an appropriate distribution of priests, or to carry out special pastoral or missionary enterprises in different regions or for different social groups."[6] Personal prelatures are very different from religious institutes and are relatively independent of local bishops once they have been invited into a diocese by a diocesan bishop.

Associations of the faithful include clergy and laity working together to promote holiness of life or doctrine, or to foster worship or other apostolic works such as charitable works to animate society with the Christian spirit.[7] Associations are distinct from religious institutes and include the Focolare movement, the Catholic Women's League, and the Saint Vincent de Paul Society.

Religious Institutes

A religious institute is a group or society whose members live together in community. They make public vows[8] as described in canon 573:

> Life consecrated through profession of the evangelical counsels is a stable form of living, in which the faithful follow Christ more closely under the action of the Holy Spirit, and are totally dedicated to God, who is supremely loved. By a new and special title they are dedicated to seek the perfection of charity in the service of God's Kingdom, for the honor of God, the building up of the Church and the salvation of the world. They are a splendid sign in the Church, as they foretell the heavenly glory. (Can. 573 §1)

Religious institutes are either diocesan or pontifical; lay or clerical; and some religious reside in monasteries.

Diocesan institutes (often referred to as "diocesan right") are those which have been canonically established by a diocesan bishop and have not subsequently received juridic recognition from the Apostolic See.[9]

Pontifical institutes (often referred to as "of pontifical right") are those which have been canonically established by the Apostolic See or which have originated as a diocesan institute but subsequently received a formal decree of approbation from the Apostolic See.[10] Most religious institutes in New Zealand and Australia are pontifical.

Both diocesan and pontifical institutes may be clerical or lay institutes. Some religious institutes such as the St. John of God Institute include priests and brothers.

Lay institutes are those recognized as such by the Church and whose purpose does not include the exercise of holy orders.[11] Some lay institutes have a membership of brothers, and all sisters are members of lay institutes.

Clerical religious institutes are those recognized as such by the Church and whose purpose includes the exercise of holy orders, and which are governed by clerics.[12] The clergy need to receive faculties from the diocesan bishop or local ordinary to minister publicly, for example, the Society of Mary.

Among the religious institutes, there are relatively independent *monasteries* of contemplative sisters, brothers, and priests, such as the Carmelites or Cistercians. They profess solemn vows and observe papal enclosure[13] and are overseen by the diocesan bishop.[14]

Some religious institutes that own hospitals and schools have created ministerial public juridic persons to manage these apostolates, but the religious institute itself retains ownership.

Ministerial Public Juridic Persons (MPJP) "can be associations of persons, as in the case of a religious institute, or an association of things, such as the assets of an educational or health care ministry. The latter has come to be referred to as a ministerial juridic person or MJP, or a ministerial public juridic person (MPJP), to indicate that it was founded primarily for a ministerial purpose rather than for the sanctification of its members as a religious institute."[15] These juridic persons submit annual reports to the Dicastery for Institutes of Consecrated Life and Societies of Apostolic Life at the Vatican.

EXEMPT RELIGIOUS INSTITUTES

Before the 1917 Code came into effect, the constitutions of religious institutes described the charism and the apostolic purposes for which the institute was founded. In general, religious were called to live a holy life by living a vowed life according to the spirit of the institute. Members of the religious institute contributed to the mission of the Church through their apostolates. The constitutions are a specific law for a religious institute and contain the procedures of governance and authority within it.

In 1881, Pope Leo XIII granted exempt religious institutes the privilege of exemption so that their religious houses were separated from the governance of the diocese.[16] These regular religious were men and women of religious orders who followed an approved rule of life and professed solemn vows.[17] Other religious men and women were members of religious congregations who professed simple vows.[18] Solemn vows are always permanent and are taken by all members of monastic and mendicant orders. These are strictly cloistered communities and most semicloistered communities. Active communities of religious orders take simple vows. Like solemn vows, simple vows are taken publicly, that is, received by the superior in the name of the Church. They may be temporary or perpetual.

People often use the terms *nun* and *sister* interchangeably. However, there is a difference between the two. A nun is a woman who lives a contemplative life in a monastery that is usually enclosed (cloistered) or semi-enclosed. Her ministry and prayer life are centered within the monastery for the good of everyone in the world. She makes perpetual *solemn* vows, living a life according to the evangelical counsels of poverty, chastity, and obedience. Solemn vows are perpetual, and if she marries, the marriage is invalid. She cannot own property, and if money is left to her in a will, it goes to the religious institute and is not retained in a special fund in case she ever leaves. A religious society of solemn vows is called an order, and its members are called nuns (examples: Benedictines, Franciscans, Dominicans).

Canon 615 of the 1917 Code stated that some religious were exempt from the governance (jurisdiction) of the local Ordinary,[19] including the diocesan bishop, and subject only to the pope except where the law stated they were not exempt:

> Religious, not excluding novices, whether men or women, with their houses and churches, excepting those nuns who are not subject to regular Superiors, are exempt from the jurisdiction of the local Ordinary, except in those cases expressed by law. (Can. 615)[20]

Canon 488 §2 defined exemption as "withdrawn from the jurisdiction of the local ordinary." This meant that they were directly accountable to the Apostolic See. Exempt religious included the Dominicans, Jesuits, Redemptorists, and members of the Saint John of God institute. Their major superiors were Ordinaries and could exercise the power of governance.[21] The bishop continued to have authority over the care of souls and liturgical matters. According to the 1917 Code, the local Ordinary included residential bishops (now called diocesan bishops).[22] Exemption always included the internal life and governance of the religious. However, exemption was always partial and did not include erection of houses, celebrating public worship, and the sacraments for laypeople.[23]

Many religious were not exempt, such as the Society of Mary, the Sisters of Saint Joseph, and the Sisters of Mercy. If money was left to one of them, the money was kept in a special trust fund until her death. It would then usually become part of the assets of the religious institute.

Vatican II taught in the Dogmatic Constitution on the Church (*Lumen Gentium*) that the pope could exempt religious from the governance of local Ordinaries, so they were pontifical and subject only to the pope.

> To meet the needs of the whole of the Lord's flock more effectively, any institute of perfection and its individual members can, for the general good of the Church, be exempted by the supreme pontiff from the jurisdiction of local ordinaries and subjected to him alone; this is possible by reason of his primacy over the universal Church. (*Lumen Gentium* 45).[24]

Although the exemption meant the religious institute had a lot of independence from the local diocesan bishop, they were still accountable to the bishop concerning the pastoral work of the religious institute:

> The object is that everything in these institutes should be well-coordinated and in the interest of the growth and perfection of religious life....This exemption, however, does not stand in the way of the religious in their respective dioceses coming canonically under the jurisdiction of the bishops, in so far as is required for the fulfilment of their pastoral duties and the well-ordered care of souls. (*Christus Dominus* 35)

Following on from this, the decree *Christus Dominus* pointed out:

> All religious, exempt and non-exempt, are subject to the authority of the local ordinaries in the following matters: the public practice of divine worship (without prejudice, however, to the diversity of rites), the care of souls, sermons preached to the people...and what concerns the good repute of the clerical state as well as the various activities involving the exercise of their sacred apostolate. (no. 35)

Therefore, Matthew Kozlowski concluded that "Vatican II did not bring about the demise of exemption but brought to it a *novus habitus mentis*."[25] This new way of thinking about exemption requires transparency, collaboration, and a completely new way of thinking without covering up problems such as abuse.[26]

MUTUAE RELATIONES

On May 14, 1978, the Congregation for Religious and Secular Institutes and the Congregation for Bishops issued "Directives for Mutual Relations between Bishops and Religious in the Church" *(Mutuae Relationes)*,[27] which seeks to establish better working relationships between bishops and religious:

> Bishops, furthermore, as members of the Episcopal College, in harmony with the will of the Supreme Pontiff, are united in this:...in determining the exemption of some institutes "from the jurisdiction of local ordinaries for the sake of the common good" (*LG*, 45) of the universal Church and to better "ensure that everything is suitably and harmoniously arranged within them, and the perfection of the religious life promoted" (*CD*, 35, 3).[28]

In these documents, there was a reminder that "the difference between the proper works of an institute and works entrusted to an institute should be kept in mind by diocesan Bishops."[29] Bishops were again reminded of this in the *Directory on the Pastoral Ministry of Bishops* no. 100:

> Following the norm of law, the bishop will respect the exemption given to certain institutes, through which the Pope as primate over the entire Church, can exempt any institute of Christian perfection and its individual members from the jurisdiction of local ordinaries and subject them to himself alone or to another ecclesiastical authority. (*Apostolorum Successores* 100)

Pope Paul VI had legislated that apostolic works entrusted to a religious institute remained "under the authority and direction of the diocesan Bishop without prejudice to the right of religious Superiors to exercise vigilance (oversight) over the life of the members of the Institute."[30] The current law is:

> In the exercise of an external apostolate towards persons outside the institute, religious are also subject to their own Superiors and must remain faithful to the discipline of the institute. If the need arises, Bishops themselves are not to fail to insist on this regulation. (Can. 678 §2)

From 1966, if abuse of a minor by a religious occurred within the context of the exercise of ministry in an entrusted work, the religious superior was obliged to inform the diocesan bishop because the work was under the bishop's authority and direction. Also, the religious institute and the bishop were obliged to collaborate. Even if the abuse occurred within a proper work of an institute, there was an obligation to inform the bishop, especially because a person was harmed and scandal[31] could be involved. The sin of scandal is described by the *Catechism of the Catholic Church* as

> an attitude or behavior which leads another to do evil. The person who gives scandal becomes his neighbor's tempter. He damages virtue and integrity; he may even draw his brother into spiritual death. Scandal is a grave offense if by deed or omission another is deliberately led into a grave offense. (*CCC* 2284)[32]

Scandal in canon law is different from sensational bad behavior as understood in society, but obviously the same activity can give rise to both understandings of scandal.

PROPER OR ENTRUSTED WORKS

A key distinction in the relationship between bishops and religious is whether the apostolate is proper or entrusted to the religious institute. The following description helps to clarify the authority of bishops: "proper works are administered[33] by a particular institute or society, with vigilance (oversight) by the diocesan bishop; entrusted works are administered by a diocesan bishop, with vigilance[34] (oversight) exercised by the major superior."[35] Benjamin Earl notes that the proper works depend on the religious superiors in accordance with their constitutions, even though as regards pastoral action they are subject to the jurisdiction of the local Ordinary according to the norm of law.[36]

He explains that the phrase "depending on the religious superiors in accordance with their constitutions" refers

> to both the spiritual patrimony of the institute and to its basic norms of governance operating in harmony. Certainly, the spiritual patrimony of the institute should be expressed in any apostolate exercised by religious, for their apostolate "consists primarily in the witness of their consecrated life.[37]

The apostolic work could be subject to the norms of the constitutions. The juridical person of the religious institute could be the owner of the apostolic work, such as the hospital or orphanage.

A clear example is when a parish is entrusted to a religious institute. The major superior proposes a priest to be the parish priest, and then it is the diocesan bishop who appoints him as the parish priest.[38] Diocesan bishops frequently entrust parishes to the care of members of religious institutes. Benjamin Earl notes that "in such cases the bishop will always retain a decisive role in the government of the work, even if the ordinary governance is entrusted to members of the religious institute."[39]

AUTONOMY OF RELIGIOUS

Members of religious institutes enjoy a real autonomy of life from diocesan bishops but are to obey the commands of their superiors:

> The evangelical counsel of obedience, undertaken in the spirit of faith and love in the following of Christ, who was obedient even unto death, obliges submission of one's will to lawful Superiors, who act in the place of God when they give commands that are in accordance with each institute's own constitutions. (Can. 601)

Members of the religious institute are to be faithful to the discipline of the institute:

> In the exercise of an external apostolate towards persons outside the institute, religious are also subject to their own Superiors and must remain faithful to the discipline of the institute. If the need arises, Bishops themselves are not to fail to insist on this regulation. (Can. 678 §2)

The vow of obedience affects every area of the life of a religious, but especially in the internal governance and charism of the institute:

> A religious institute is a society in which, in accordance with their own law, the members pronounce public vows and live a fraternal life in common. (c. 607 §2)

THE AUTHORITY OF THE DIOCESAN BISHOP

In the 1917 code, the diocesan bishop was called a residential bishop. He governed his diocese with the power granted to him in canon law: "Residential Bishops are ordinary and immediate pastors in the dioceses committed to them" (c. 334 §1).

The power and authority of the diocesan bishop changed dramatically when Vatican II taught that he was the vicar of Christ in his own diocese (*Lumen Gentium* 27). The Decree on the Life and Ministry of Bishops then taught that bishops could dispense from all disciplinary laws except those reserved by the pope:

> [From] the general law of the church all diocesan bishops are given the power of granting dispensations in particular cases to the faithful over whom they hold canonical authority, whenever they judge it to be for their spiritual good. This power does not extend to cases which have been specially reserved by the supreme authority of the church. (*Christus Dominus* 8b)[40]

Prior to the Council, diocesan bishops could only dispense in those matters that the law allowed them to dispense. James Provost explained:

> Note, canon 381 §1 states that the diocesan bishop possesses "*all* power which is required," not "*full* power." Only the Roman Pontiff and the college of bishops in union with the Roman Pontiff are subjects of "full power" within the

Church (cc. 331 and 336, respectively). As such, there is a clear distinction between the power that is enjoyed by the supreme authority and that which is all power to exercise his office.[41]

The diocesan bishop enjoys ordinary power of governance,[42] which is executive, legislative, and judicial.[43] He must maintain and uphold church discipline and has authority over the external apostolate of religious which "consists primarily in the witness of their consecrated life"[44] fully living their vowed life of poverty, chastity, and obedience.

DIOCESAN BISHOPS' AUTHORITY AND RELIGIOUS

The authority of diocesan bishops over members of religious institutes is summarized by Kozlowski:

> All members are subject to the diocesan bishop....The extent of the authority that a diocesan bishop exercises over a member of a religious institute, then, is largely dependent on the member's engagement in the external apostolate in conjunction with the nature of the apostolic work (i.e., is the work proper to the institute or is it entrusted to the institute or one of its members by the diocesan bishop?). At the same time, the member must still obey the legitimate commands of his/her religious superiors (c. 601) and remain faithful to the discipline of the institute (c. 678 §2). Also, this same superior has authority over a religious' exercise of an external apostolate. The extent of the religious superior's authority is also affected by the nature of the work (i.e., proper or entrusted). In short, a religious who exercises an external apostolate is subject to a dual authority structure which consists of the diocesan bishop and religious superior.[45]

The most common apostolate that religious institutes are involved with are schools. The power of the bishop in relation to schools is outlined by Richard Hill:

> According to the 1983 Code, whether the school is a proper or entrusted work: "The bishop has the right to establish general policies for all Catholic schools (C 806, §1), to supervise religious formation and education imparted in schools (C 804, §1), to approve the appointment of those who are to teach religion and to require their removal if he judges this necessary for reasons of religion or morals (C 805)." If the school is a proper work of the institute, "the right of the religious to direct or manage these schools remains intact (C 806, §1)."[46]

On the relationship between canons 683 §1[47] and 806 §1,[48] Cito states that the bishop's function of vigilance "encompasses everything that could reasonably cause harm to the Catholic character of the educational institution." The local Ordinary, including the diocesan bishop, can remove the faculties of any cleric, or if there is an investigation into an alleged crime,[49] the cleric can be prohibited from the exercise of sacred ministry by the local Ordinary.[50]

When an individual religious is causing grave scandal, canon law provides for a diocesan bishop to expel him or her from the diocese:

> For the gravest of reasons, a diocesan Bishop can forbid a member of a religious institute to remain in his diocese, provided the person's major superior has been informed and has failed to act; the matter must, however, immediately be reported to the Holy See. (Can. 679)

The reason could be that the religious is having an affair with someone or is behaving in another gravely inappropriate manner.

TERMINATING AN APOSTOLATE OF RELIGIOUS INSTITUTES

There is no canonical process to terminate an apostolate of a religious institute.[51] However, if religious violate universal or particular law in an apostolate, they can be removed.

> In matters concerning the care of souls, the public exercise of divine worship, and other works of the apostolate, religious are subject to the authority of the bishops, whom they are bound to treat with sincere submission and reverence. (Can. 678 §1)

The bishop grants faculties for a religious to function publicly in the Church.[52] He can also remove those faculties or prohibit the exercise of public ministry if required.[53]

Usually, religious institutes are the ones who terminate an apostolate because of shortage of members. In such cases, there should be negotiation about the timing and the process for withdrawal from the apostolate.

Sometimes the diocesan bishop may initiate the termination of the apostolate of a religious institute. The most common situation would be a bishop deciding to "take back" a parish for it to be staffed by diocesan priests. The bishop can easily do this because a parish belongs to the structure of a diocese. There should also be an agreement or contract made between the religious institute and the diocese when the parish was entrusted to the religious institute.[54] There should always be a contract between the diocesan bishop and the religious institute for any religious carrying out an apostolate in the diocese.[55] This contract may affect how and when the apostolate is terminated.

When a diocesan bishop carries out a visitation of an apostolate of a religious institute, such as a school, and discovers abuses, he is directed how to proceed by canon 683 §2: "If the diocesan Bishop becomes aware of abuses, and a warning to the religious Superior having been in vain, he can by his own authority deal with the matter." The bishop is to demand that the religious superior correct the abuse. If the superior fails to act in the time given, then the diocesan bishop is to deal with the matter himself. If the abuse is systemic, the bishop will have to take recourse to the Dicastery for Institutes of Consecrated Life and Societies of Apostolic Life and the Dicastery for the Doctrine of the Faith. This could lead to a canonical investigation and potential suppression of the religious institute or a section of it. In Australia, for example, the Society of Saint Gerard Majella, a diocesan institute in New South Wales, was suppressed after sexual abuse was found to be systemic in the institute.[56] In 1773, the Jesuits, a pontifical institute, was suppressed for largely political reasons by Pope Clement XIV. The decision of Pope Clement XIV was not promulgated in Prussia and Russia, so the Jesuit order survived the suppression order in those territories. The Jesuit order was restored officially by Pope Pius VII in 1814.[57]

RELIGIOUS INSTITUTES RESERVED TO THE APOSTOLIC SEE

Kozlowski lists the actions concerning religious institutes that are reserved to the Apostolic See:

> By law, the following actions are reserved to the authority of the Apostolic See: to merge and to unite institutes, confederations, and federations, whether of pontifical or diocesan right (c. 582) to suppress an institute and to decide what to do with the temporal goods of the suppressed institute, whether of pontifical or diocesan right (c. 584);[58] to approve new forms of consecrated life (c. 605); to grant an indult of exclaustration for nuns (c. 686 §2); to dispense a candidate from the age requirement for the presbyterate or the diaconate if he is more than one year younger than the required age (c. 1031 §4); to dispense from all irregularities for receiving or exercising orders received if the matter has been brought to the judicial forum (c. 1047 §1); to dispense from the irregularity for ordination for the public delicts of apostasy, heresy, or schism, or attempted marriage (c. 1047 §2, 1°); to dispense from the irregularity for ordination for public or occult delicts of voluntary homicide or procurement of a completed abortion or positively cooperating in either delict (c. 1047 §2, 2°); to dispense from the impediment to ordination for married men (c. 1047 §2, 3°); to dispense in public cases from the irregularity to exercise an order already received for attempted marriage and even in occult cases from the irregularity of voluntary homicide or procurement of a completed abortion or positively cooperating in either delict (c. 1047 §3); and to remit the *latae sententiae* excommunication for the delicts of desecrating the Eucharist (c. 1367), striking the pope (c. 1370), absolving an accomplice in a sin against the sixth commandment (c. 1378 §1), consecrating a bishop without a pontifical mandate (c. 1382), and directly violating the sacramental seal (c. 1388 §1). The law also specifies that the judgment of a supreme moderator of a religious institute of pontifical right is reserved to the Roman Rota (c. 1405 §3, 2°). Any judge below the level of the Roman Rota is absolutely

> incompetent (c. 1406 §1) and so would render an irremediably null sentence (c. 1620, 1°).[59]

In 2001, Pope John Paul II in the *motu proprio Sacramentorum Sanctitatis Tutela*[60] required all clerical religious institutes to report to the Congregation for the Doctrine of the Faith, from October 11, 2001, onward, the receipt of any reports or allegations of sexual abuse of a minor by a cleric. The requirement to report included all historical allegations that had a semblance of truth about them as well as all those the major superior decided were unfounded. If the accused cleric was deceased, the major superior still needed to report the allegation and what he had done as a result of the allegation.

VOS ESTIS LUX MUNDI

In 2019, Pope Francis introduced new legislation in his *motu proprio Vos Estis Lux Mundi*. This law came into effect on June 1, 2019. It had been unclear whether religious brothers or sisters committed a canonical crime or delict when they sexually abused a minor. These brothers or sisters were to be dismissed from the religious institute according to canon 695.[61] Now any religious sister or brother who abuses a minor has committed a canonical crime if they sexually abuse someone according to the expanded definition in *Vos Estis Lux Mundi*:

> Art. 1 – Scope of application. §1. These norms apply to reports regarding clerics or members of Institutes of Consecrated Life or Societies of Apostolic Life and concerning: a) delicts against the sixth commandment of the Decalogue consisting of: i. forcing someone, by violence or threat or through abuse of authority, to perform or submit to sexual acts; ii. performing sexual acts with a minor or a vulnerable person; iii. the production, exhibition, possession or distribution, including by electronic means, of child pornography, as well as by the recruitment of or inducement of a minor or a vulnerable person to participate in pornographic exhibitions; b) conduct carried out by the subjects referred to in article 6, consisting of actions or omissions intended to interfere with or avoid civil investigations or canonical investigations, whether administrative or penal, against a cleric or a religious regarding the delicts referred to in letter a) of this paragraph. (VELM 1)

This is the first time that religious brothers and sisters have been explicitly included in documents concerning sexual abuse. A lacuna in the law has been rectified. The norms also encompass members of societies of apostolic life such as the Columbans. Priests and deacons of societies of apostolic life have always been subject to the norms of *Sacramentorum Sanctitatis Tutela*,[62] but their sisters or brothers were not.

"Sexual Abuse" includes "forcing someone, by violence or threat or through abuse of authority, to perform or submit to sexual acts" (VELM 1). Now crimes of sexual abuse by religious brothers and sisters must be reported to the local Ordinary and the religious major superior.[63]

This ensures that there is adequate transparency and accountability within the Church.

Compulsory Reporting within the Church

In his *motu proprio Vos Estis Lux Mundi* (2019), Pope Francis required that priests, deacons, and religious must report sexual abuse when they know it has happened or they believe that it is happening:

> §1. Except as provided for by canons 1548 §2 CIC and 1229 §2 CCEO, whenever a cleric or a member of an Institute of Consecrated Life or of a Society of Apostolic Life has notice of, or well-founded motives to believe that, one of the facts referred to in article 1 has been committed, that person is obliged to report promptly the fact to the local Ordinary. (VELM 3)

Religious Leaders Failing to Act

In article 6 of *Vos Estis Lux Mundi*, Pope Francis also reserved to the Dicastery for Institutes of Consecrated Life and Societies of Apostolic Life the crimes of a religious superior failing to act in a case of sexual abuse, or failing to observe canon law or civil laws on reporting and failing to cooperate with civil or canonical investigations:

> The procedural norms referred to in this title concern the delicts referred to in article 1, carried out by: a) Cardinals, Patriarchs, Bishops and Legates of the Roman Pontiff; b) clerics who are, or who have been, the pastoral heads of a particular Church or of an entity assimilated to it, Latin or Oriental, including the Personal Ordinariates, for acts committed *durante munere*; c) clerics who are or who were entrusted with the pastoral leadership of a Personal Prelature, for acts committed *durante munere*; d) clerics who are or who were leaders of public clerical associations with the faculty of incardination, for acts committed *durante munere*; e) those who are or who were Supreme Moderators of Institutes of Consecrated Life or of Societies of Apostolic Life of Pontifical right, as well as of monasteries *sui iuris*, for acts committed *durante munere*; f) lay faithful who are or who were Moderators of international associations of the faithful recognized or erected by the Apostolic See, for acts committed *durante munere*. (VELM 6)

The provisions of articles 1 b), c), d), e), and f) are a dramatic change in approach by the Church. It is now a crime for religious leaders to fail to observe canon law or civil laws on reporting and failing to cooperate with or obstructing civil investigations. Effectively the Church is canonizing aspects of civil laws concerning what constitutes sexual abuse and grooming, as well as civil procedural laws concerning this reporting.[64] This has significance in many countries because of laws concerning grooming, obtaining phone numbers of children, photographing children, and so on.

Historic failures of not dealing with complaints are also now encompassed by this legislation. Article 1 b), c), and

d) specifically mentions those "who have been in the past leaders" and refers to moderators of institutes of consecrated life, societies of apostolic life, and monasteries concerning acts or omissions while they were in office in the past.

This law specifically applies canon 1378, which had already included acts or failures to act as crimes when they constituted an abuse of an office or position:

> §1. A person who, apart from the cases already foreseen by the law, abuses ecclesiastical power, office, or function, is to be punished according to the gravity of the act or the omission, not excluding by deprivation of the power or office, without prejudice to the obligation of repairing the harm. §2. A person who, through culpable negligence, unlawfully and with harm to another or scandal, performs or omits an act of ecclesiastical power or office or function, is to be punished according to the provision of can. 1336 §§2–4, without prejudice to the obligation of repairing the harm. (Can. 1378)[65]

These provisions remove any doubts about the application of this canon concerning sexual abuse cases. The local Ordinary would mean the diocesan bishop, apostolic or diocesan administrator.[66] The revised Book VI addressed reporting requirements:

> A person who neglects to report an offence, when required to do so by a canonical law, is to be punished according to the provision of canon 1336 §§2–4, with the addition of other penalties according to the gravity of the offence. (Can. 1371 §6)[67]

The new provision in the revised Book VI makes it a crime to fail to report an offense.

Civil Law

Vos Estis Lux Mundi states:

> Compliance with state laws. These norms apply without prejudice to the rights and obligations established in each place by state laws, particularly those concerning any reporting obligations to the competent civil authorities. (VELM 19)

Also, not observing civil law requirements is explicitly covered in the *motu proprio*:

> Article 1 – Scope of application. §1. These norms apply to reports regarding clerics or members of Institutes of Consecrated Life or Societies of Apostolic Life and concerning: ...b) conduct carried out by the subjects referred to in article 6, consisting of actions or omissions intended to interfere with or avoid civil investigations or canonical investigations, whether administrative or penal, against a cleric or a religious regarding the delicts referred to in letter a) of this paragraph.

Although the Doctrine of the Faith's circular letter in 2011 made it clear the Church must obey civil laws regarding abuse and reporting,[68] Archbishop Scicluna claimed that "compliance with state laws" had become universal canon law for the first time in the *motu proprio Vos Estis Lux Mundi.* Archbishop Scicluna explained it was unacceptable for people to try to protect the Church now, because "the good of the church requires truth and transparency, which includes respecting civil law." He added that he hoped people felt "empowered to go to the police" to denounce a crime,[69] and he said people have an obligation[70] to report already existing crimes, negligence, and inappropriate behavior to church authorities.[71] Furthermore, "If people have the right and the duty to denounce something illicit" in the case of abuse, "they also have the right to denounce if, after one year, nothing has been done."[72]

RESPONSIBILITY AND LIABILITY FOR REPAIR OF HARM TO ABUSE VICTIMS

Some diocesan bishops believed that canon 384 justified them in showing priests leniency in dealing with complaints about their abuse or misconduct:

> He is to have special concern for the priests, to whom he is to listen as his helpers and counsellors. He is to defend their rights and ensure that they fulfil the obligations proper to their state. He is to see that they have the means and the institutions needed for the development of their spiritual and intellectual life. He is to ensure that they are provided with adequate means of livelihood and social welfare, in accordance with the law. (Can. 384)

While bishops have a responsibility to defend and care for their priests, it is vital that they do not take one canon alone without considering the whole Code of Canon Law and all other canonical documents.

Bishops also have a responsibility to care for all the faithful in their dioceses. Diocesan bishops are responsible for caring for victims:

> In exercising his pastoral office, the diocesan Bishop is to be solicitous for all Christ's faithful entrusted to his care, whatever their age, condition or nationality, whether they live in the territory or are visiting there. He is to show an apostolic spirit also to those who, because of their condition of life, are not sufficiently able to benefit from ordinary pastoral care, and to those who have lapsed from religious practice. (Can. 383 §1)

In *Vos Estis Lux Mundi,* Pope Francis explained what it meant for diocesan bishops "to be solicitous for all Christ's faithful committed to his care":

> Article 5 – Care for persons. §1. The ecclesiastical Authorities shall commit themselves to ensuring that those who state that they have been harmed, together with their families, are to be treated with dignity and respect, and, in particular, are to be: a) welcomed, listened to and supported, including through provision of specific services; b) offered spiritual assistance; c) offered medical assistance, including therapeutic and psychological assis-

> tance, as required by the specific case. (VELM 1)

It must be acknowledged that in dealing with sexual abuse victims, so many aspects are case specific. General statements do not always serve a just outcome. Religious institutes have a parallel responsibility to care for those their members have abused.[73]

Rights and Obligations of Clerical and Religious Abusers

What is just for abusers is not simple in practice. Abusers have the right to sufficient income for their support if they have not been dismissed from the clerical state or a religious institute.[74] However, if they have been dismissed from the clerical state or their religious institute, any support they receive is given out of charity.

Justice for victims is related to justice for abusers. Morally, abusers should not be getting more income/housing/ and so on than their victims, and this is quite possible, for example, if clergy are receiving both a stipend and superannuation. If the abuser has assets, the abuser must be forced to compensate their victim by the Ordinary or tribunal:

> Whoever unlawfully causes harm to another by a juridical act, or indeed by any other act which is malicious or culpable, is obliged to repair the damage done. (Can. 128)

Natural law and canon law recognize this obligation enshrined in canon 128. The Church, because of its mission, must place particular emphasis on the obligation to repair moral and spiritual harm.[75] This harm to victims must be repaired. Cases vary enormously and the impact of the abuse also varies greatly, and this must be recognized in each case.

Sometimes abusers receive a punishment of a life of prayer and penance from the Dicastery for the Doctrine of the Faith. What this means must be defined in detail by the Conference of Bishops for their territory to ensure that justice is real, and that the punishment does not become a farce.

Lawyers may argue that dioceses and religious institutes are not legally liable for crimes of their clergy, religious, and lay employees. There is no doubt, however, that there is a moral responsibility and liability.

Obligations of Dioceses

In 2009, the Congregation for the Clergy reminded bishops that ecclesiastical discipline includes the obligations of continence:[76]

> The bishop has, among other things, the duty to remind priests of their obligation to perfect and perpetual continence for the sake of the kingdom of heaven, an obligation freely and willingly assumed by them at the moment of their ordination. Moreover, the bishop must always be attentive that the priest is faithful in carrying out his proper ministerial duties (cf. Canons 384, 392).[77]

However, the priest is not considered an employee or agent of the bishop and is appointed to a parish to do pastoral work such as that outlined in canons 528–29. The Congregation for the Clergy declared:

> The diocesan priest, who is not merely the passive executor of commands received from the bishop, enjoys autonomy in making decisions both in his ministry and in his personal and private life. Thus, he is personally responsible for his personal actions and for those carried out in the scope of his ministry. Consequently, a bishop cannot be held juridically responsible for the acts which a diocesan priest carries out in transgression of the canonical norms, universal or particular. This principle is not new and has always been part of the patrimony of the church, means, among other things, that the criminal action of a priest, and its penal consequences as well as any eventual payment of damages, is imputable to the priest who has committed the offense and not to the bishop or to the diocese of which the bishop is the legal representative (cf. Canon 393).[78]

However, *Vos Estis Lux Mundi* has modified this stance by the Congregation for the Clergy in article 5.[79] Dioceses have a responsibility to care for victims of diocesan priests from their diocese.[80] Incardination in a diocese connects the cleric to the diocese, which must provide for him in return for his commitment to serve there.[81] If a priest abuser belonged to two dioceses, the dioceses should compensate/help in a proportional manner according to the number of years the priest worked in each diocese. When a diocesan priest offends, he holds the primary responsibility to pay his legal expenses. If he is judged innocent, his diocese has a responsibility to recompense him.

Bishops have more power and responsibility over an entrusted work of a religious institute than over a proper work. This is because they hold the power to appoint to positions or offices. Consequently, a diocesan bishop appoints a religious priest as a parish priest.[82]

Issues do arise about the bishop's liability because of his supervisory role over associations of the faithful:

> §1. All associations of Christ's faithful are subject to the supervision of the competent ecclesiastical authority. This authority is to ensure that integrity of faith and morals is maintained in them and that abuses in ecclesiastical discipline do not creep in. The competent authority has therefore the duty and the right to visit these associations, in accordance with the law and the statutes. Associations are also subject to the governance of the same authority in accordance with the provisions of the canons which follow. §2. Associations of every kind are subject to the supervision of the Holy See. Diocesan associations are subject to the supervision of the local Ordinary, as are other associations to the extent that they work in the diocese. (Can. 305)

Canon 305's "supervision" [*vigilantia*] is not "governance" or "administration." The diocesan bishop's right of visitation or vigilance over ecclesiastical entities is limited according to the statutes of the entity and that right certainly does not envision day-to-day decision-making. Rather, the role of the diocesan bishop's supervision as provided for in canon 305 consists in the right of review and approval of statutes, and the right to intervene in case of malfeasance or commission of a delict or abuse of office.

If abuse is committed during work time by *lay staff* employed by a diocesan bishop, the abuser has the responsibility to repair the damage done to victims. If the abuser cannot or will not repair the damage, the diocese has a moral responsibility to repair the damage done to victims.

Obligations of Religious Institutes

If members of religious institutes (brothers, sisters, or clerics) abuse others, their religious institutes have the responsibility to repair the damage done to victims, whether it takes place in an entrusted or a proper work.[83]

Bishops do not have the power to appoint office holders in a proper work of a religious institute, but merely approve appointees of a religious institute.[84] However, a bishop is usually only informed whom the religious institute has appointed and needs to trust their decision-making. Because the religious institute appoints the office holders, the religious institute holds the liability for any subsequent abuse.

Similarly, if perpetrators are members of societies of apostolic life, their society bears the responsibility to repair the damage done to victims.[85]

If the religious institute does not help the victim or repair the harm done, the diocesan bishop must pressure the religious institute or the Ministerial Public Juridic Person (MPJP) to meet their obligations to repair the damage done to victims. The Apostolic See can force any religious institute to meet their obligations. If a religious institute no longer exists, the diocese must help the victims.

If abuse is committed by lay employees of a religious institute in their proper work, the abuser has the responsibility to repair the damage done to victims. If the abuser cannot or will not repair the damage, the religious institute has the responsibility to repair the damage done to victims.

Obligations of Integrated Schools

Catholic schools in New Zealand, for example, have all been integrated into the state education system. This system was changed in 1989 by what is referred to as "Tomorrow's Schools." The government review as part of the Tomorrow's Schools reforms states:

> Until the Tomorrow's Schools reforms of 1989, the governance and administration of New Zealand's compulsory education system was highly centralised....Since the 1989 reforms, each school has been operating as a largely self-managing statutory Crown entity with responsibility for a wide range of functions that were previously centralised, such as employing staff and developing school policies.[86]

Proprietors of integrated schools in New Zealand, including bishops and religious institutes, have four representatives on school boards, but they are not the majority on the board. The board of trustees in an integrated school appoints the teachers and other staff. If abusers are laypeople (teachers, caretakers, and so forth) appointed by the board, the board is responsible for placing them in that position. Neither a religious institute nor a diocese makes the appointment and so they are not legally responsible for compensating victims of those appointed by the board of trustees.

CHART OF MUTUAL RIGHTS AND DUTIES

To understand better the mutual rights and duties between diocesan bishops/ local Ordinaries, societies of apostolic life, and religious institutes as required by law, it is worth consulting the chart[87] compiled by Elizabeth McDonough, OP, in "Relationship between Bishops and Religious: Mutual Rights and Duties."

CONCLUSION

The 1983 Code and *Mutuae Relationes* emphasize the importance of bishops and religious superiors implementing canon law, consulting, (c. 678) collaborating, and acting in a transparent manner.[88] As Benjamin Earl elucidates:

> The canon insists on mutual consultation between bishops and religious superiors. Clearly this mutual consultation is particularly important when it comes to determining the appropriate form an apostolic work should take, whether that be at the moment of establishing a presence of the institute in the diocese,[89] at a moment of notable changes in the apostolate,[90] or at the moment when an institute must withdraw from a particular place.[91]

It is a grave scandal that in the past religious institutes have not been sufficiently transparent and accountable. It is now a crime if members of institutes and religious superiors fail to report sexual abuse complaints to the local Ordinary and to the Dicastery for the Doctrine of the Faith when the complaints concern clerics. Complaints about lay religious must be reported to the local Ordinary, but mandatory dismissals are to be dealt with by their major superiors according to canon 695. Failures to act by Ordinaries or religious superiors must also be reported to the competent Dicasteries.

Abuse of authority was a crime according to the 1917 Code. Abuse of vulnerable people has been a crime since *Vos Estis Lux Mundi* became law in 2019. Tribunals established by diocesan bishops are to judge allegations of crimes of religious against vulnerable people or by abuse of authority. In the past, many of these cases have too often been rationalized as consenting adult situations that do not involve a crime. The imbalance of power was never considered.

Bishops and religious superiors have failed to implement canon law in the past and caused the sexual abuse scandal to become a grave crisis in the Church. If canon law had been implemented, the situation would not be as notorious as it is. It is incumbent on church leaders now to change and fully implement the revised legislation. This requires trust between bishops and religious, as well as the creation of a culture that is committed to a safe Church committed to repairing the harm done to victims in a victim-centered approach that provides justice for all and the reform of the offender.

6

MANDATORY REPORTING OF SEXUAL ABUSE

Law concerning sexual abuse has existed for most of the history of the Church. In the 1983 Code, canon 1395 concerning sexual abuse of minors stated:

> A cleric who in another way has committed an offence against the sixth commandment of the Decalogue, if the delict was committed by force or threats or publicly or with a minor below the age of sixteen years, is to be punished with just penalties, not excluding dismissal from the clerical state if the case so warrants. (Can. 1395 §2)

There was a time limit of five years for lodging a complaint about an offense until the law was changed in 2001.[1]

After the revelation of the extent of the problem of clerical sexual abuse in North America and in many other countries, Pope John Paul II issued *motu proprio* the apostolic letter *Sacramentorum Sanctitatis Tutela*, on April 30, 2001.[2] He legislated several offenses as more grave crimes, including sexual abuse of minors, absolution of an accomplice in a sin against the sixth commandment, and solicitation. Pope John Paul II required Ordinaries to report each case they were informed of to the Congregation for the Doctrine of the Faith.[3]

It did not matter when the alleged events had taken place. Failure to report knowledge of these offenses was a crime of failure to act according to canon 1389 of the 1983 Code. The equivalent canon is now:

> §1. A person who, apart from the cases already foreseen by the law, abuses ecclesiastical power, office, or function, is to be punished according to the gravity of the act or the omission, not excluding by deprivation of the power or office, without prejudice to the obligation of repairing the harm. §2. A person who, through culpable negligence, unlawfully and with harm to another or scandal, performs or omits an act of ecclesiastical power or office or function, is to be punished according to the

provision of can. 1336 §§2–4, without prejudice to the obligation of repairing the harm. (Can. 1378)

PENAL LAW CHANGES

Over the years, there have been modifications to the norms of *Sacramentorum Sanctitatis Tutela* so that the sexual abuse of minors includes pornography and other offenses against the sixth commandment. Pope Francis revised Book VI of the Code of Canon law in 2021 so that canon 1398 was specifically concerned with sexual abuse:

> §1. A cleric is to be punished with deprivation of office and with other just penalties, not excluding, where the case calls for it, dismissal from the clerical state, if he: 1° commits an offence against the sixth commandment of the Decalogue with a minor or with a person who habitually has an imperfect use of reason or with one to whom the law recognizes equal protection; 2° grooms or induces a minor or a person who habitually has an imperfect use of reason or one to whom the law recognizes equal protection to expose himself or herself pornographically or to take part in pornographic exhibitions, whether real or simulated; 3° immorally acquires, retains, exhibits or distributes, in whatever manner and by whatever technology, pornographic images of minors or of persons who habitually have an imperfect use of reason. §2. A member of an institute of consecrated life or of a society of apostolic life, or any one of the faithful who enjoys a dignity or performs an office or function in the Church, who commits an offence mentioned in §1 or in can. 1395 §3 is to be punished according to the provision of can. 1336 §§2–4, with the addition of other penalties according to the gravity of the offence. (Can. 1398)

The predecessor of canon 1398 was canon 1395 in the section under "Offenses against Special Obligations," that is, as an offense against the obligation to observe celibacy. Victims and the 2017 *Final Report* of the Australian Royal Commission recommended that in the penal law there should be a canon specifically relating to sexual abuse.[4] Pope Francis has responded to this recommendation with the new canon 1398 in the section of the Code appropriately entitled "Offenses against Human Life, Dignity and Liberty."

Pope Francis had used the term *sexual acts* in *Vos Estis Lux Mundi* rather than "delicts against the Sixth Commandment," which was used in *Sacramentorum Sanctitatis Tutela.*

Sexual abuse is defined in *Vos Estis Lux Mundi* (VELM) art. 1 §1a:

> Art. 1 – Scope of application. §1. These norms apply to reports regarding clerics or members of Institutes of Consecrated Life or Societies of Apostolic Life and Moderators of international associations of the faithful recognized or erected by the Apostolic See concerning:
>
> a) *a delict against the sixth commandment of the Decalogue committed through violence or threat or through abuse of authority, or

by forcing someone to perform or submit to sexual acts;

** a delict against the sixth commandment of the Decalogue committed with a minor or with a person who habitually has imperfect use of reason or with a vulnerable adult;

*** the immoral acquisition, possession, exhibition or distribution, in any way or by any means, of pornographic images of minors or of persons who habitually have imperfect use of reason;

**** the recruitment or inducement of a minor or of a person who habitually has imperfect use of reason or of a vulnerable adult to pose in a pornographic manner or to participate in real or simulated pornographic exhibitions;

b) conduct carried out by the subjects referred to in art. 6, consisting of actions or omissions intended to interfere with or avoid civil investigations or canonical investigations, whether administrative or penal, against one of the subjects indicated in §1 regarding the delicts referred to in letter a) of this paragraph. (VELM 1)

To force someone encompasses compelling the person by physical, moral, or intellectual means, or an abuse of authority or position.

This change from sexual acts to delicts makes a significant difference to the crimes encompassed by the legislation. The term *sexual acts* is in accord with secular legislation and the terminology of the United Nations. However, "delicts against the Sixth Commandment" is the traditional term in canon law and encompasses the intention to commit a crime. The revised Book VI returns to the use of the traditional term of "offense against the sixth commandment." This term is also used by the *Catechism of the Catholic Church*, in paragraphs 2351–56, where it is made clear that these offenses include adultery, rape, and the accessing of pornography.

The meaning of "Sexual acts with a minor or vulnerable adult" is clarified by the Dicastery for the Doctrine of the Faith in its *Vademecum: On Certain Points of Procedure in Treating Cases of Sexual Abuse of Minors Committed by Clerics*:

1. The delict in question includes every external offense against the sixth commandment of the Decalogue committed by a cleric with a minor (cf. canon 1398 §1, 1° CIC; art. 6, 1° SST).
2. The typology of the delict is quite broad; it can include, for example, sexual relations (consensual or non-consensual), physical contact for sexual gratification, exhibitionism, masturbation, the production of pornography, inducement to prostitution, conversations and/or propositions of a sexual nature, which can also occur through various means of communication.[5]

"Sexual Abuse" includes "forcing someone, by violence or threat or through abuse of authority, to perform or submit to sexual acts." By including "abuse of authority" in this description, the cases of people such as the former Cardinal McCarrick in the United States are encompassed. Jurisprudence of the Dicastery for the Doctrine of the Faith will interpret exactly what this "abuse of authority" means in its decisions on individual cases.

Any ordained cleric or religious has significant spiritual authority over lay people. If a cleric has a ministerial relationship with a person with whom he has sex, the cleric would be guilty of sexual abuse because he is abusing his authority. This would mean a sexual relationship between a bishop and a member of the faithful from his diocese; a priest and a parishioner; a priest-lecturer and a student; and a seminary staff member with a seminarian would all be crimes of sexual abuse.

PREVENTING ABUSE

In his address to the Irish bishops on October 28, 2006, Pope Benedict XVI gave a succinct and compelling account of the response that the Catholic Church needed to give:

> In your continuing efforts to deal effectively with this problem, it is important to establish the truth of what happened in the past, to take whatever steps are necessary to prevent it from occurring again, to ensure that the principles of justice are fully respected and, above all, to bring healing to the victims and to all those affected by these egregious crimes.[6]

Establishing the truth about sexual abuse is vital for victims. They need justice, and the Church must do everything it possibly can to prevent more victims of known perpetrators. Removing perpetrators from access to potential victims is vitally important.

MANDATORY REPORTING

In 2019, Pope Francis in *Vos Estis Lux Mundi* first introduced mandatory reporting of sexual abuse by clerics and religious within the Church:

> §1. Except as provided for by canons 1548 §2 CIC and 1229 §2 CCEO, whenever a cleric or a member of an Institute of Consecrated Life or of a Society of Apostolic Life has notice of, or well-founded motives to believe that, one of the facts referred to in article 1 has been committed, that person is obliged to report promptly the fact to the local Ordinary where the events are said to have occurred or to another Ordinary among those referred to in canons 134 CIC and 984 CCEO, except for what is established by §3 of the present article. §2. Any person can submit a report concerning the conduct referred to in article 1, using the methods referred to in the preceding article, or by any other appropriate means. §3. When the report concerns one of the persons indicated in article 6, it is to be addressed to the Authority identified based upon articles 8 and 9. The report can always be sent to the Holy See directly or through the Pontifical Representative. §4. The report shall include as many particulars as possible, such as indications of time and place of the facts, of the persons involved or informed, as well as any other circumstance that may be useful

in order to ensure an accurate assessment of the facts. §5. Information can also be acquired ex officio. (VELM 3)

Most importantly, the person submitting the report was guaranteed protection:

Art. 4 – Protection of the person submitting the report. §1. Making a report pursuant to article 3 shall not constitute a violation of office confidentiality. §2. Except as provided for by canons 1390 CIC and 1452 and 1454 CCEO, prejudice, retaliation or discrimination as a consequence of having submitted a report is prohibited and may constitute the conduct referred to in article 1§1, letter b). §3. An obligation to keep silent may not be imposed on any person with regard to the contents of his or her report. (VELM 4)

Mandatory reporting was taken into account with the changes in Book VI of the Code of Canon Law. All clergy and religious brothers and sisters must report sexual abuse by clergy and religious brothers and sisters to the local Ordinary (usually a diocesan bishop). They must report even suspicions that abuse is happening. This includes a cleric or religious abusing their authority by having sexual contact with anyone. This requirement is now reinforced by canon 1371 §6 in the revised penal law which provides penalties for clergy and religious who fail to report an offense as required by canon law:

A person who neglects to report an offence, when required to do so by a canonical law, is to be punished according to the provision of canon 1336 §§2–4, with the addition of other penalties according to the gravity of the offence. (Can. 1371 §6)

All major superiors (including provincials, and leaders of societies of apostolic life) must report to the local Ordinary (usually a diocesan bishop) all allegations of sexual abuse that have happened in the past, including who the victim and the perpetrator were, and what action was taken as a result.

The Dicastery for Legislative Texts explains:

103. Omission of the duty to communicate news of a delict (can.1371 §6) A further new delict is that which is typified by §6 of can. 1371 regarding the duty to communicate to the competent ecclesiastical Authority any news of a delict that has become known in the external forum. Obviously, news received in the context of the sacrament of confession and in the internal forum in general are excluded. See also *Apostolic Penitentiary*, Note on the importance of the internal forum and the inviolability of the sacramental seal of 29 June 2019, *AAS* 111 (2019), 1113–1121.

As one will recall, the motu proprio *Vos Estis Lux Mundi*, of 7 May 2019, established the duty of clerics and consecrated persons to communicate verisimilar news of delicts against the sixth commandment committed by other clerics or consecrated persons to the competent ecclesiastical Authority, as well as the behaviour of complicit silence or concealment of such delicts

> by the Bishops or Supreme moderators of Institutes in the various ecclesiastical extrajudicial processes in which they must participate. The delict is outlined in a general way in order to be able to understand not only the matters specifically considered by *Vos Estis Lux Mundi* (sexual abuse or silence in this regard in administrative practices), but also any other obligations to report that the norms of the Church may impose. Obviously, the condition for committing the delict is that the subject is obliged by the canonical order to notify said information, which, in the case of *Vos Estis Lux Mundi*, specifically concerns clergy and consecrated persons. Consequently, the delict can have different forms of gravity. In any case the ecclesiastical authority is necessarily bound to initiate a sanctioning provision in these cases, having to punish the offender with an expiatory penalty among those indicated in can. 1336 §§2–4 (cf. nn. 45–47), to which other penalties can be added according to the gravity of the delict.[7]

The requirement to report is explained in detail in article 3 of *Vos Estis Lux Mundi*:

> §1. Except for when a cleric learns of information during the exercise of ministry in the internal forum, whenever a cleric or a member of an Institute of Consecrated Life or of a Society of Apostolic Life learns, or has well-founded motives to believe, that one of the acts referred to in art. 1 has been committed, that person is obliged to report it promptly to the local Ordinary where the events are said to have occurred or to another Ordinary among those referred to in canons 134 CIC and 984 CCEO, except for what is established by §3 of the present article. (VELM 3)

The local Ordinary means the diocesan bishop, apostolic or diocesan administrator.[8] Pope Francis has reinforced this obligation of religious to report abuse by telling religious priests and brothers to "not be ashamed to denounce" one of their confreres if an abuse is known, because they must "protect the others":[9]

> "Please remember this well: Zero tolerance on abuse against children or disabled persons; zero tolerance," he said. "We are religious men, we are priests who bring people to Jesus, not 'eat' people with our concupiscence. And the abuser destroys, he 'eats'—so to speak—the abused with his concupiscence."[10]

Clearly, Pope Francis considers protecting abusers to be the worst outcome of clericalism[11] and this culture must change.

A priest cannot report sexual abuse when it is confessed to him by a perpetrator in confession:

> The sacramental seal is inviolable; therefore it is absolutely forbidden for a confessor to betray in any way a penitent in words or in any manner and for any reason. (Can. 983 §1)

> A confessor who directly violates the sacramental seal incurs a *latae sententiae* excommunication reserved to the

> Apostolic See; he who does so only indirectly is to be punished according to the gravity of the offence. (Can. 1386 §1)

However, the priest can and should help a victim to report or complain about the abuse when they come to him in confession seeking help.

COMPLAINTS ABOUT BISHOPS AND OTHER CHURCH LEADERS

If a complaint involves a bishop or religious superior personally abusing someone or failing to act on abuse complaints, then the report would go to the metropolitan,[12] the papal nuncio, or directly to the Holy See. Persons making complaints are protected in canon law, and any discriminatory action taken against them is a crime in canon law. There is no requirement in *Vos Estis Lux Mundi* that the acts of the investigation be shared with the accused bishop or religious leader before notifying the Dicastery for the Doctrine of the Faith about the complaint or accusation.

This requirement is reinforced by the Pontifical Commission for the Protection of Minors' *Universal Guidelines Framework* (UGF), which states:

> Each Metropolitan must put in place procedures for managing allegations against Bishops and Church Authorities. This includes actions or omissions which result in abuse, in line with VELM articles 6–17.[13]

ANONYMOUS COMPLAINTS

Reports might be anonymous or only suspicions that sexual abuse is taking place. The Dicastery for the Doctrine of the Faith explained:

> At times, a *notitia de delicto* can derive from an anonymous source, namely, from unidentified or unidentifiable persons. The anonymity of the source should not automatically lead to considering the report as false. Nonetheless, for easily understandable reasons, great caution should be exercised in considering this type of *notitia*, and anonymous reports certainly should not be encouraged....Likewise, when a *notitia de delicto* comes from sources whose credibility might appear at first doubtful, it is not advisable to dismiss the matter *a priori*. (*Vademecum* 11–12)

Experience teaches that anonymous complaints often have a basis in fact, especially when the complaint specifies an exact time and place when the alleged offense occurred. Investigations of these anonymous complaints must also be reported to the Dicastery for the Doctrine of the Faith, including those that the Ordinary decides lack a semblance of truth.[14]

FAILURE TO ACT

Pope John Paul II was conscious that a priest who sexually abused a child harmed not only the victim but the whole Church. In 2001, he appointed the Congregation for the Doctrine of the Faith to supervise investigations into credible complaints of sexual abuse of children and how they were handled[15] and authorized the Congregation to order penal trials for accused priests. Effectively, the Apostolic See established a system of accountability. Now when any Ordinary (provincial or diocesan bishop) receives a complaint of sexual abuse of a minor, he must notify the Dicastery for the Doctrine of the Faith that he has received a complaint. Article 10 of *Sacramentorum Sanctitatis Tutela* states:

> §1. Whenever the Ordinary or Hierarch receives a report of a more grave delict, which has at least the semblance of truth, and after having completed the preliminary investigation according to the norm of can. 1717 CIC and can. 1468 CCEO, he is to communicate the matter to the Dicastery for the Doctrine of the Faith which, unless it calls the case to itself due to particular circumstances, will direct the Ordinary or Hierarch how to proceed further. (SST, 10)

The Dicastery will then instruct the bishop about how the complaint is to be handled and will appoint a tribunal of its own or appoint a local tribunal to carry out a penal trial. This requirement to report more grave crimes to the Dicastery for the Doctrine of the Faith is reinforced by its *Vademecum* in 2022:

> 69. In accordance with art. 10 §1 SST, once the preliminary investigation has concluded, whatever its outcome, the Ordinary or Hierarch is obliged to send, without delay, an authentic copy of the relative acts to the DDF. Together with the copy of the acts and the duly completed form found at the end of this handbook, he is to provide his own evaluation of the results of the investigation (*votum*) and to offer any suggestions he may have on how to proceed (if, for example, he considers it appropriate to initiate a penal procedure and of what kind; if he considers sufficient the penalty imposed by the civil authorities; if the application of administrative measures by the Ordinary or Hierarch is preferable; if the prescription of the delict should be declared or its derogation granted). (*Vademecum* 60)

The Dicastery for the Doctrine of the Faith directs that only in a case where a report lacks a semblance of truth can the alleged crime be deemed impossible:

> Given the sensitive nature of the matter (for example, the fact that sins against the sixth commandment of the Decalogue rarely occur in the presence of witnesses), a determination that the *notitia* lacks the semblance of truth (which can lead to omitting the preliminary investigation) will be made only in the case of the manifest impossibility of the commission of a delict according to the norms of canon law. For example, if it turns out that at the time of the delict of which he is accused, the person was not yet a cleric; if it comes to light that the presumed victim was not a minor (on this point, cf. no. 3); if it is a well-known fact that the person accused could not have been present at the place of the delict when the alleged

> actions took place....Even in these cases, however, it is advisable that the Ordinary or Hierarch communicate to the DDF the *notitia de delicto* and the decision made to forego the preliminary investigation due to the manifest lack of the semblance of truth. (*Vademecum* 18–19)

The media have reported many instances from all over the world of bishops and other religious leaders failing to investigate or adequately deal with complaints of sexual abuse. In response, and as already noted, Pope Francis promulgated the *motu proprio* "You are the Light of the World" (VELM 2019). It was revised in 2023. The definition of abuse in *Vos Estis Lux Mundi* article 1 b) also included religious leaders failing to act on complaints of sexual abuse of minors while they were in office.[16] It is now a crime for religious leaders to fail to observe civil law on reporting crimes and failing to cooperate with or obstructing civil investigations.[17] Effectively, the Church is canonizing aspects of civil law regarding what constitutes sexual abuse and grooming, as well as civil procedural laws on reporting.[18] This has significance in many countries because of civil laws regarding grooming, obtaining the phone numbers of children, photographing children without parental consent, and so on.

Historic failures of bishops and other religious leaders not dealing properly with complaints are now encompassed by the legislation in *Vos Estis Lux Mundi*. Article 6 b), c), and d) includes previous leaders by stating "who have been in the past leaders," referring to moderators of institutes of consecrated life societies of apostolic life and monasteries concerning acts or omissions while they were in office. They can now be held accountable for their failures to act properly.

Bishops have a duty to act on complaints:

> §1. Since the Bishop must defend the unity of the universal Church, he is bound to foster the discipline which is common to the whole Church, and so press for the observance of all ecclesiastical laws. §2. He is to ensure that abuses do not creep into ecclesiastical discipline. (Can. 392)

The bishop has an obligation to ensure that universal law is observed and, if necessary, to issue a particular law concerning matters such as celibacy and continence as provided for in canon 277. This includes laws on safeguarding, safe ministerial practices, code of conduct, and professional development on these matters.

Vos Estis Lux Mundi clarified canon law such as canon 1389 (now c. 1378) which had already categorized acts or failures to act crimes when they constituted an abuse of an office or position.

The provisions of *Vos Estis Lux Mundi* removed any doubt about the application of this canon concerning sexual abuse cases. Failure to act constitutes an abuse of office. When religious superiors fail to act in a case of sexual abuse, the diocesan bishop must insist that the religious superior act.

> §1. In matters concerning the care of souls, the public exercise of divine worship, and other works of the apostolate, religious are subject to the authority of the Bishops, whom they are bound to treat with sincere submission and reverence. §2. In the exercise of an external apostolate towards persons outside the institute, religious are also subject to their own Superiors and must remain faithful to the discipline of the institute. If the need arises, Bishops themselves are not to fail to insist on this regulation. (Can. 678)

The bishop has a clear obligation to act concerning sexual abuse in Catholic schools:

> In his own diocese, the local Ordinary has the right to appoint or to approve teachers of religion and, if religious or moral considerations require it, the right to remove them or to demand that they be removed. (Can. 805)

Moral considerations would include sexual abuse or misconduct.

If the religious superior still fails to act, the diocesan bishop must inform the Holy See:

> For the gravest of reasons, a diocesan Bishop can forbid a member of a religious institute to remain in his diocese, provided the person's major Superior has been informed and has failed to act; the matter must, however, immediately be reported to the Holy See. (Can. 679)

Clearly, a bishop or a religious superior failing to act properly on a complaint of sexual abuse is committing a canonical crime or delict. The *Vademecum* reminds bishops that they can be removed for negligence, failing to act, or failing to deal properly with a complaint:

> According to canon 1717 CIC and canon 1468 CCEO, responsibility for the preliminary investigation belongs to the Ordinary or Hierarch who received the *notitia de delicto*, or to a suitable person selected by him. The eventual omission of this duty could constitute a delict subject to a canonical procedure in conformity with the Code of Canon Law and the Motu Proprio *Come una madre amorevole*, as well as art. 1 §1, b VELM. (*Vademecum* 21)

The *motu proprio Come una Madre Amorevole* (As a Loving Mother), issued by Pope Francis on June 4, 2016, contains the procedures to remove a bishop for negligence, and *Vos Estis Lux Mundi* informs bishops that they could be removed for failing to deal with complaints of sexual abuse.

Furthermore, canon 128 provides for redress for a person who has been harmed by a failure to act, and to be recompensed for the harm[19] they incurred as a result: "Whoever unlawfully causes harm to another by a juridical act, or indeed by any other act which is malicious or culpable, is obliged to repair the damage done." Myriam Wijlens notes that "canon 128 is not only directed to individuals who might cause damage, but includes damage caused by ecclesiastical officials."[20] Therefore, a bishop or religious superior who fails to act can be held accountable for their failure(s) to act, especially when these actions lead to other persons being harmed or abused.

VULNERABLE PEOPLE

In *Vos Estis Lux Mundi*, Pope Francis legislated that abuse of vulnerable people was a crime:

> §1. These norms apply to reports regarding clerics or members of Institutes of Consecrated Life or Societies of Apostolic Life and concerning: a) delicts against the sixth commandment of the Decalogue consisting of: i. forcing someone, by violence or threat or through abuse of authority, to perform or submit to sexual acts; ii. performing sexual acts with a minor or a vulnerable person. (VELM 1)

The revised penal law has been criticized for omitting any mention of "vulnerable." Bishop Arrieta, the secretary for the revision process, said at the press conference after the promulgation of the changed penal law that vulnerable people were encompassed by the phrase "one to whom the law recognizes equal protection" in canon 1398.[21] Bishop Arietta also added that "vulnerable" is not accepted in many countries as a legal category of persons who should receive special protection.[22]

Canon 1398 §1 states:

> A cleric is to be punished with deprivation of office and with other just penalties, not excluding, where the case calls for it, dismissal from the clerical state, if he: 1° commits an offence against the sixth commandment of the Decalogue with a minor or with a person who habitually has an imperfect use of reason or with one to whom the law recognizes equal protection.

A vulnerable person was defined in *Vos Estis Lux Mundi* as "any person in a state of infirmity, physical or mental deficiency, or deprivation of personal liberty which, in fact, even occasionally, limits their ability to understand or to want or otherwise resist the offence" (VELM 1 §2, b).

The Pontifical Commission for the Protection of Minors defines a vulnerable adult as:

> any person aged 18 years and over who is at increased risk of experiencing abuse, such as people: who are elderly; with a disability; who suffer from mental illness; who have diminished capacity; who have cognitive impairment; who have suffered previous abuse; who are experiencing transient risks; who in receiving a ministry are subject to a power imbalance; who identify as First Nations and/or Indigenous; who are from a culturally and linguistically diverse background; who are of diverse sexuality; who have any other impairment or adversity that makes it difficult for them to protect themselves from abuse.[23]

Cases of vulnerable people are not within the competence of the Dicastery for the Doctrine of the Faith. The *Vademecum* of the DDF states:

> The revision of the Motu Proprio SST, promulgated on 21 May 2010, states that a person who habitually has the imperfect use of reason is to be considered equivalent to a minor (cf. art. 6 §1, 1° SST). With regard to the use of the term "vulnerable adult," elsewhere described as "any person in a state of infirmity, physical or mental deficiency, or deprivation of personal liberty which, in fact, even occasionally limits their ability to understand or to want or otherwise resist the offence" (cf. art. 1 §2, b VELM), it should be noted that this definition includes other situations than those pertaining to the competence of the CDF, which remains limited to minors under eighteen years of age and to those who "habitually have an imperfect use of reason." Other situations outside of these cases are handled by the competent Dicasteries (cf. art. 7 §1 VELM). (*Vademecum* 5)

This would mean that cases of allegations of clerics abusing vulnerable people would be handled either by the Dicastery for Evangelization for mission countries or the Dicastery for Clergy. Allegations against religious brothers and sisters would be handled by the Dicastery for Institutes of Consecrated Life and Societies of Apostolic Life.

ABUSE OF AUTHORITY

The revised penal law reiterates that abuse of authority as a cleric is a crime. It is recognized that many so-called consenting adult relationships are not ones with equal consent and that vulnerable people are often manipulated by people with positions of power and authority. In the revised Book VI, canon 1389 has become canon 1378, which states:

> §1. A person who, apart from the cases already foreseen by the law, abuses ecclesiastical power, office, or function, is to be punished according to the gravity of the act or the omission, not excluding by deprivation of the power or office, without prejudice to the obligation of repairing the harm. §2. A person who, through culpable negligence, unlawfully and with harm to another or scandal, performs or omits an act of ecclesiastical power or office or function, is to be punished according to the provision of canon 1336 §§2–4, without prejudice to the obligation of repairing the harm.

Abuse of authority includes culpable negligence and failing to act. The revised canon points directly to penalties that may be imposed on an offender and makes explicit mention of their obligation to repair the harm they have caused.[24] A penalty is not to be remitted until there has been reparation of harm:

> Remission must not be granted until, in the prudent judgement of the Ordinary, the offender has repaired any harm caused. The offender may be urged to make such reparation or restitution by one of the penalties mentioned in can. 1336 §§2–4; the same applies also when the offender is granted remission of a censure under can. 1358 §1. (Can. 1361 §4)

This provision gives church authorities real power to demand restitution or reparation for offenses causing harm to others. The Ordinary must not remit a penalty before he prudently judges that the offender has repaired any harm caused.

UNIVERSAL GUIDELINES FRAMEWORK

The *Universal Guidelines Framework* (UGF) reinforces the obligation to report information concerning sexual abuse to both Church and civil authorities when it states:

> 4.3.1 All reports of sexual abuse should be reported to the civil authorities. The Church Body maintains documented evidence of their cooperation with civil authorities in responding to abuse allegations.
>
> 4.3.2 There are clear and accessible mechanisms in place to ensure the reporting of all abuse allegations to the appropriate civil and Church Authorities. This should stipulate reporting to the local Ordinary where the alleged events took place.
>
> 4.3.3 Each Metropolitan must put in place procedures for managing allegations against Bishops and Church Authorities. This includes actions or omissions which result in abuse, in line with VELM articles 6–17.

Protocols and abuse procedures of each bishops' conference must enshrine the duty to report and the procedures for doing so.

MANDATORY REPORTING OF SEXUAL ABUSE BY EMPLOYEES

Bishops via employment contracts should also make it obligatory for all diocesan and parish employees to report to the local Ordinary any sexual abuse by clerics, religious, diocesan, or parish employees they know of, or suspect is happening or has happened. Laypeople in these positions are often in a very privileged position to know about sexual abuse activities because of what the faithful share with them.

The Pontifical Commission for the Protection of Minors, *Universal Guidelines Framework* supports this:

> The Church Body's Complaints Handling Policy and procedures empower and support personnel to raise, in good faith, concerns and allegations about unacceptable behaviour towards children and adults by other personnel and include provisions for the protection of whistle-blowers from prejudice, retaliation or discrimination. (UGF 4.2.10)

CONCLUSION

Canon law is clear. When clergy and members of religious institutes and societies of apostolic life, except for information learnt in the internal forum, learn, or have well-founded reasons to believe, that sexual abuse has been committed, that person is obliged to report it promptly to the local Ordinary where the events are said to have occurred or to another Ordinary. That Ordinary is then obliged by canon law and conscience to take the appropriate actions.

7

REQUIREMENT TO REPORT SEXUAL ABUSE

Sometimes clergy and religious are informed about a sexual abuse offense by someone in the external forum and the informant does not want the bishop or other authorities to be told about it. An issue arises about respecting the wishes of the victim.

This scenario highlights the need for people to be informed about the requirement of clergy and religious to report. Tribunal and other church websites should inform people about the obligation of clergy, religious, and other church employees to report information about sexual abuse. The priest or religious learning about the sexual abuse needs to understand the effects of trauma on the victim/witness and how the abuse has affected their sense of trust. It may help if the process is reframed more as a helping process.

It is essential to acknowledge that the person has a reason(s) for not wanting to report and to understand why the person does not want to report to church authorities. Possibly the person fears that they won't be believed; their trust in the Church could be shattered; they may have already experienced cover-up by the Church; there might be someone in church leadership they currently do not trust; the abuser may have been in a highly placed position; they may be afraid for their family (in some Asian countries it could affect whether a brother gets ordained); or may not yet have told their family.

There needs to be an open conversation to come to understand their position. Understanding the reason may allow for a different discussion and move it into a conversation about the tribunal/church reporting process. It is often helpful when it is explained to them how the reporting process works and what and who is involved. It is important that the person has ongoing help and contact with someone who can support them. If the person does not want to report or have further contact, it is important to document what was said and pass that on to church authorities.

While an individual person with knowledge of sexual abuse may for personal reasons not want the information passed on to church or civil authorities, the common good of the Church is at stake with this information about sexual abuse:

> §1. In exercising their rights, the Christian faithful, both as individuals and gathered together in associations, must take into account the common good of the Church, the rights of others, and their own duties toward others. §2. In view of the common good, ecclesiastical authority can direct the exercise of rights which are proper to the Christian faithful. (Can. 223)

Canon 223 specifies that individuals must consider "their own duties toward others." The person with knowledge of the abuse and the priest or religious to whom it has been revealed do not know whether there has been another complaint against the accused priest or religious. Often there are other victims of abusers. The accused priest or religious may have denied the first complaint. Now, when another report is submitted, this information may enable the first alleged victim's complaint to be upheld, so that this victim now receives justice. Everyone in the Church has an obligation to help victims. Besides crimes against minors or persons habitually lacking the use of reason, sexual abuse crimes include abuse of authority and position, taking advantage of vulnerable persons, and the failure to act as required by the law.[1]

The word *mandatory* comes from Latin *mandatum* meaning "something commanded." Mandatory reporting demonstrates that the Church is serious about eliminating the evil of sexual abuse. Pope Francis is conscious that actions speak louder than words and added a second paragraph to canon 1311 including the necessity for penal law and its three aims of "the restoration of justice, the reform of the offender, and the repair of scandal."

Canon 223 also speaks of the obligation of individual members of the faithful to consider the "rights of others." This includes preventing others from becoming victims. Sexual abuse does enormous damage to victims who may self-harm, lose jobs, or become addicted to substances. Sometimes abuse causes broken marriages and relationships. An abusive priest or religious needs help, treatment, and possibly monitoring to ensure that every reasonable action is taken to guarantee that there is no further abuse in future.

Civil investigations in many countries today often reveal cover-ups by church leaders fifty years ago. The local Church must learn the lesson of what has been happening in other countries and not be foolish enough to think that scandals of cover-ups of sexual abuse by church officials and leaders will not be exposed in their own country. In thirty years, there may be an external examination of actions taken today.

In 2018, Pope Francis began his "Letter to the People of God" with the words:

> "If one member suffers, all suffer together with it" (1 Cor 12:26). These words of Saint Paul forcefully echo in my heart as I acknowledge once more the suffering endured by many minors due to sexual abuse, the abuse of power and the abuse of conscience perpetrated by a significant number of clerics and consecrated persons. Crimes that inflict deep wounds of pain and powerlessness, primarily among the victims, but also in their family members and in the larger community of believers and nonbelievers alike. Looking back to the past, no effort to beg pardon and to seek to repair the harm done will ever be sufficient. Looking ahead to the future, no effort must be spared to create a culture able to prevent such situations from happening, but also to prevent the possibility of their being covered up and perpetuated. The pain of the victims and their families is also our pain, and so it is urgent that we once more reaffirm our commitment to ensure the protection of minors and of vulnerable adults.[2]

As noted in an earlier chapter, Pope Francis first established the duty of clerics and consecrated persons to report information about delicts against the sixth commandment to the competent ecclesiastical authority in *Vos Estis Lux Mundi*. Mandatory reporting is facilitated by an instruction on the Confidentiality of Legal Proceedings issued on December 6, 2019.[3] This means that when, for example, evidence of sexual abuse by clergy, religious, or church employees is disclosed in a marriage annulment case, it must be reported to church authorities. If civil authorities have mandatory reporting laws, they must be obeyed. The instruction states:

> Office confidentiality shall not prevent the fulfilment of the obligations laid down in all places by civil laws, including any reporting obligations, and the execution of enforceable requests of civil judicial authorities.[4]

While paragraph 4 only speaks about civil reporting requirements, it has the same implications for reporting obligations within the Church. (c. 19)

In 2022, the Dicastery for the Doctrine of the Faith's *Vademecum* addressed the issue of what must be done when information (*notitia*)[5] is received about a possible delict (canonical crime). The Dicastery said "it need not be a formal complaint" and that

> this *notitia* can come from a variety of sources: it can be formally presented to the Ordinary or Hierarch, orally or in writing, by the alleged victim, his or her guardians or other persons claiming to have knowledge about the matter; it can become known to the Ordinary or Hierarch through the exercise of his duty for vigilance; it can be reported to the Ordinary or Hierarch by the civil authorities through channels provided for by local legislation; it can be made known through the communications media (including social media); it can come to his knowledge through hear-

> say, or in any other adequate way. (See *Vademecum* 9–10)

I once had an experience in which a family complained to me about a priest having a minor stay overnight at his presbytery. The family feared retribution and did not want their names known. I lodged the complaint anonymously with the professional standards office. There was plenty of detailed information in the file so that it could not be ignored. The professional standards office informed the bishop who dealt with the priest. The next Sunday the priest's homily was devoted to an attack on those who "dobbed him in,"[6] confirming the need in some cultural settings to lay an anonymous complaint.

The Dicastery for the Doctrine of the Faith requires anonymous complaints to be taken seriously (*Vademecum* 11). This illustrates the importance of dealing adequately with complaints after the mistakes of the past. The *Vademecum* reiterates that the seal of confession is an exception to the obligation of reporting sexual abuse:

> It must be pointed out that a report of a *delictum gravius* received in confession is placed under the strictest bond of the sacramental seal (cf. canon 983 § 1 CIC; canon 733 § 1 CCEO; art. 4 § 1, 5° SST). A confessor who learns of a *delictum gravius* during the celebration of the sacrament should seek to convince the penitent to make that information known by other means, in order to enable the appropriate authorities to take action. (*Vademecum* 14)

The failures of bishops and other church leaders all over the world to act upon and report abuse is a grave scandal. The *Vademecum* advises:

> Even in cases where there is no explicit legal obligation to do so, the ecclesiastical authorities should make a report to the competent civil authorities if this is considered necessary to protect the person involved or other minors from the danger of further criminal acts. (17)

This advice to report sexual abuse to civil authorities even when there is no legal obligation to do so demonstrates a zero tolerance for any abusive actions. Pope Francis reiterated the legislation for mandatory reporting in *Vos Estis Lux Mundi* (2023):

> Art. 3 – Reporting. §1. Except for when a cleric learns of information during the exercise of ministry in the internal forum, whenever a cleric or a member of an Institute of Consecrated Life or of a Society of Apostolic Life learns, or has well-founded motives to believe, that one of the acts referred to in art. 1 has been committed, that person is obliged to report it promptly to the local Ordinary where the events are said to have occurred or to another Ordinary among those referred to in canons 134CIC and 984 CCEO, except for what is established by §3 of the present article. (VELM 17)

Mandatory reporting includes reporting religious leaders who fail to act:

> §3. When the report concerns one of the persons indicated in art. 6, it is to be addressed to the Authority identified on the basis of articles 8 and 9. The report can always be sent to the competent Dicastery directly or through the Pontifical Representative. If the first option is chosen, the Dicastery will inform the Pontifical Representative about the matter....§5. Information can also be acquired *ex officio*. (VELM 3)

Vos Estis Lux Mundi (2023) slightly broadens the exception to mandatory reporting as indicated in VELM (2019), when it describes the exception as "ministry in the internal forum." This means that as well as information disclosed under the seal of confession, information revealed in spiritual direction is included in the exception. Note that there is special legislation concerning spiritual direction in seminaries.[7]

If there were many exceptions to the law, or if exceptions to the law were made for less serious reasons, these exceptions would defeat the purpose of having mandatory reporting legislation. Mandatory reporting would not exist in practice.

In 2021, Pope Francis legislated the crime of failing to report offenses.[8] This legislation is for the good of victims and the common good of the Church so that it is a crime for a priest or a religious not to report sexual abuse. This crime emphasizes the serious legal obligation each priest and religious holds to report sexual abuse when they learn about it. Priests and religious must report knowledge of sexual abuse to the local Ordinary where the alleged events took place.

8

REPORTING TO CIVIL AUTHORITIES

In recent years, there have been many instances where the Catholic Church has faced criticism for not fully cooperating with civil authorities in addressing cases of abuse. These cases have highlighted the need for greater transparency, accountability, and the establishment of clear protocols to ensure effective collaboration between the Church and civil authorities. As noted in the previous chapter, any instance of abuse or failure to address abuse must be taken seriously and dealt with appropriately.

Cooperation between the Catholic Church and civil authorities is an important aspect of ensuring the well-being of society and upholding the rule of law. It is important to note that most clergy members and individuals within the Catholic Church are dedicated to serving the community and upholding moral values. However, instances of abuse or misuse of canon law can occur in certain situations, and it is crucial to address such concerns and promote transparency, accountability, and justice.

Canon law, which governs the internal affairs of the Catholic Church, is separate from civil law, which is the legal framework established by civil authorities. While the Catholic Church recognizes the authority of civil laws, it also maintains its own set of rules and regulations to guide its members and internal operations.

Abuse of canon law can take different forms, such as cases in which the Church may not fully cooperate with civil authorities in investigating allegations of sexual abuse or other criminal activities committed by clergy. This lack of cooperation can hinder the pursuit of justice and may result in the protection or concealment of offenders.

To address these concerns, many dioceses and religious orders have implemented new policies and procedures to ensure cooperation with civil authorities, reporting allegations promptly, and providing support to victims. Additionally, the Vatican has taken steps to improve transparency and accountability, such as issuing guidelines for handling cases of abuse and establishing a dedicated office to oversee these matters.

The goal should always be to ensure justice for victims, prevent further abuse, and restore trust in the Church. Open dialogue, collaboration, and a commitment to upholding the principles of justice and accountability are crucial in addressing any instances of abuse or misuse of canon law and promoting a safer and more just society.

DOCTRINE OF THE FAITH LETTER (2011)

Observing the civil reporting laws in countries was first addressed canonically on May 3, 2011, in a circular letter[1] sent by the Congregation for the Doctrine of the Faith to Episcopal Conferences stating:

> e) Cooperation with Civil Authority. Sexual abuse of minors is not just a canonical delict but also a crime prosecuted by civil law. Although relations with civil authority will differ in various countries, nevertheless it is important to cooperate with such authority within their responsibilities. Specifically, without prejudice to the sacramental internal forum, the prescriptions of civil law regarding the reporting of such crimes to the designated authority should always be followed. This collaboration, moreover, not only concerns cases of abuse committed by clerics, but also those cases which involve religious or lay persons who function in ecclesiastical structures.[2]

VOS ESTIS LUX MUNDI

Although the revised penal law does not provide a penalty for not reporting to civil authorities, *Vos Estis Lux Mundi* requires bishops, religious, and clergy to obey civil reporting laws except if the knowledge came "in the exercise of his ministry in the internal forum" (VELM 2023 updated version, art. 3 §1).

> Article 20 – Compliance with state laws. These norms apply without prejudice to the rights and obligations established in each place by state laws, particularly those concerning any reporting obligations to the competent civil authorities.

Bishops and religious superiors can be removed from office or punished for the delict of covering up sexual abuse and not cooperating with civil investigations.

Not observing civil law requirements is also explicitly covered in *Vos Estis Lux Mundi*:

> Article 1 – Scope of application. b) conduct carried out by the subjects referred to in art. 6, consisting of actions or omissions intended to interfere with or avoid civil investigations or canonical investigations, whether administrative or penal, against one of the subjects indicated in §1 regarding the delicts referred to in letter a) of this paragraph.

Although the Doctrine of the Faith's circular letter in 2011 made it clear that the Church must obey civil laws regarding abuse and reporting,[3] Archbishop Scicluna indicated that *Vos Estis Lux Mundi* was the first time that "compliance with state laws" had become universal law.

Archbishop Scicluna explained that it was unacceptable for people to continue trying to protect the Church because "the good of the church requires truth and transparency, which includes respecting civil law." He added that he hoped people felt "empowered to go to the police" to denounce a crime. People have an obligation to report criminal actions, negligence, and inappropriate behavior to church authorities. Furthermore, "if people have the right and the duty to denounce something illicit" in the case of abuse, "they also have the right to denounce if, after one year, nothing has been done."[4]

The obligation to observe civil reporting laws is clear.[5] However, the Vatican maintains that mandating reporting to civilian authorities would imperil Catholics in some countries where they already face oppression. In some places, reporting abuse could result in victims being harshly dealt with and the clergy being persecuted.[6] Occasionally, there are media reports of rape victims being jailed or punished, such as, for example, a rape victim being stoned in Somalia in 2008.[7] Also, privacy laws in some countries conflict with universal mandatory reporting.[8]

RELIGIOUS LEADERS FAILING TO ACT

As already noted in chapter 5, *Vos Estis Lux Mundi* article 1 b) makes it a delict for religious leaders to fail to act on complaints of sexual abuse:

Furthermore, historic failures of not dealing with complaints are now also encompassed by canon law. The provisions of articles 1 b), c), d), e), and f) are a dramatic change in approach by the Church. It is now a delict or crime for religious leaders to fail to observe civil law on reporting and failing to cooperate with or obstructing civil investigations.[9]

After *Vos Estis Lux Mundi* was promulgated, the Dicastery for the Doctrine of the Faith went further in its *Vademecum* and encouraged reporting even when there is not a legal obligation to do so:

> Even in cases where there is no explicit legal obligation to do so, the ecclesiastical authorities should make a report to the competent civil authorities if this is considered necessary to protect the person involved or other minors from the danger of further criminal acts. (17)

Church authorities must do everything possible to ensure there are no more victims. This law specifically applies canon 1378 (c. 1389 1983), which had already made acts or failures to act delicts when they constituted an abuse of an office or position:

> §1. A person who, apart from the cases already foreseen by the law, abuses ecclesiastical power, office, or function,

> is to be punished according to the gravity of the act or the omission, not excluding by deprivation of the power or office, without prejudice to the obligation of repairing the harm. §2. A person who, through culpable negligence, unlawfully and with harm to another or scandal, performs or omits an act of ecclesiastical power or office or function, is to be punished according to the provision of can. 1336 §§2–4, without prejudice to the obligation of repairing the harm. (Can. 1378)[10]

These provisions remove any doubt about the application of this canon concerning sexual abuse cases.

CONFIDENTIALITY AND CHURCH OFFICIALS

In canon law, a clear distinction is made between the knowledge of abuse that victims, witnesses, and their families have, and knowledge that church officials have in their capacity as delegates, investigators, judges, and so on. Church officials must observe the highest confidentiality (secret of office) concerning information they learn in an official capacity.

Canon law makes it very clear that there is no restriction on victims, witnesses, and their families making known the abuse that was suffered. The *Vademecum* states:

> It should also be noted that accusations, processes and decisions relative to delicts mentioned in art. 6 SST are subject to the secret of office. This does not prevent persons reporting—especially if they also intend to inform the civil authorities—from making public their actions. Furthermore, since not all forms of *notitiae de delicto* are formal accusations, it is possible to evaluate whether or not one is bound by the secret, always keeping in mind the respect for the good name of others referred to in no. 44. (47)
>
> Here too, consideration should be given to whether the Ordinary or Hierarch is obliged to inform the civil authorities of the reception of the *notitia de delicto* and the opening of the preliminary investigation. Two principles apply: a/ respect for the laws of the state (cf. art. 20 VELM); and b/ respect for the desire of the alleged victim, provided that this is not contrary to civil legislation. Alleged victims should be encouraged—as will be stated below (no. 56)—to exercise their duties and rights vis-à-vis the state authorities, taking care to document that this encouragement took place and to avoid any form of dissuasion with regard to the alleged victim. Relevant agreements (concordats, accords, protocols of understanding) entered into by the Apostolic See with national governments must always and in any event be observed. (48)
>
> When the laws of the state require the Ordinary or Hierarch to report a *notitia de delicto*, he must do so, even if it is expected that on the basis of state laws no action will be taken (for example, in cases where the statute of limitations has expired or the definition of the delict may vary). (49)
>
> Whenever civil judicial authorities issue a legitimate executive order

requiring the surrender of documents regarding cases, or order the judicial seizure of such documents, the Ordinary or Hierarch must cooperate with the civil authorities, always respecting any possible agreements, where they exist. If the legitimacy of such a request or seizure is in doubt, the Ordinary or Hierarch can consult legal experts about available means of recourse. In any case, it is advisable to inform the Papal Representative immediately. (50)

In cases where it proves necessary to hear minors or persons equivalent to them, the civil norms of the country should be followed, as well as methods suited to their age or condition, permitting, for example, that the minor be accompanied by a trusted adult and avoiding any direct contact with the person accused. (51)

Vos Estis Lux Mundi protects not only the seal of confession, but also knowledge learned in the internal forum:

> Except for when a cleric learns of information during the exercise of ministry in the internal forum, whenever a cleric or a member of an Institute of Consecrated Life or of a Society of Apostolic Life learns, or has well-founded motives to believe, that one of the acts referred to in art. 1 has been committed, that person is obliged to report it promptly to the local Ordinary where the events are said to have occurred or to another Ordinary among those referred to in canons 134 CIC and 984 CCEO, except for what is established by §3 of the present article. (VELM 3 §1)

PROTECTION OF WHISTLEBLOWERS

The person making the allegation (report) is protected from prejudice, retaliation, or discrimination because of submitting that report. This brings the church legislation into line with most civil jurisdictions. *Vos Estis Lux Mundi* states:

> §1. Making a report pursuant to article 3 shall not constitute a violation of office confidentiality. §2. Except as provided for by canons 1390 CIC and 1452 and 1454 CCEO, prejudice, retaliation or discrimination as a consequence of having submitted a report is prohibited and may constitute the conduct referred to in article 1 §1, letter b). §3. An obligation to keep silent may not be imposed on the person claiming to have suffered as a result of a delict or on the witnesses with regard to the contents of their report, without prejudice to the provisions of article 5 §2. (VELM 4)

Persons making a report could easily be members of a religious institute or diocesan clergy. Paragraph 4 makes it clear that no obligation to silence or secrecy can be imposed on a person making a report or witnesses who give testimony about criminal actions. This eliminates nondisclosure agreements, as well as making it clear that the person making the report is free to report to any police or civil authority concerning the abuse.

The pontifical secret[11] does not apply to accusations, trials, and decisions involving the offenses referred to in:

a) Article 1 of the *motu proprio Vos Estis Lux Mundi* (May 7, 2019 and as updated March 25, 2023); or
b) Article 6 of the *Normae de Gravioribus Delictis* reserved to the judgement of the Congregation for the Doctrine of the Faith, in accordance with the *motu proprio Sacramentorum Sanctitatis Tutela* of Saint John Paul II (April 30, 2001), and subsequent amendments.
c) In the cases referred to in VELM 1, the information is to be held and handled ensuring its security, integrity and confidentiality in accordance with the prescriptions of canons 220, 471, 2° CIC and 244 §2, 2° CCEO, for the sake of protecting the good name, image and privacy of all persons involved.
d) The person who submits the report, the person who alleges to have been harmed and the witnesses shall not be bound by any obligation of silence regarding matters involving the case.

Nor does the pontifical secret apply when such offenses were committed in conjunction with other offenses. Furthermore, office confidentiality shall not prevent the fulfillment of the obligations laid down in all places by civil laws, including any reporting obligations and the execution of enforceable warrants/requests of civil judicial authorities.

Removing the word "secret" from procedures for handling abuse cases eliminates confusion for victims and others reporting cases to civil authorities. Now information about sexual abuse by clergy and religious that is learned during a marriage annulment case can and must be reported to the local Ordinary where the alleged events took place. Tribunals should make it clear on their websites and explanatory literature that tribunal officials have this obligation to report information about sexual abuse crimes.

SEAL OF CONFESSION

Priests must make it clear to penitents when sexual abuse is not covered by the seal of confession. The priest must advise the penitent/victim to seek help and to inform civil authorities. The Apostolic Penitentiary advises confessors with adult victims in the confessional:

> If a penitent is present who has been a victim of the evil of others, it will be the concern of the confessor to instruct them regarding their rights, as well as about the concrete juridical instruments to use to denounce the fact in civil and/or ecclesiastical forum and invoke his justice.[12]

The priest must be careful to uphold the seal of confession. If the child victim restates to the confessor outside confession what had earlier been stated in confession, the knowledge is now in the external forum and not only in the internal sacramental forum. Care must be taken not to confuse what is under the seal and what is not under the seal. Once the priest has been told about the abuse outside confession, the priest could then accompany the child to speak to its parents and/or could help the child to inform civil authorities.

In 2020, the Holy See replied to a recommendation made by the Australian Royal Commission concerning the seal of confession:

> Concerning absolution, the confessor must determine that the faithful who confess their sins are truly sorry for them and that they have a purpose of amendment (cfr. CIC, can. 959). Since repentance is, in fact, at the heart of this sacrament, absolution can be withheld only if the confessor concludes that the penitent lacks the necessary contrition (cfr. CIC, can. 980). Absolution then, cannot be made conditional on future actions in the external forum.[13]

When delaying absolution the confessor could:

> a) Ask the penitent to seek help from a psychologist/psychiatrist before granting absolution.
> b) Defer or refuse to grant absolution until he judges the sincerity of the penitent's intention to amend his/her life.[14]

A penitent can be encouraged to hand himself in to civil authorities. However, a confessor cannot require a penitent to hand himself into civil authorities and the granting of absolution cannot be conditional on a perpetrator handing himself in.[15] A parallel example is a confessor should not require an unfaithful husband to tell his wife of the affair. The *Note* issued by the Apostolic Penitentiary on July 1, 2019, explains this:

> If an abuser/penitent later discloses abuse outside the sacrament of Penance, obviously the knowledge is now in the external forum (not in the internal sacramental forum)—but care must be taken not to confuse what is under the seal of confession and what is not. The matter is in the external forum and must be dealt with accordingly.

If a priest learns of the abuse from a source outside the confessional, the seal of confession does not apply to the information he has learned in the external forum. The priest must do what he can to prevent further sexual abuse of minors. Because of the complexity of such situations, bishops, major superiors of clerical religious institutes, and members of sexual abuse protocol committees should not hear the confessions of priests to avoid any potential conflict of interest.

Upholding the seal of confession is a serious obligation for priests. The seal is not just to protect the privacy of the penitent. It is founded on the necessity to protect the dignity of the sacrament. Montini explains:

> The sacramental seal is to protect (even) the sacrament itself, and, therefore, the removal of the confessor from the seal is not at the discretion of the penitent. If at all the seal is at the discretionary power of the penitent, then the latter may be indirectly subject to such pressures (moral, social, etc.) so that the confessor is freed from the bond of the secrecy, which in reality

> would be equivalent to shift the actual guardian of the sacramental seal.[16]

The seal of confession applies to mortal and venial sins. The sacrament of Penance is the only way the faithful receive forgiveness of their sins in normal circumstances. Therefore, priests must be very careful not to discourage the faithful from going to receive the sacrament of Penance or Reconciliation by giving the impression that the seal of confession is not absolute.

When there is doubt about whether information is under the seal or not, the priest must keep the information confidential under the seal of confession. If, however, the person who came to confession divulges the information again to the priest outside the context of the confession, it is clear that the information divulged in the external forum is not under the seal of confession. Priests having a clear understanding of these principles should always be able to help victims who divulge in confession that they have been abused.

CONCLUSION

The law is clear that all the clergy, religious, and laypeople have an obligation to cooperate with civil authorities and obey civil laws, except when the seal of confession is at stake. Clergy and religious do not have an obligation in canon law to report to the local Ordinary anything learned in the internal forum both in the sacrament of Penance and in spiritual direction.

9

SCANDAL IN CANON LAW

"Scandal" in the media involves prominent figures being involved in sensational activities, especially those involving inappropriate relationships. We are bombarded with stories about royalty, political figures, movie stars, and the like.

SCANDAL IN THE BIBLE

The Catholic Church's understanding of "scandal" comes from the Greek word for a stumbling block. The term for "stumbling block" in biblical Hebrew is *mikšōl* (מִכְשׁוֹל) and in the Septuagint is translated into *koine* Greek as *skandalon* (σκανδαλον), in the sense of a "cause of moral stumbling." In both languages, it is associated with stumbling and that which causes one to fall. The *Encyclopedia of Catholicism* explains it as follows:

> Scandal...incites others to do evil, or provides others with an occasion for morally wrongful conduct. How we act or do not act may encourage or discourage the virtuous conduct of those who belong to the same families, institutions, and communities. Giving scandal amounts to doing wrong against our neighbours, because love for our neighbour dictates that we encourage one another to virtuous conduct.[1]

Scandal may have to be dealt with on a case-by-case basis because an action in and of itself may not be sinful. St. Paul urges the Corinthians not to eat meat offered in pagan temples out of loving concern for those with weak consciences (cf. 1 Cor 8:9). St. Paul "is concerned about the influence their thinking may have on fellow Christians."[2] Charity obliges one to refrain from conduct that could be foreseen to lead others to do wrong. In his Letter to the Romans, St. Paul considers this an offense against charity:

> Let us therefore no longer pass judgment on one another but resolve instead never to put a stumbling block or hindrance in the way of another. I know and am persuaded in the Lord Jesus that nothing is unclean in itself; but it is unclean for anyone who thinks

> it unclean. If your brother or sister is being injured by what you eat, you are no longer walking in love. Do not let what you eat cause the ruin of one for whom Christ died. (Rom 14:13–15)[3]

St. Paul reminds the strong to love and give Christlike love to their weaker brothers and sisters. The strong should not cause others to take offense, and they "are asked to do nothing that will make the weak brother or sister stumble."[4]

SCANDAL AS A SIN

Thomas Aquinas defined scandal as "the less right [*minus rectum*] word or action giving the occasion of fall."[5] The *New Catholic Encyclopedia* explains:

> According to St. Thomas (II-II:43:1) scandal is a word or action evil in itself, which occasions another's spiritual ruin. It is a word or action, that is either an external act—for an internal act can have no influence on the conduct of another—or the omission of an external act, because to omit what one should do is equivalent to doing what is forbidden; it must be evil in itself, or in appearance.[6]

St. Thomas teaches that scandal must be an act in the external forum. It must be observable, listened to, or reported by a witness. It must be a sin or have the appearance of being a sin. Raoul Naz explains that "scandal constitutes a disturbance of the social order, as it has the effect of provoking a violation of the law. Therefore, it is considered in the external forum."[7]

The *Catechism of the Catholic Church* defines *sin* as

> an offense against reason, truth, and right conscience; it is failure in genuine love for God and neighbour caused by a perverse attachment to certain goods. It wounds the nature of man and injures human solidarity. It has been defined as "an utterance, a deed, or a desire contrary to the eternal law." (*CCC* 1849)[8]

Scandal gives the occasion for another person to sin by influencing their action(s). The *Catechism of the Catholic Church* explains:

> Scandal is an attitude or behavior which leads another to do evil. The person who gives scandal becomes his neighbor's tempter. He damages virtue and integrity; he may even draw his brother into spiritual death. Scandal is a grave offense if by deed or omission another is deliberately led into a grave offense. (*CCC* 2284)

Scandal cannot cause another's sin because when one sins one must have free will and choose to do what is wrong. However, scandal may have the potential or intent to lead another to sin and is scandal per se. Otherwise, scandal is *per accidens* because the person influenced is already inclined to commit the sin.

SCANDAL AS A CRIME

A crime or delict in canon law is "an external and morally imputable violation of a law to which a canonical sanction is attached."[9] To commit a crime, a person must have sinned. Not all grave sins are crimes, but grave sins that seriously affect the individual or the church community are sometimes classified by the Church as crimes.

In canon law, scandal is a sin as well as a crime and differs from sensational bad behavior understood as scandal by the media. Obviously, however, the same grave sin can give rise to both understandings of scandal. "Scandal" has not been defined in the Code of Canon Law. Consequently, there is a risk of arbitrary or inappropriate action by ecclesiastical authority.[10]

Scandal may be "direct, that is, foreseen and intended; or indirect, that is, foreseen but not intended."[11] In direct scandal, the sinner violates charity to one's neighbor and commits a personal sin. St. Alphonsus Liguori, the patron saint of moral theologians, followed the teaching of Thomas Aquinas on scandal and linked it to the command of love of neighbor.[12] "St. Alphonsus Liguori explains that direct scandal is a sin both against charity and against the virtue that is violated by the one who is scandalized [*Theologia Moralis*, lib. III, n. 45]."[13] Active scandal intended to lead another directly into sin, while it was indirect scandal if the perpetrator only intended to commit the sin and did not intend to influence anyone else.

Thomas Aquinas distinguished between active scandal, whereby the perpetrator of the scandal performs a wrong action or verbally supports the action thereby giving scandal, and passive scandal, which is received by a person who witnessed the sin and is influenced by it.

SCANDAL BY A PERSON IN AUTHORITY

When the scandal is given by a person in authority, the scandal, according to the *Catechism of the Catholic Church,* is so much worse:

> Scandal takes on a particular gravity by reason of the authority of those who cause it or the weakness of those who are scandalized. It prompted our Lord to utter this curse: "Whoever causes one of these little ones who believe in me to sin, it would be better for him to have a great millstone fastened round his neck and to be drowned in the depth of the sea" (Matt 18:6–7). Scandal is grave when given by those who by nature or office are obliged to teach and educate others. Jesus reproaches the scribes and Pharisees on this account: he likens them to wolves in sheep's clothing. (§2285)

Elements of scandal in the negative sense are: (1) acts or omissions that harmfully affect the Christian community; (2) the passive failure to act by ecclesiastical authority; and (3) the threat to and undermining of essential values of the community.[14]

Scandal can also be given when a religious institute or a diocesan bishop fails to act on a complaint(s) of sexual abuse and does not apply the canonical laws or observes the civil laws as they are obliged to.[15] The *Catechism of the*

Catholic Church notes that "scandal can be provoked by laws or institutions, by fashion or opinion" (§2286). From an institutional perspective, church leaders create scandal when they allow a culture of clericalism to develop and exist:

> Therefore, they are guilty of scandal who establish laws or social structures leading to the decline of morals and the corruption of religious practice, or to social conditions that, intentionally or not, make Christian conduct and obedience to the Commandments difficult and practically impossible. (§2286)

As the *Catechism of the Catholic Church* teaches:

> Anyone who uses the power at his disposal in such a way that it leads others to do wrong becomes guilty of scandal and responsible for the evil that he has directly or indirectly encouraged. Temptations to sin are sure to come; but woe to him by whom they come. (§2287)

Failure to act by using the power attached to one's office can at times cause great scandal as illustrated by the sexual abuse crisis. This failure of church leaders to act and take decisive action against perpetrators led to a permissive environment allowing scandalous actions to be more prevalent. Pope Francis acknowledged this reality when he promulgated the revised penal law for the Church in 2021:

> In the past, much damage has been caused by a lack of perception of the intimate relationship which exists in the Church between the exercise of charity and recourse—when circumstances and justice require it—to penal sanctions. He says this trend represented a way of thinking which made correction more difficult, often giving rise to scandal and confusion among the faithful.[16]

THE 1917 CODE

The legislator of the 1917 Code was conscious of the damage caused to the faithful by public scandal. Raoul Naz explains that "scandal constitutes a disturbance of the social order, as it has the effect of provoking a violation of the law. Therefore, it is considered in the external forum."[17] Perpetrators of scandal were barred from receiving the Eucharist until they reformed:

> All those publicly unworthy are to be barred from the Eucharist, such as excommunicates, those interdicted, and those manifestly infamous, unless their penitence and emendation are shown and they have satisfied beforehand the public scandal [they caused]. (Can. 855 §1)

A distinction was made between those who caused public scandal and those who were unknown perpetrators of sins/crimes:

> But occult sinners, if they ask secretly and the minister knows they are unrepentant, should be refused; but not, however, if they ask publicly and they

> cannot be passed over without scandal. (Can. 855 §2)

An obvious example of this would be someone who was in an invalid marriage going to receive communion at Sunday Mass. The minister might know their marital situation, but many in the community would not, so the minister should not refuse to give communion to the person.

Scandal was considered so serious under the 1917 Code that the superior was allowed to punish someone giving scandal even if there was no sanction specified in the law:[18]

> Even though a law has no sanction attached to it, the legitimate Superior may nevertheless punish its transgression by a just penalty, even without a previous mentioning of the penalty if scandal perhaps was given or the special gravity of the transgression makes it necessary; otherwise, a defendant cannot be punished unless he was first warned with mention of the penalty, [whether] automatic or formal, in case of transgression, and nevertheless violated the law. (Can. 2222 §1)

Furthermore, to avoid scandal, a cleric was not to be promoted if a superior was uncertain of his suitability:

> Likewise the legitimate Superior, even though it is only probable that a delict has been committed or a penal action for a certainly committed delict has been prescribed, has not only the right but also the duty of not promoting a cleric of whose suitability he is not sure and, in order to avoid scandal, of prohibiting the cleric from the exercise of sacred ministry, and even of removing him from office according to the norm of law; and all these things in this case do not have the nature of a penalty. (Can. 2222 §2)

When there has been the probable commission of a crime, or it is extinguished by prescription, the legitimate superior is to avoid scandal by not promoting the cleric, prohibiting him from the exercise of sacred ministry, and removing him from office.[19] These prohibitions against scandal were according to the 1917 Code of Canon Law in the context of which clerics were forbidden to go to dances,[20] gamble for high stakes, participate in fox hunts, or enter taverns.[21] Clerics were to avoid any activity that was unbecoming to their state of life.

THE 1983 CODE

After Vatican II, the Synod of Bishops in 1967 approved ten principles for the revision of the Code of Canon Law. Three of the principles directly concerned penal law. The second principle stated: "There is to be coordination between the external and internal forum, which is proper to the Church and has been operative for centuries, so as to preclude any conflict between the two."[22]

In the 1983 Code the integrity of the internal forum has been respected even though the distinction between the internal and external forums has not been maintained completely. A priest who is under a penalty forbidding him to celebrate sacraments may provide for Christ's faithful when they are in danger of death. If the censure has not been declared, the cleric may provide sacraments and acts of governance if a member of Christ's faithful asks for them. However, in the case of a priest who has attempted marriage[23] and is therefore suspended, this priest may not celebrate the Eucharist or other sacraments at the request of Christ's faithful outside the circumstance of danger of death.[24]

The Synod of Bishops wanted penalties minimized and the third principle concluded with the statement that "unduly rigid norms are to be set aside and rather recourse is to be taken to exhortations and persuasions where there is no need of a strict observance of the law on account of the public good and general ecclesiastical discipline."[25] The ninth principle stated: "As an external, visible and independent society, the Church cannot renounce penal law. Penalties are generally to be *ferendae sententiae* (imposed) and are to be inflicted and remitted only in the external forum."[26]

The 1983 Code avoided all the detailed prohibitions of the 1917 Code and simply required clerics to avoid all those things that were unbecoming to their state so that they should always conduct themselves in a way to maintain the respect of the community at large.[27] The code stated that clerics were to avoid giving scandal (c. 277) and acknowledged that "scandal" could be given by uncompleted offenses in canon 1328 §2. Scandal given by clergy and religious is particularly grave when they perpetrate sexual abuse especially of minors but is also given by violations of canons 1394 and 1395.

Automatic Penalties

"*Latae sententiae* (automatic) penalties are to be reduced to a few cases and are to be inflicted only for the most serious offences."[28] This is reflected in canon 1318:

> *Latae sententiae* penalties are not to be established, except perhaps for some outstanding and malicious offences which may be either more grave by reason of scandal or such that they cannot be effectively punished by *ferendae sententiae* penalties; censures, however, especially excommunication, are not to be established, except with the greatest moderation, and only for offences of special gravity.

Compared to the 1917 Code, the 1983 Code dramatically reduced the number of automatic penalties but provided for them in cases of grave scandal.

"Scandal" is included in twenty-four canons of the present Code of Canon Law,[29] thirteen of them in Book VI on "Penal Sanctions in the Church."[30] More detailed prescriptions for "scandal" were made in nine canons in the 2021 revisions of penal law.[31]

A key addition in the revision of penal law in 2021 was the addition of a second paragraph to canon 1311:

> The one who is at the head of a Church must safeguard and promote the good of the community itself and of each of Christ's faithful, through pastoral char-

> ity, example of life, advice and exhortation and, if necessary, also through the imposition or declaration of penalties, in accordance with the provisions of the law, which are always to be applied with canonical equity and having in mind the restoration of justice, the reform of the offender, and the repair of scandal. (Can. 1311 §2)

This paragraph noted that one of the key purposes of imposing penalties is to repair scandal. The *Code of Canons of the Eastern Churches* had already explained the purpose of penal law in canon 1401: "sinners are to be recalled to right Christian living, the innocent faithful are to be protected from bad behaviour, ecclesiastical communion is to be promoted."[32] Fred Easton noted that, apart from reforming offenders, "the canon states the imposition of penalties is also appropriate because it can heal the wounds caused by the delict."[33] Imposing penalties can help those injured and upset by the commission of crimes.

Attempted Crimes

The legislator of the 1983 Code was conscious that scandal could be given even if the perpetrator attempted and did not actually complete the crime. Consequently, a lesser penalty was prescribed for attempted but not completed crimes if scandal resulted:

> §1. One who in furtherance of an offence did something or failed to do something but then, involuntarily, did not complete the offence, is not bound by the penalty prescribed for the completed offence, unless the law or a precept provides otherwise. §2. If the acts or the omissions of their nature lead to the carrying out of the offence, the person responsible may be subjected to a penance or to a penal remedy, unless he or she had spontaneously desisted from the offence which had been initiated. However, if scandal or other serious harm or danger has resulted, the perpetrator, even though spontaneously desisting, may be punished by a just penalty, but of a lesser kind than that determined for the completed crime. (Can. 1328)

This canon was unchanged in the 2021 revision of penal law. Although the offender did not manage to complete the crime, the scandal caused could be almost as bad as if the crime was committed. A. Brown, in a sentence dated January 5, 2000, concerning a priest soliciting homosexual sex, explained the impact of "scandal" on a penalty for an attempted crime:

> The important change is that the present law prescribes a lesser penalty for such situation (penance or penal remedies) but only when the perpetrator has spontaneously desisted from the crime before it was completed. Unless there was scandal involved or grave harm or danger resulted from the attempted crime, then there is apparently no punishment to be given. On the other hand, if there was scandal, grave harm, or danger as a result of the attempted crime, the determination of the punishment is left to the Judge's discretion.[34]

An example would be a cleric who arranges to meet a fourteen-year-old at a park but gets arrested by the police before the meeting happens.

Private Associations and Religious Institutes

The law provides for the suppression of private associations if their activity causes scandal to the faithful:

> A private association of Christ's faithful is extinguished in accordance with the norms of the statutes. It can also be suppressed by the competent authority if its activity gives rise to grave harm to ecclesiastical teaching or discipline, or is a scandal to the faithful. (Can. 326 §1)

Private associations would include a group such as the Saint Vincent de Paul Society, which does not act officially on behalf of the Church as public associations do.

Religious institutes act officially on behalf of the Church. Members of religious institutes can be dismissed for causing "grave scandal arising from the culpable behavior of the member":

> A member can be dismissed for other causes, provided they are grave, external, imputable and juridically proven. Among such causes are: habitual neglect of the obligations of consecrated life; repeated violation of the sacred bonds; obstinate disobedience to the lawful orders of Superiors in grave matters; grave scandal arising from the culpable behaviour of the member; obstinate attachment to, or diffusion of, teachings condemned by the magisterium of the Church; public adherence to materialistic or atheistic ideologies; the unlawful absence mentioned in Can. 665 §2, if it extends for a period of six months; other reasons of similar gravity which are perhaps defined in the institute's own law. (Can. 696 §1)

The process involves an administrative procedure protecting the rights of the accused member. However, if the scandal is grave, the local superior can immediately expel a member from the religious house:

> In a case of grave external scandal, or of extremely grave and imminent harm to the institute, a member can be expelled forthwith from the house by the major Superior. If there is danger in delay, this can be done by the local Superior with the consent of his or her council. The major Superior, if need be, is to introduce a process of dismissal in accordance with the norms of law, or refer the matter to the Apostolic See. (Can. 703)

Taking such action should be rare and undertaken only in exceptional circumstances.[35] The scandal must be grave and external. It could be related to publicity in the media or the filing of criminal charges.

Marriages and Funerals

Provision is made in the section of the Code on marriage so that an Ordinary is not bound to observe secrecy about a marriage if scandal may arise:

> The obligation of observing the secret mentioned in Canon 1131 no. 2 ceases for the local Ordinary if from its observance a threat arises of grave scandal or of grave harm to the sanctity of marriage. This fact is to be made known to the parties before the celebration of the marriage. (Can. 1132)

Examples justifying secret marriages include:

> One can find an example of these reasons that has become a classic: the state of secret concubinage of two people who are publicly considered to be man and wife. Other cases may be added to this example: the disparity of the social conditions of the spouses, the unreasonable opposition from family members, certain prohibitions imposed by civil laws.[36]

Apartheid laws forbidding mixed-race marriages would also fit into this category.

The 1983 Code makes provision for funerals to be denied to people when scandal would be given to the faithful:

> §1. Church funerals are to be denied to the following, unless they gave some signs of repentance before death: 1/ notorious apostates, heretics and schismatics; 2/ those who for anti-Christian motives chose that their bodies be cremated; 3/ other manifest sinners to whom a Church funeral could not be granted without public scandal to the faithful. §2. If any doubt occurs, the local Ordinary is to be consulted and his judgement followed. (Can. 1184)

The denial of a large public funeral and a requiem Mass often happens when a leading mafia person dies. A priest is permitted to celebrate a graveside service for such a person.[37]

PROCEDURES BEFORE A MEDICINAL PENALTY IS IMPOSED

An offender must be warned before a medicinal penalty is imposed:

> A censure cannot validly be imposed unless the offender has beforehand received at least one warning to purge the contempt[38] and has been allowed suitable time to do so. (Can. 1347 §1)

A person can be corrected and warned if the person is in danger of committing an offense or if there is serious suspicion that an offense has been committed. As part of the 2021 revision of penal law, paragraphs 4 and 5 were added to canon 1339 detailing the procedure for the issuing of penal precepts and imposition of penalties:

> §1. When someone is in a proximate occasion of committing an offence or when, after an investigation, there is a serious suspicion that an offence has been committed, the Ordinary either personally or through another can give that person warning. §2. In the case of behaviour which gives rise to scandal or serious disturbance of public order, the Ordinary can also correct the person, in a way appropriate to the particular conditions of the person and of

> what has been done. §3. The fact that there has been a warning or a correction must always be proven, at least from some document to be kept in the secret archive of the curia. §4. If on one or more occasions warnings or corrections have been made to someone to no effect, or if it is not possible to expect them to have any effect, the Ordinary is to issue a penal precept in which he sets out exactly what is to be done or avoided. §5. If the gravity of the case so requires, and especially in a case where someone is in danger of relapsing into an offence, the Ordinary is also to subject the offender, over and above the penalties imposed according to the provision of the law or declared by sentence or decree, to a measure of vigilance determined by means of a singular decree. (Can. 1339)

The addition of paragraphs 4 and 5 to the existing canon of the 1983 code that included provision to deal with behavior causing scandal means that a more detailed procedure is implemented including "warnings and corrections" as well as the issuing of a penal precept that "sets out exactly what is to be done or avoided."

The offender must be given at least one warning, and then a detailed precept must be given in writing to the offender setting out exactly what is to be done or avoided. Canon 1339 §3 states: "The fact that there has been a warning or a correction must always be proven, at least from some document to be kept in the secret archive of the curia."

The Ordinary has a duty of vigilance, and the canon makes it clear that the Ordinary has an obligation to investigate allegations as well as an obligation to impose penalties on offenders. Paragraph 5 also speaks of "vigilance." This means Ordinaries have a grave obligation to have a detailed safety plan for offenders and to do everything reasonably possible to prevent the offender from reoffending and creating more victims. Lack of supervision of offenders has been a source of grave scandal around the world.

OBLIGATORY PENAL PROCESS AND PENALTY TO REPAIR SCANDAL

The Ordinary must begin a judicial process, either judicial or extrajudicial if there is no other way to repair the scandal caused by a crime:

> The Ordinary must start a judicial or an administrative procedure for the imposition or the declaration of penalties when he perceives that neither by the methods of pastoral care, especially fraternal correction, nor by a warning or correction, can justice be sufficiently restored, the offender reformed, and the scandal repaired. (Can. 1341)

This provision acknowledges that scandal may require a penal process to be initiated.

The changes to penal law in 2021 include some optional penalties that are now obligatory. For example, canon

1344 requires the imposition of a penalty when there is "an urgent need to repair scandal":

> Even though the law may use obligatory words, the judge may, to his own conscience and prudence: 1/ defer the imposition of the penalty to a more opportune time, if it is foreseen that greater evils may arise from a too hasty punishment of the offender, unless there is an urgent need to repair scandal. (Can. 1341)

The scandal could be publicity about the gravity and number of crimes committed by the offender.

PENALTY FOR SCANDAL REDUCED, SUSPENDED, OR REMOVED

The Code of Canon Law makes several special provisions when a person is in danger of death. This includes the application of penalties:

> If a penalty prohibits the reception of the sacraments or sacramentals, the prohibition is suspended for as long as the offender is in danger of death. (Can. 1352 §1)

Consequently, the personal and spiritual needs of an offender are provided for when the person is in danger of death. Therefore, an excommunicated or interdicted person can receive the sacraments when they are seriously ill and in danger of death.

When a member of the faithful requests a sacrament from a priest who is excommunicated, interdicted, or suspended, but the penalty has not been declared and is not notorious or well-known, the priest can celebrate the sacrament such as the sacrament of Penance:

> The obligation of observing a *latae sententiae* penalty which has not been declared and is not notorious in the place where the offender actually is, is suspended either in whole or in part to the extent that the offender cannot observe it without the danger of grave scandal or loss of good name. (Can. 1352 §2)

This is regarded as more important than causing grave scandal or loss of his reputation. The requirement to observe the penalty is suspended by the circumstances.

Sometimes the perpetrator of an offense is exempted from a penalty, but even so, because the perpetrator has caused scandal, lesser penalties or penances may be imposed:

> §1. The perpetrator of a violation is not exempted from penalty, but the penalty prescribed in the law or precept must be diminished, or a penance substituted in its place, if the offence was committed by: …§3. In the circumstances mentioned in § 1, the offender is not bound by a *latae sententiae* penalty, but may have lesser penalties or penances imposed for the purposes of repentance or repair of scandal. (Can. 1324)

These lesser penalties could include fines or penances such as a curfew imposed on the perpetrator each evening.

REMISSION OF RESERVED PENALTIES

The remission of several penalties is reserved to the Apostolic See. These include excommunications for the absolution of an accomplice (cc. 977, 1385) and the violation of the seal of confession (c. 1386).

> §1. Without prejudice to the provisions of canons 508 and 976, a confessor can in the internal sacramental forum remit a *latae sententiae* censure of excommunication or interdict which has not been declared if it is difficult for the penitent to remain in a state of grave sin for the time necessary for the competent Superior to provide. §2. In granting the remission, the confessor is to impose upon the penitent, under pain of again incurring the censure, the obligation to have recourse within one month to the competent Superior or to a priest having the requisite faculty, and to abide by his instructions. In the meantime, the confessor is to impose an appropriate penance and, to the extent demanded, to require reparation of scandal and harm. The recourse, however, may be made even through the confessor, without mention of a name. §3. The same duty of recourse, when the danger has ceased, binds those who in accordance with can. 976 have had remitted an imposed or declared censure or one reserved to the Holy See. (Can. 1357)

It may be difficult for the offender to have recourse for their crime because of the time delay in getting a response. A priest may grant absolution for the sin(s) of the offender and have recourse to the Penitentiary as well. The dicastery will impose an appropriate penance and require any action that is necessary to repair the scandal the offender has caused.

UPHOLDING CLERICAL CONTINENCE AND CELIBACY

The 1983 Code legislated that clerics were to behave prudently to observe continence so that they did not give scandal:

> §1. Clerics are obliged to observe perfect and perpetual continence for the sake of the kingdom of heaven and therefore are bound to celibacy which is a special gift of God by which sacred ministers can adhere more easily to Christ with an undivided heart and are able to dedicate themselves more freely to the service of God and humanity. §2. Clerics are to behave with due prudence towards persons whose company can endanger their obligation to observe continence or give rise to scandal among the faithful. §3. The diocesan bishop is competent to establish more specific norms concerning this matter and to pass judgment in particular cases concerning the observance of this obligation. (Can. 277)

Clerics have an obligation to be prudent so that they do not endanger their obligation to abstain from sexual activity or scandalize the faithful.

PARTICULAR CRIMES

The Code includes several particular crimes that only clergy can commit but that give rise to grave scandal.

Apostasy, Heresy, and Schism

Apostasy, heresy, and schism are defined in canon 751. Canon 1364 addresses the penalties for these crimes:

> §1. An apostate from the faith, a heretic or a schismatic incurs a *latae sententiae* excommunication, without prejudice to the provision of can. 194 §1 no 2; he or she may also be punished with the penalties mentioned in canon 1336 §§2–4. §2. If a long-standing contempt or the gravity of scandal calls for it, other penalties may be added, not excluding dismissal from the clerical state. (Can. 1364)

Perpetration of these crimes by clerics and religious would usually cause grave scandal. Consequently, other penalties may be imposed, including dismissal from the clerical state.

Clerical Marriage and Cohabitation

If a cleric or religious attempts marriage or maintains a long-term affair or cohabitation with one person or a series of persons, grave scandal is caused:

> §1. A cleric who attempts marriage, even if only civilly, incurs a *latae sententiae* suspension, without prejudice to the provisions of canon 194 §1 no. 3, and 694 §1 no. 2. If, after warning, he has not reformed or continues to give scandal, he must be progressively punished by deprivations, or even by dismissal from the clerical state. §2. Without prejudice to the provisions of canon 694 §1 no. 2, a religious in perpetual vows who is not a cleric but who attempts marriage, even if only civilly, incurs a *latae sententiae* interdict. (Can. 1394)

When the cleric or religious does not stop causing scandal, canon 1394 makes provision for other penalties to be imposed, including dismissal from the clerical state or dismissal from the religious institute:

> §1. A cleric living in concubinage, other than in the case mentioned in canon 1394, and a cleric who continues in some other external sin against the sixth commandment of the Decalogue which causes scandal, is to be punished with suspension. To this, other penalties can progressively be added if after a warning he persists in the offence, until eventually he can be dismissed from the clerical state. § 2. A cleric who has offended in other ways against the sixth commandment of the Decalogue, if the offence was committed in public, is to be punished with just penalties, not excluding dismissal from the clerical state if the case so warrants. § 3. A cleric who by force, threats or abuse of his authority commits an offence against the sixth commandment of the

> Decalogue or forces someone to perform or submit to sexual acts is to be punished with the same penalty as in §2. (Can. 1395)

This canon makes provision for progressively more severe penalties to be imposed on an offender. Ultimately, if the offender continues to disobey precepts and commits crimes, he is to be dismissed from the clerical state.

Violation of Divine or Canon Law and the Prevention and Repair of Scandal

It is very difficult for a legislator to legislate for every possible crime. Consequently, the final canon of Book VI on "Penal Sanctions in the Church" provides for a penalty in extraordinary circumstances, including "the special gravity of the violation requires it and necessity demands that scandals be prevented or repaired."

> Besides the cases prescribed in this or in other laws, the external violation of divine or canon law can be punished, and with a just penalty, only when the special gravity of the violation requires it and necessity demands that scandals be prevented or repaired. (Can. 1399)

This all-encompassing canon includes all offenses against divine and ecclesiastical law. The most common application of this canon is for offenses against the sixth commandment. No warning is required for the imposition of an expiatory penalty to restore justice and repair scandal.

Obligatory and Proportionate Penalties for Scandal

Even when there has been a judicial process, it may be necessary to impose expiatory penalties (c. 1336) such as removal from office to repair the scandal that has been caused.

> If the competent authority imposes or declares a censure in a judicial process or by an extra-judicial decree, it can also impose the expiatory penalties it considers necessary to restore justice or repair scandal. (Can. 1335 §1)

Penalties must be proportionate to the scandal caused and the gravity of the crime:

> If a penalty is indeterminate, and if the law does not provide otherwise, the judge in determining the penalties is to choose those which are proportionate to the scandal caused and the gravity of the harm; he is not however to impose graver penalties, unless the seriousness of the case really demands it. He may not impose penalties which are perpetual. (Can. 1349)

Therefore, graver penalties are not to be imposed unless the seriousness of the crime warrants them.

THE FAILURE OF CHURCH LEADERS TO ACT

This issue was treated in some length and detail in chapter 6. The revised penal law reiterates that abuse of authority as a cleric is a crime. It is recognized that many so-called consenting adult relationships are not ones with equal consent, and often vulnerable people are manipulated by people with positions of power and authority. In the revised Book VI, canon 1389 has been moved to become canon 1378:

> §1. A person who, apart from the cases already foreseen by the law, abuses ecclesiastical power, office, or function, is to be punished according to the gravity of the act or the omission, not excluding by deprivation of the power or office, without prejudice to the obligation of repairing the harm. §2. A person who, through culpable negligence, unlawfully and with harm to another or scandal, performs or omits an act of ecclesiastical power or office or function, is to be punished according to the provision of can. 1336 §§2–4, without prejudice to the obligation of repairing the harm. (Can. 1378)

Abuse of authority includes culpable negligence and failing to act, which has caused enormous scandal in recent years. The canon indicates which penalties may be imposed on an offender and makes explicit mention of the offender's obligation to repair the harm he/she caused.[39] In the 2021 revision of penal law, a new paragraph was added to canon 1371. This provision includes cases such as clerics or religious not reporting abuse to the local Ordinary and Ordinaries not reporting cases of clerical sexual abuse of minors to the Dicastery for the Doctrine of the Faith:

> §6. A person who neglects to report an offence, when required to do so by a canonical law, is to be punished according to the provision of can. 1336 §§2–4, with the addition of other penalties according to the gravity of the offence. (Can. 1371)

The failures of church leaders have caused almost as much scandal as the original crimes of abuse. The chief motivation of church leaders to keep crimes secret and do nothing is to conceal the failures of clerics from the faithful, thereby causing loss of trust and scandal among the faithful.

THE JURISPRUDENCE OF THE SIGNATURA

In 2002, Cardinal Pompedda of the Apostolic Signatura explained "scandal" in a decision in a penal case as follows:

> It is required that the majority of the people who are familiar with the person, his function, and his activity suffer a negative impression, that is, they are led in a certain measure to something wrong.[40]

Cardinal Raymond Burke, who was also of the Apostolic Signatura, developed this explanation as he notes that "the first and properly theological meaning of scandal is to do or omit something which leads another into error or sin. The second meaning is to do or omit something which causes wonderment (*admiratio*) in others."[41] Burke explained that giving communion to the obstinate, serious sinner is scandal in the first meaning of scandal; while denying communion to the occult sinner gives scandal in the second sense.[42]

CONCLUSION

Perpetrators of crimes cause enormous harm to victims. The resulting scandals from the crimes also cause great harm to the whole Church. With modern media, each report of abuse crimes around the world affects the faithful in every country. People cannot understand why church leadership has failed to deal with perpetrators appropriately, with catastrophic results for individual victims and the whole Church. The failures of bishops and superiors of religious institutes to act appropriately has undermined the credibility of the Church and resulted in many people ceasing to practice the faith. Both clergy and laity feel shame and isolation from the cover-ups by church leaders that have resulted in a loss of confidence in the institutional Church. The church leaders have not been transparent and have lost credibility. Jesus taught that only "the truth will make you free" (John 8:32) to be of service to the Church. Any attitude that covers up the truth is our enemy.[43] Because of the incalculable harm of sexual abuse and other crimes, there must be appropriate penalties to restore justice and repair the scandal that has resulted.

10

SPIRITUAL ABUSE AS A DELICT

Many cases of spiritual abuse are being reported around the world, and consideration needs to be given to spiritual abuse as a delict or crime in canon law. It is currently not considered to be such. The *Universal Guidelines Framework* (UGF) states:

> Spiritual abuse means abuse of a person that invokes a person's religious beliefs and faith to perpetrate harm. Spiritual abuse can occur as a secondary experience of abuse when abuse is perpetrated by someone in a position of spiritual authority and trust within the Church and can negatively impact a person's spirituality.[1]

This description is very generic. The New Zealand Royal Commission Report into Abuse in Care did not see spiritual abuse only as a secondary experience and described it as

> where an abuser uses spirituality to gain power and control over a victim or has the result of harming the spiritual wellbeing of an individual. Spiritual abuse can co-occur with or enable physical, sexual or emotional abuse, and can intensify the impacts of that abuse by giving it a spiritual dimension, for example, feeling guilty or "sinful" after sexual abuse.[2]

Individual cases demonstrate the different aspects and dimensions of spiritual abuse. Spiritual abuse can be the primary way an abuser gets power and control over the victim. It can be a key part of grooming a victim, enabling abuse, and then exacerbating the effects of abuse by affecting the victim's relationship with God. Samuel Fernandez also describes spiritual abuse in a more experiential manner.[3]

Lisa Oakley and Justin Humphrey draw attention to how the abuser often befriends, manipulates, and exploits the victim, requiring secrecy and silence, as the victim is controlled by appeals to such things as obedience and use of sacred texts.[4] This could result in the voice of God being replaced with the voice of the abuser. This abuse can have long-lasting effects, not only on the spiritual well-being of the victim, but it can also erode trust in religious leaders. This may result in people eventually ceasing to participate in worship and the sacraments, leading to a profound emptiness and despair from the loss of God. The victim may then feel toxic guilt and shame, creating a profoundly crippling sense of fear. Ultimately, that will destabilize someone's spiritual security, resulting in post-traumatic stress disorder (PTSD) and the loss of belief in God and the Church. This often manifests in intergenerational trauma that results in generations of families no longer in the Church.[5]

Some examples of spiritual abuse are:

- Stopping a person from practicing their religious/spiritual devotions
- Denying sacraments or significantly delaying sacraments for no good reason
- Implementing unrealistic expectations before they can receive the sacraments
- Using authority to unfairly punish or humiliate
- Forcing a person to keep silent about abuse
- Telling a person that they are not good enough and will go to hell
- Turning a parish against a person until that person leaves
- Forcing a person to attend meetings they don't want to
- Forbidding a person to go to anyone else for confession
- Forbidding them to attend any other parish
- Intrusive sexual questioning of a woman in the sacrament of Penance
- Threatening to "go after" the person's family or doing it.[6]

EXAMPLES OF SPIRITUAL ABUSE

Rape: Bishop Franco Mulakkal

In June 2018, in Kottayam, Kerala, a forty-four-year-old religious sister filed a complaint of rape at Kottayam police station against Bishop Franco Mulakkal of Jalandhar diocese. This was the first time the authorities in India had arrested a bishop for a case of rape. The sister accused Mulakkal of raping her thirteen times during visits to her convent.[7] The victim wrote to church authorities in January 2017, to the apostolic nuncio in India in January 2018, and then to Pope Francis in May 2018. On October 16, 2018, Mulakkal was released on conditional bail pending trial and is no longer the bishop of the diocese. On October 22, 2018, a prime witness, Father Kuriakose Kattuthara, who had testified against Mulakkal, was found dead in his room in Jalandhar. The death of Kattuthara was said to be caused by health conditions. However, family members are reported to believe that his death was related to his support for the rape victim.[8]

Sister Julie George explained the power imbalance between bishops and religious: "Congregations founded by bishops are completely suppressed and oppressed by the bishop. That was the kind of convent this survivor lived in. Even financial expenditure or how much money a sister can get per month was completely decided by that bishop."[9] Father Augustine Vattoli, one of the few priests who supported the victim, stated that "the church in India is all powerful" and they will do anything in their power to throw out those who stand against them.[10] S. Harishankar, the former Kottayam police superintendent, stated that "her entire existence itself is dependent on the accused. He is the one who gets to decide if she should remain dead or alive."[11]

Sexual Manipulation: Marko Rupnik

The Dicastery for the Doctrine of the Faith has been investigating allegations against Fr. Marko Rupnik, the former Jesuit whom several religious sisters have accused of psychological and sexual abuse. He was dismissed from the Society of Jesus in June 2023.

Anna, a former religious sister, has stated:

> Father Marko asked me to have threesomes with another sister of the community, because sexuality had to be, in his opinion, free from possession, in the image of the Trinity where, he said, "the third person would welcome the relationship between the two."[12]

Ms. Kovac, another victim of Rupnik, told reporters about the "spiritual abuse and abuse of conscience" she endured and other abuses she had learned about, which were carried out by someone who was considered a revered figure in the religious community.[13]

Spiritual Abuse: Thomas Walshe

Stephen E. de Weger and Jodi Death give this example of spiritual abuse in which Father Thomas Walshe had sex with an eighteen-year-old seminarian who later claimed he was assaulted while drunk and unconscious. Father Walshe strenuously denied committing any abuse and complained that it was "completely consensual." However, the independent commissioner for the Melbourne Response, the Catholic organization for investigating and dealing with allegations of clergy sexual abuse in the Melbourne Archdiocese, accepted that "Father Walshe had sexually abused the then 18-year-old seminarian." Archbishop Denis Hart of Melbourne, however, concluded that it "was a consensual homosexual relationship that only breached the teachings of the church and vow of celibacy taken by both men… it was not illegal, it was not child abuse and there was no finding that it was nonconsensual (Jacks and Vedelago 2016)."[14] Archbishop Hart summarized the sexual activity of Fr. Walshe as "legal," "consensual," "sexual abuse." This is an illogical, contradictory summation of the case. This case involves spiritual abuse and abuse of authority.

Exorcisms: Sons of the Holy Redeemer

In New Zealand there is a controversy involving the Sons of the Holy Redeemer, a diocesan religious institute of the Diocese of Aberdeen in Scotland. The Sons of the Holy Redeemer only celebrate

Mass in Latin. The focus of news reports has been on exorcism. Newshub reported abusive behavior in a television program on TV3.[15] The New Zealand Herald newspaper stated:

> According to a Newshub report tonight, some people who received exorcisms in the church were tied up by the neck and screamed at, while pleading for the rituals—which could last several hours—to stop. This would go on for several hours.
>
> A leader at the church disputed the claims to Newshub and said the participants had agreed only the exorcist could decide when the exorcism would stop, and occasionally a safety harness would be used.[16]

A ritual book for exorcisms was published in 1614. After Vatican II, the 1614 ritual was replaced by a new ritual on January 26, 1999. A slightly amended edition was issued in 2004. Then *De Exorcismis et Supplicationibus Quibusdam*,[17] *editio typica* was printed in November 2014. The final text of *Exorcisms and Related Supplications* (ERS) was confirmed by the Holy See in December 2016 and implemented in the dioceses of the United States as of June 29, 2017.[18]

The current ritual has very different procedures and prayers from the former ritual. People should not be tied up. This ritual makes it clear that a person can be exorcized only after thorough medical, psychological, and psychiatric testing. It is only then that an exorcist makes the final decision whether the person is genuinely possessed by the devil.

Unlawful Exercise of Sacred Ministry

When exorcisms are not carried out according to liturgical law, and are unlawful sacred ministry, canon 1389 would apply:

> A person who, apart from the cases mentioned in canons 1379–1388, unlawfully exercises the office of a priest or another sacred ministry, is to be punished with a just penalty, not excluding a censure. (Can. 1389)

Arietta notes that this canon is similar to the previous canon 1384 in the 1983 Code of Canon Law. He comments, "It defines as an offence any conduct not dealt with in cc. 1379–1388 that constitutes unlawful exercise of priestly function or other sacred ministry. This includes a wide range of behavior contravening mandatory liturgical norms or those regulating the manner of celebrating the sacraments (for example, administering collective absolution without observing the prescriptions of c. 961)."[19] Besides unlawful general absolution, officiating at a marriage of divorced person(s) without a declaration of nullity, exorcising a mentally ill person, or tying people up to be exorcised would be violations of canon 1389, because these things should not be taking place.

SPIRITUAL ABUSE AND THE SACRAMENT OF PENANCE

Solicitation and absolution of an accomplice in a sin against the sixth commandment obviously includes spiritual abuse:

> A priest who acts against the prescription of can. 977 incurs a *latae sententiae* excommunication reserved to the Apostolic See. (Can. 1384)

The attempt to grant absolution except when the penitent is in danger of death is invalid.[20] The delict carries an automatic excommunication and is reserved to the judgment of the Dicastery for the Doctrine of the Faith in article 4 of *Sacramentorum Sanctitatis Tutela.*[21] When such a case is reported to the Ordinary, he must inform the Dicastery for the Doctrine of the Faith and follow their directions.[22]

> Canon 1385. A priest who in confession, or on the occasion or under the pretext of confession, solicits a penitent to commit a sin against the sixth commandment of the Decalogue, is to be punished, according to the gravity of the offence, with suspension, prohibitions and deprivations; in the more serious cases he is to be dismissed from the clerical state.

The *Penal Sanctions User Guide* explains that this offense by a priest can occur during the sacramental confession, and before or after the confession itself. The Ordinary must communicate information concerning the delict to the Dicastery for the Doctrine of the Faith and carry out their instructions. The penalty will depend on the gravity of the case and may be dismissal from the clerical state.[23]

There are some complaints about the intrusive questioning of women concerning sexual matters during the sacrament of Penance. The questioning in these cases often goes on for a long time and usually does not meet the criteria for solicitation. However, being asked in detail about sexual activities is very traumatic for the penitent. The priest does not question men in this way, so it is clearly the spiritual abuse of women that is not properly encompassed by the current legislation.

ABUSE OF AUTHORITY

Abuse of authority has long been recognized as a crime in canon law. The Council of Trent decreed in 1563:

> Bishops must visit their dioceses personally...and that neither they nor any of their party accept anything for expenses during the visitation, even from money left for pious uses... except what is legally owed to them... nor to intrude on the revenues from stable goods and funds, unless they have a right to do so.[24]

The decree of the Council of Trent was summarized in the 1917 Code:

> Abuse of ecclesiastical power, in the prudent judgment of the legitimate Superior, shall be punished according to the gravity of the fault, with due regard for the prescriptions of those canons that establish certain penalties for various offenses. (Can. 2404; 1917 CIC)

The council decree was a source of canon 2404. Therefore, Augustine in his commentary emphasizes the financial crimes emanating from abuse of authority:

> There may be overzealous, or imprudent, or revengeful prelates, who are too ready to inflict penalties, especially censures, before they have lawful proofs against the culprit. Then there is "the root of all evil," (1 Tim 6) avarice, which may prompt some to be too lenient in granting favors, absolutions or dispensations, or in meting out penalties. Another abuse of power would be to demand pecuniary contributions on the occasion of episcopal or canonical visitations."[25]

In his commentary, Beste indicates that abuse of authority includes ordinary, jurisdiction, administrative, or governing authority.[26]

The 1983 Code

When the 1983 Code was promulgated, abuse of authority was included in canon 1389, which replaced canon 2404:

> §1. One who abuses ecclesiastical power, office, or function, is to be punished according to the seriousness of the act or the omission, not excluding deprivation from office, unless a penalty for such abuse has already been established by a law or a precept. §2. One who, through culpable negligence illegitimately places or omits an act of ecclesiastical power, ministry or function which damages another person is to be punished with a just penalty. (Can. 1389)

The failure to act, using one's power, ministry, or function, must be a deliberate failure or blameworthy negligence. Pope Francis emphasizes how church authority must be exercised in a spirit of service, and so this canon penalizes both abuse of power and function as well as negligence that results in harm to other people. Canon 1389 §2 makes it clear that the office holder's negligence and failure to act is also a crime and he may be punished for it. Furthermore, the one neglecting to act could well be liable to compensate the one harmed:

> Whoever illegitimately inflicts damage upon someone by a juridic act or by any other act placed with malice or negligence is obliged to repair the damage inflicted. (Can. 128)

Bishops have a responsibility to care for all the faithful in their dioceses. This includes a responsibility to care for victims of incardinated diocesan priests[27]:

> §1. In exercising the function of a pastor, a diocesan bishop is to show himself

> concerned for all the Christian faithful entrusted to his care, of whatever age, condition, or nationality they are, whether living in the territory or staying there temporarily; he is also to extend an apostolic spirit to those who are not able to make sufficient use of ordinary pastoral care because of the condition of their life and to those who no longer practice their religion. (Can. 383)

Diocesan bishops must care for victims.

Vos Estis Lux Mundi (2019)

In 2019, Pope Francis promulgated the *motu proprio Vos Estis Lux Mundi*, in which he stated that "the crimes of sexual abuse offend Our Lord, cause physical, psychological and spiritual damage to the victims and harm the community of the faithful." Significantly, Pope Francis acknowledged that crimes of sexual abuse cause spiritual damage to the victims and harm the community of the faithful.

Vos Estis Lux Mundi stated:

> Art. 5 – Care for persons. §1. The ecclesiastical Authorities shall commit themselves to ensuring that those who state that they have been harmed, together with their families, are to be treated with dignity and respect, and, in particular, are to be: a) welcomed, listened to and supported, including through provision of specific services; b) offered spiritual assistance; c) offered medical assistance, including therapeutic and psychological assistance, as required by the specific case.

Victims are to be offered spiritual assistance, which is obviously necessary if they have suffered spiritual harm. But spiritual harm is not classified as a crime; it is recognized as an effect of the crime of sexual abuse.

In its *Vademecum*, the Dicastery for the Doctrine of the Faith reiterated the obligation to offer all kinds of help and support, including spiritual help:

> The ecclesiastical authorities must ensure that the alleged victim and his or her family are treated with dignity and respect, and must offer them welcome, attentive hearing and support, also through dedicated services, as well as spiritual, medical and psychological help, as required by the specific case (cf. art. 5 VELM). The same can be done with regard to the accused. One should, however, avoid giving the impression of wishing to anticipate the results of the process. (*Vademecum* 55)

Revised Penal Law (2021)

As noted earlier, in 2021 Pope Francis revised the penal law of the Church, Book VI. The former canon 1389 became canon 1378 in the revision:

> §1. A person who, apart from the cases already foreseen by the law, abuses ecclesiastical power, office, or function, is to be punished according to the gravity of the act or the omission, not excluding by deprivation of the power or office, without prejudice to the obligation of repairing the harm. §2. A person who, through culpable negligence, unlawfully and with harm to another or scandal, performs or

> omits an act of ecclesiastical power or office or function, is to be punished according to the provision of can. 1336 §§2–4, without prejudice to the obligation of repairing the harm. (c. 1378)

The *Penal Sanctions in the Church: User Guide* explains that this canon addresses the abuse of power (c. 1378 §1) and culpable negligence in the exercise of one's duty (c. 1378 §2).

> The delict of abuse of power or office defined by can. 1378 §1 includes in a general form any arbitrariness or excess committed by the holder of some managerial power, of an office or of a ministry, either by actions or by equally voluntary omissions. The law considers the so-called "abuse of power" as an autonomous delict, punishable in itself. It is different from other specific types of delicts which necessarily include as a constituent element some sorts of abuse of power or authority, such as the case of those considered, for example, in nn. 113, 136, 151.[28]

In both paragraphs of canon 1378, there was the addition of the obligation for the perpetrator to repair the harm that he caused. This is in accord with canon 128 and the new canon 1361 §4.[29] The second paragraph also specifies the expiatory penalties that may be inflicted according to the revised canon 1336. Arietta notes that "since the canon deals with offences not specified elsewhere, there is an indeterminate penalty in paragraph one."[30]

COMPLAINTS ABOUT BISHOPS OR THEIR FAILURE TO ACT

Sacramentorum Sanctitatis Tutela

As already noted, in 2001, the Congregation for the Doctrine of the Faith promulgated *Sacramentorum Sanctitatis Tutela*, which was revised in 2010.[31] This legislation already required accountability and transparency from bishops and religious superiors. However, there were no sanctions for Ordinaries who failed to act, and the law was not generally enforced.

Pope Francis issued the *motu proprio Come una Madre Amorevole* (As a Loving Mother) in June 2016.[32] Bishops must protect the faithful, especially minors and the vulnerable, from abusers. Provision is made for removing ministers who fail to act from their ecclesiastical office "for grave reasons" and cause grave harm to others, either to physical persons or to the whole community (cf. Art. 1 §1). Regarding the application of these norms, it is further determined that in the case of sexual abuse of minors and vulnerable adults, "it is enough that the lack of diligence be grave" (Art. 1 §3).

When a bishop or major Superior has failed to act when informed about spiritual abuse committed through abuse of authority and taking advantage of vulnerable persons, these provisions would apply.

Vulnerable People

Sometimes complaints of spiritual abuse are just dismissed or not taken seriously. Myriam Wijlens recounts:

> In some files I could read that when hints had been voiced by women, they were often put aside with the written comment: "The woman is problematic and, yes, she is a single parent" or "She wants to draw attention," "She just wants to make herself important." (Similar comments can also be found in the McCarrick report). Therefore, bishops and the other faithful who believe that bishops and/or priests have a special gift to judge the true nature of a person need to learn that their ability is fallible.[33]

Ignoring or covering up of spiritual abuse has been all too common in the Church. There has been much publicity about the cases of Cardinals Barbarin (France), McCarrick (United States), and Pell (Australia), among others. Following this publicity and questions raised about dealing with accusations against bishops, Pope Francis devoted a significant part of his *motu proprio Vos Estis Lux Mundi,* Title II, articles 6ff. to procedures for dealing with complaints against bishops and other religious leaders who failed to act on complaints of abuse as in article 1 of *Vos Estis Lux Mundi*:

> Article 1 §1. These norms apply to reports regarding clerics or members of Institutes of Consecrated Life or Societies of Apostolic Life and concerning: a) delicts against the sixth commandment of the Decalogue consisting of: i. forcing someone, by violence or threat or through abuse of authority, to perform or submit to sexual acts; ii. performing sexual acts with a minor or a vulnerable person.

Pope Francis legislated that abuse of vulnerable people was a crime. Spiritual abuse could easily be abuse of vulnerable people, as we saw in those earlier examples. Spiritual abuse of vulnerable people is not within the competence of the Dicastery for the Doctrine of the Faith. The *Vademecum* of the DDF states:

> The first revision of the Motu Proprio SST, promulgated on 21 May 2010, stated that a person who habitually has the imperfect use of reason is to be considered equivalent to a minor. This extension of the category of those considered equivalent to minors was confirmed without modification in the second revision of SST in 2021 (cf. art. 6, 1° SST). With regard to the use of the term "vulnerable adult", elsewhere described as "any person in a state of infirmity, physical or mental deficiency, or deprivation of personal liberty which, in fact, even occasionally limits their ability to understand or to want or otherwise resist the offence" (cf. art. 1 §2, b VELM), it should be noted that this definition includes other situations than those pertaining to the competence of the DDF, which remains limited to minors under eighteen years of age and to those who "habitually have

> an imperfect use of reason". Other situations outside of these cases are handled by the competent Dicasteries (cf. art. 7 §1 VELM). (*Vademecum* 5)

Philip Milligan, the dicastery canon lawyer, insisted that lay groups must understand who is considered a "vulnerable adult" when it comes to sexual abuse. He noted that seemingly "consensual sexual activity between adults can, because of the state of mind or the situation of one of the persons, actually be a situation of sexual abuse."[34] This could encompass a person being abused by a formator, novice master, or superior.

The bishop has the right to appoint and remove teachers of religion. While civil law may prevent the bishop from doing this in many situations, the diocesan bishop does have rights to remove members of religious institutes for spiritual abuse in an apostolic work:

> For his own diocese, the local ordinary has the right to appoint or approve teachers of religion and even to remove them or demand that they be removed if a reason of religion or morals requires it. (Can. 805)

Apart from schools, canon law provides this right in other ministries:

> If a custom or an express prescript of universal or particular law is lacking in a certain matter, a case, unless it is penal, must be resolved in light of laws issued in similar matters, general principles of law applied with canonical equity, the jurisprudence and practice of the Roman Curia, and the common and constant opinion of learned persons. (Can. 19)

If the religious institute does not help the victim of spiritual abuse or repair the harm done, the diocesan bishop must strongly exhort the religious institute or the Ministerial Public Juridic Person (MPJP) to meet their obligations to repair the damage done to victims. The bishop can force the individual religious to leave his diocese.[35] Also, the Apostolic See can force any religious institute to meet their obligations.

INTERNAL AND EXTERNAL FORUM

Church teaching and canon law require a careful distinction between actions and information in the external and internal forum. A confessor is absolutely forbidden to use knowledge that he has gained from the sacrament of Penance (c. 984 §1). This applies to information he learned in confession before he was in leadership (c. 984 §2).[36] There have been instances in recently founded religious associations or movements where members are required to have spiritual direction and reception of the sacrament of Penance only from members of the association or movement. This is an unsafe practice that traditional orders, such as the Carmelites, carefully avoid and legislate against in their constitutions.

FOUNDING A DIOCESAN RELIGIOUS INSTITUTE

There have been many instances of various forms of spiritual abuse in religious institutes founded since Vatican II. In 2016, Pope Francis decreed that for the validity of the establishment of a religious institute the diocesan bishop must obtain prior approval of the Apostolic See in writing.[37] In 2020, this became even stricter, so that "prior consultation with the Holy See is to be understood as necessary *ad validitatem* before establishing a diocesan Institute of consecrated life, otherwise risking nullity of the decree of establishment of this said Institute."[38] In third-world countries, there are many instances of religious institutes being established without proper structures. I am aware of one public association of nine hundred perpetually professed members who claim to be a religious institute that is accepted as such by millions of people. This group does not have constitutions or statutes.

Pope Francis, in an audience on February 7, 2022, in the presence of the Cardinal Prefect and Archbishop Secretary of the Dicastery for the Institutes of Consecrated Life and the Societies of Apostolic Life, specifically approved the following provision:

> The diocesan bishop, before erecting—by decree—a public association of the faithful with a view to becoming an Institute of Consecrated Life or a Society of Apostolic Life of diocesan right, must obtain the written permission of the Dicastery for Institutes of Consecrated Life and Societies of Apostolic Life.[39]

This rescript was promulgated on June 15, 2022, and became effective immediately. The rescript reinforced the 2020 legal requirements to establish a diocesan religious institute.

REPORTING SPIRITUAL ABUSE

The Church clearly needs a system to handle and receive complaints of spiritual abuse, just as they have systems to receive complaints of sexual abuse.

It is not difficult to see how a whole range of questions will also arise around spiritual abuse. Hence, it is possible to learn from the insights and experiences gained from the sexual abuse crises. For example, a very first step could consist of setting up a system that receives and handles complaints about spiritual abuse.

Bishops need to be more cautious and careful before groups are recognized as associations.[40] Many church leaders do not take the problem of spiritual abuse seriously enough. Myriam Wijlens points out:

> Just as Church leaders and believers are struggling to recognise sexual abuse as a systemic problem, it is likely that this will also be the case for spiritual abuse. The situation for the latter is aggravated by the fact that spiritual

> abuse constitutes no specific offence be it in canon or state law.[41]

The leaders in these associations, groups, and religious institutes have the first and primary responsibility to prevent abuse, whether it is spiritual, sexual, emotional, psychological, and so on.

VISITATION AND OVERSIGHT

No association may call itself "Catholic" without the consent of the Church authority.[42] Since diocesan bishops recognize or establish these associations or religious institutes and allow or permit one approved in another diocese to have a house or be active in their diocese, a great deal of responsibility lies with them. Bishops also have the power to recommend to the faithful that they join them and be members.[43] But bishops also have the right and duty to respond to information about abuses, including spiritual abuse.

The diocesan bishop has the right and duty in canon law to visit diocesan religious institutes at least once every five years.[44] He also has this right if a diocesan religious institute from another diocese has a house in his diocese. He must also visit their apostolic works or arrange for someone to visit them on his behalf. There are more limits to a bishop visiting pontifical religious institutes,[45] but if there are abuses, the bishop must order the superior to deal with them. The diocesan bishop can also deal with abuses on his own authority because he oversees all apostolic works.[46] The diocesan bishop should also inform the bishop in which the diocesan religious institute was founded, as well as the supreme moderator, about any abuse, including spiritual abuse.

CONCLUSION

A grave sin that is also categorized as a delict or crime in canon law and punished "because it represents conduct which, in addition to being a personal sin in the moral order, damages essential aspects of the spiritual society which is the Church."[47] There is no specific crime of spiritual abuse in the current norms. However, cases of spiritual abuse potentially involve several other canonical crimes such as unlawful exercise of sacred ministry, abuse of authority, abuse of vulnerable people, and bishops failing to act on information *notitia de delicto* received.

Unfortunately, cases of spiritual abuse are being reported all over the world, especially in new religious institutes and new associations of the faithful. Pope Francis has been doing his best to control this spiritual abuse by legislation concerning new associations of the faithful and new diocesan religious institutes. It is important that leaders of associations and institutes are alert to the possibility of spiritual abuse and other forms of abuse. Diocesan bishops need to carefully implement the legislation and carefully fulfill their duties to visit and supervise the associations and institutes operating within their dioceses.

11

THE CRIME OF SOLICITATION AND CANON LAW

The sexual abuse crisis is the biggest crisis for the Catholic Church since the Reformation. There have been cover-ups and scandals as the extent and seriousness of the problem was denied. Initially, it was perceived to be a problem only in the United States of America.

To understand the juridical situation, John Beal and Roch Page remind us that we need to see canonical laws "in their text and context."[1] The changes from Vatican II caused a great deal of upheaval in the Catholic Church, especially among clergy. Over one hundred thousand priests left active ministry and many requested dispensations from the pope.[2] There was confusion about which laws were in force after Vatican II. As the 1917 Code was revised, there was a desire to reduce and simplify the penal laws of the Church.[3] There were reports of divisions among officials of the Roman Curia and ignorance of canon law because it was not properly taught in seminaries after Vatican II.

PRIESTS LEAVING MINISTRY

Prior to Vatican II, if a priest left active ministry, the traditional approach had been to investigate if he had been validly ordained. The 1917 Code did not acknowledge the possibility of a dispensation from celibacy. However, norms for dispensations from celibacy were issued by the then Sacred Congregation of the Sacraments on June 9, 1931. These norms presumed there had been an unsuccessful attempt to declare the ordination invalid.[4]

In preparation for Vatican II, the Preparatory Commission for the Discipline of the Sacraments had prepared a *Schema* for discussion at the Council[5] on priests who had left ministry and on declaring their ordinations null or granting dispensations from celibacy. After the first session of Vatican II, all the *schemata* were revised. As a consequence, the *Schema de Sacerdotibus Lapsis* was not presented to the bishops at the Council. The documents of Vatican II make no reference to dispensations from celibacy because Pope Paul VI (June 21, 1963–August 6, 1978) informed the Council that he would address the issue of celibacy.[6]

Paul VI issued new norms for the dispensation from celibacy on February 2, 1964.[7] He reserved such dispensations to himself[8] and then published his encyclical letter, *On Priestly Celibacy*, on June 24, 1967.[9] Many priests had requested dispensations from celibacy, so simplified norms were promulgated on January 13, 1971.[10] These norms combined the approaches of declaring orders invalid and granting dispensations from the obligations of priestly ordination. The process adopted was administrative in nature rather than judicial. For the first time a priest could be reduced to the lay state and dispensed from the obligations that arose from sacred orders, including celibacy, in a single process. There was no mention of declaring a priest's ordination invalid "without having to prove coercion by grave fear," since canon 214 §2 of the 1917 Code was effectively abrogated.[11] Bishops could have priests *ex officio* dismissed from the clerical state for scandalous behavior such as sexual abuse.[12]

In June 1991, the Undersecretary of the Congregation for the Clergy estimated that since Vatican II about 60,000 priests had been granted dispensations from celibacy. Most of them would have been granted during the pontificate of Paul VI.[13] Between 1964 and 2004, the number of priests who officially left the ministry was 69,063.[14] The Vatican was very concerned about how these numbers were undermining the permanence of priestly commitment.

Pope John Paul I (August 26, 1978–September 28, 1978) granted a few dispensations from celibacy using the 1970 norms during his thirty-three days as pope.

Pope John Paul II (October 16, 1978–April 2, 2005) placed a moratorium on dispensations from celibacy at the beginning of his pontificate. His first Holy Thursday letter addressed to priests, April 8, 1979, expressed concern for priests who were struggling with celibacy. However, he affirmed the need for celibacy as "a matter here of *keeping one's word to Christ and the Church...* through a conscious and free commitment to celibacy for the whole of one's life."[15] He also pointed out that married people "*have the right to expect from us*, Priests and Pastors, good example and *the witness of fidelity to one's vocation until death*."[16]

Pope John Paul II established a group to study the norms for dispensations from celibacy. After the group reported back to him, new norms were prepared and published by the Sacred Congregation for the Doctrine of the Faith on October 14, 1980.[17] The norms exclusively concerned a dispensation from celibacy, and there was no mention of "reduction to the lay state." The norms addressed two groups of priests: those who had left active ministry a long time ago and wanted to regularize their situation; and those who should not have been ordained in the first place because they lacked the equivalent of due discretion as for marriage, or whose formators were unable to judge their suitability for ordination. Commentators consider the 1980 process quasi-judicial.[18] Dispensed clergy were said to lose the clerical state rather than be reduced to the lay state.

By virtue of his 1988 apostolic constitution *Pastor Bonus*, Pope John Paul II transferred the competency for processing dispensations from celibacy from the Congregation for the Doctrine of the Faith to the Congregation for Divine Worship and the Discipline of the Sacraments. In 1991, the Congregation for Divine Worship and the Discipline of the Sacraments issued a letter, "Documents Necessary for the Instruction of a Case for the Dispensation from the Obligation of Priestly Ordination." This dicastery retained its competency until 2005.

Joseph Fessio, a former student of Cardinal Ratzinger's and founder of the publishing house Ignatius Press, said of the Vatican perspective: "Look at it from the perspective of priestly commitment. You want to get married? You're still a priest. You're a sex offender? Well, you're still a priest. Rome is looking at it from the objective reality of the priesthood."[19] The Vatican focus was on getting priests to maintain their commitment to be priests forever. It was not until 1991 that Pope John Paul II for the first time *ex officio* dismissed from the clerical state notorious pedophile priests.[20]

Pope Benedict XVI (July 13, 2005–February 28, 2013) changed the approach to dispensations from celibacy. He transferred the competency for processing cases from the Congregation for Divine Worship and the Discipline of the Sacraments to the Congregation for Clergy effective from August 1, 2005.[21] On April 18, 2009, Cardinal Hummes, the then Prefect of the Congregation for Clergy, wrote to all bishops noting that priests should be celibate or else they should be dispensed from their obligations. Pope Benedict wanted the situation of priests who had left active ministry regularized. Special faculties were granted to the Congregation for Clergy to present to the Holy Father cases for the dismissal of priests and deacons who were living in a scandalous or irregular state or violating canons 1394 or 1395, which included the crime of pedophilia.

Ordinaries were granted the faculty to apply for dispensations for these clergy in accord with canon 1399. The Congregation for Clergy had a special faculty to handle cases of clerics who had abandoned ministry for at least five years. The procedure to be used was very simple and streamlined and was included in the letter.[22] On March 31, 2009, similar special faculties were granted to the Congregation for the Evangelization of Peoples.[23]

THE 1917 CODE

Sexual abuse by clergy has been severely punished for most of the history of the Catholic Church.[24] The apostolic constitution *Sacramentum Poenitentiae*, issued by Pope Benedict XIV in 1741, was an appendix to the 1917 Code of Canon Law.

The 1917 Code in respect of sexual abuse by clergy in canon 2359 §2 stated:

> If they engage in a delict against the sixth precept of the Decalogue with a minor below the age of sixteen, or engage in adultery, debauchery, bestiality, sodomy, pandering, incest with blood-relatives or affines in the first degree, they are suspended, declared infamous, and are deprived of any office, benefice, dignity, responsibility, if they have such, whatsoever, and in more serious cases they are to be deposed.

More specific norms were issued in "On the Method of Proceeding in Cases of Solicitation" (*Crimen Sollicitationis*) in 1922. This instruction was approved *in forma specifica* by Pope Pius XI and signed by Cardinal Merry del Val, the Cardinal Secretary of the Holy Office. Although the document was printed by Vatican Press, it was not promulgated in the normal way in the *Acta Apostolicae Sedis*. Nicholas Cafardi notes:

> In fact, the first page of the instruction says it is to be "diligently kept in the secret archives of the [diocesan] curia for internal use, and is not to be published or commented on in any canonical commentary." While the instruction is addressed to "All Patriarchs, Archbishops, Bishops, and Other Local Ordinaries, including of the Oriental Rites" it was evidently not circulated to them. Instead, the text was available by request to bishops who needed to know its contents to deal with such crimes.[25]

The Holy Office was given competence to deal with cases administratively or in a judicial process.[26]

The Holy Office reissued *Crimen Sollicitationis* in 1962 with minor changes to the 1922 text to include religious priests. Pope John XXIII approved the revised document, with Cardinal Ottaviani acting as Secretary of the Holy Office and signing it. The first page of the document said it was to be

> diligently kept in the secret archives of the [diocesan] curia for internal use, and is not to be published or commented on in any canonical commentary. Again, the instruction is addressed to "All Patriarchs, Archbishops, Bishops, and Other Local Ordinaries, including of the Oriental Rites." And again, the only bishops who received it were those who contacted the Holy See about the crimes covered by the instruction. Although there had been a plan to distribute the document to the bishops attending the Second Vatican Council, that never happened.[27]

The Holy See is careful about the naming of documents. The first few Latin words of an official document become its name and express what the document is all about.[28] As the title indicated, *Crimen Sollicitationis* dealt almost entirely with the crime of solicitation—that is, the solicitation of sex by a priest hearing confession.

The final section[29] of both the 1922 and the 1962 versions of *Crimen Sollicitationis* reads: "What is established herein on the crime of solicitation is also valid, *mutatis mutandis*, for the worst crime *crimen pessimum* [of pedophilia]." The worst crime is defined in section 73 as "obscene behaviour with pre-adolescent children of either sex or with brute animals."[30] There are 289 words in the English translation of the final section of *Crimen Sollicitationis*, which was 4 percent of the total document of 7,112 words. It is simply not true, as some have claimed, that this document is aimed at covering up pedophilia.[31]

The contents of *Crimen Sollicitationis* are explained by Nicholas Cafardi:

> What was established "herein" on the crime of solicitation? One thing the document established was that the Holy Office had jurisdiction over these crimes, and was, in this document, telling local bishops how to handle them. More than anything, the instruction is a dry statement of the rules of criminal procedure that apply when a priest has been accused of solicitation. And that what the Holy Office says about the crime of solicitation also applies to the crime of the sexual abuse of children by a priest.[32]

The teaching of the Church in reference to such crimes is centuries old. The Didache of the second century commanded Christians: "Do not murder; do not commit adultery; do not practice pederasty, do not fornicate."[33] Polycarp (c. 69–155), the second bishop of Smyrna, wrote to the Philippians that "the younger men must be blameless in all things, caring of purity before everything and curbing themselves from every evil...whether whoremongers nor effeminate persons nor defilers of themselves with men and boys shall inherit the Kingdom of God."[34] Athenagoras of Athens [c. 133–190] was a significant apologist and Christian thinker in the second century. He defended the Christian concept of purity and described pederasts as enemies of the Church.[35] Canon 71 of the Council of Elvira (305–306) in Spain condemned those who rape little boys.[36] The First Council of Neocaesarea (ca. 315) enacted legislation that punished priests for violating the sixth commandment by adultery or fornication.[37]

Although the instruction *Crimen Sollicitationis* was not promulgated, it was not intended to provide a cover-up for the crimes it addressed, because it clearly established the procedures to be followed in dealing with such crimes, including sexual abuse of children. Nevertheless, most bishops and priests and all laity were unaware of its existence. While secret laws do not make sense, there is no doubt that the secrecy surrounding this document has made dealing with the sexual abuse crisis more difficult. Notwithstanding, once the 1983 Code of Canon Law came into effect on November 27, 1983, bishops and Ordinaries, to whom clerics were subject, had the norms of canons 1717–19, which provided for the preliminary investigation of a possible crime or once they became aware of a possible crime, to follow.

JURIDICAL STATUS

Distinguishing between different kinds of documents is very important, because the kind of document it is helps determine its binding force in canon law.

Pope Benedict XV (September 3, 1914–January 22, 1922) explained the status of instructions:

> The ordinary function [of the congregations as regards general decrees] will therefore be not only to see that the prescriptions of the Code are religiously observed, but also to issue *Instructions*, as need arises, whereby those prescriptions may be more fully explained and appropriately enforced. These documents are to be drawn up in such a manner that they shall not only be in reality explanations and complements to the canons, but also that they may be clearly seen to be such.[38]

This statement is clear. In practice, however, other legislators beneath the pope can make some contents of instructions equivalent to law because they complement *lacunae* in the canons of the Code. Francis Morrisey observes:

> It is this form of document, along with the declaration, that has given rise to the greatest difficulty in interpretation in the post-conciliar era. Since the texts are not strictly speaking legislative—at least according to their nature—their application certainly allows for more leeway than would a decree.[39]

Canon 34 §1 of the 1983 Code makes instructions binding on those implementing the law:

> Instructions clarify the prescripts of laws and elaborate on and determine methods to be observed in fulfilling them. They are given for the use of those whose duty it is to see that laws are executed and oblige them in the execution of the laws. Those who possess executive power legitimately issue such instructions within the limits of their competence.[40]

The contents of instructions are subservient to the law and depend on the existence of the law to retain their binding force.[41]

Pope John XXIII approved *Crimen Sollicitationis in forma specifica.* It states that His Holiness Pope John XXIII, in an audience granted to the Most Eminent Cardinal Secretary of the Holy Office on March 16, 1962, graciously approved and confirmed this instruction, ordering those responsible to observe it and to ensure that it is observed in every detail.[42]

In 2001, Pope John Paul II confirmed this when he explained: "It is to be kept in mind that an Instruction of this kind had the force of law since the Supreme Pontiff, according to the norm of canon 247 §1 of the *Codex Iuris Canonici* promulgated in 1917, presided over the Congregation of the Holy Office, and the Instruction proceeded from his own authority, with the Cardinal at the time only performing the function of secretary."[43]

When Congregations of the Roman Curia issue documents, most of them have general approval (*in forma communi*) from the pope before they are promulgated. Significant documents are sometimes approved by the pope *in forma specifica*. This approval gives the document legislative force.[44] Although *Crimen Sollicitationis* was approved *in forma specifica*, it retained the canonical status of an instruction.

THE 1983 CODE

Canon 277 of the 1983 Code legislated that clerics are to be celibate, that is, not marry, and that they be continent, that is, that they abstain from sexual activity. Canon 1395 §2 determined pedophilia as a crime along with some other sexual offenses:

> A cleric who in another way has committed an offence against the sixth commandment of the Decalogue, if the delict was committed by force or threats or publicly or with a minor below the age of sixteen years, is to be punished with just penalties, not excluding dismissal from the clerical state if the case so warrants.

There was a time limit of five years for laying a complaint about an offense until the law was changed in 2001.[45]

WHICH LAW APPLIED?

The Congregation for the Doctrine of the Faith handled dispensations from celibacy during the 1980s. Cardinal Ratzinger, the Prefect of this Congregation, was shocked by the scandalous actions of some priests. He did not think that they should get dispensations from celibacy as a favor but should instead be punished. Therefore, Cardinal Ratzinger wrote to Cardinal Castillo Lara, President of the Pontifical Commission for the Authentic Interpretation of the Code of Canon Law, on February 19, 1988, asking for a simpler penal process to dismiss clergy:

> Your Eminence, this Dicastery, in the course of examining petitions for dispensation from priestly obligations, has to deal with cases of priests who, in the exercise of their ministry, have been guilty of grave and scandalous conduct, for which the Code of Canon Law, after due process, provides for the imposition of specific penalties, not excluding reduction to the lay state.
>
> These provisions, in the judgement of this Dicastery, ought in some cases, for the good of the faithful, to take precedence over the request for dispensation from priestly obligations, which, by its nature, involves a "grace" in favour of the petitioner. Yet in view of the complexity of the penal process required by the Code in these circumstances, some Ordinaries are likely to experience considerable difficulty in implementing such a penal process.
>
> I would be grateful to Your Eminence, therefore, if you were to communicate your valued opinion regarding the possibility of making provision, in specific cases, for a more rapid and simplified penal process.[46]

Three weeks later, Cardinal Castillo Lara of the Pontifical Commission replied in a letter dated March 10, 1988:

> I can well understand Your Eminence's concern at the fact that the Ordinaries involved did not first exercise their

judicial power in order to punish such crimes sufficiently, even to protect the common good of the faithful. Nevertheless the problem seems to lie not with juridical procedure, but with the responsible exercise of the task of governance.

In the current Code, the offences that can lead to loss of the clerical state have been clearly indicated: they are listed in canons 1364 §1, 1367, 1370, 1387, 1394 and 1395. At the same time the procedure has been greatly simplified in comparison with the previous norms of the 1917 Code: it has been speeded up and streamlined, partly with a view to encouraging the Ordinaries to exercise their authority through the necessary judgement of the offenders "ad normam iuris" and the imposition of the sanctions provided.

To seek to simplify the judicial procedure further so as to impose or declare sanctions as grave as dismissal from the clerical state, or to change the current norm of can. 1342 §2 which prohibits proceeding with an extra-judicial administrative decree in these cases (cf. can. 1720), does not seem at all appropriate. Indeed, on the one hand it would endanger the fundamental right of defence—and in causes that affect the person's state—while on the other hand it would favour the deplorable tendency—owing perhaps to lack of due knowledge or esteem for the law—towards ambivalent so-called "pastoral" governance, which ultimately is not pastoral at all, because it tends to obscure the due exercise of authority, thereby damaging the common good of the faithful.

At other difficult times in the life of the Church, when there has been confusion of consciences and relaxation of ecclesiastical discipline, the sacred Pastors have not failed to exercise their judicial power in order to protect the supreme good of the "salus animarum."[47]

Cardinal Castillo Lara then proceeded to report that cases for the so-called dismissal *ex officio* from the clerical state had already been considered and decided upon.[48] Instead, bishops should implement the penal law. The cardinal's reply was not helpful. The response did not face the reality and enormity of the pedophilia problem.

The wording in Cardinal Ratzinger's letter would seem to indicate that he did not seem to think that the Congregation for the Doctrine of the Faith was competent to handle pedophilia cases. Perhaps this is because canon 6 of the 1983 Code had abrogated many penal laws.[49]

In 1988, Pope John Paul II restructured the Roman Curia with the promulgation of the apostolic constitution *Pastor Bonus*,[50] which replaced *Regimini Ecclesiae Universae*.[51] Article 52 of *Pastor Bonus* gave exclusive penal jurisdiction to the Congregation for the Doctrine of the Faith. This ensured that the Congregation for the Doctrine of the Faith was not only competent with regard to offenses against the faith or in the celebration of the sacraments, but also with regard to "more serious offences against morals." However, there was no public statement or advice to bishops about dealing with pedophilia and there was no action from the Congregation.

The existence of the instruction *Crimen Sollicitationis* was not a complete secret. The officers of the Canon Law Society of America visited the Congregation for the Doctrine of the Faith in 1996. In its June 1996 Newsletter, the president reported:

> The norms on solicitation cases issued in 1962 are currently under review by a commission within the CDF. New norms are required in light of the revision of canon law. In the interim, the 1962 norms should be followed with obvious adaptations.[52]

On January 28, 1998, Archbishop Philip Wilson, then the Bishop of Wollongong, wrote to the Congregation for the Doctrine of the Faith asking if *Crimen Sollicitationis* was restricted to confession. On February 28, 1998, Archbishop Bertone, the Secretary of the Congregation for the Doctrine of the Faith, replied to Bishop Wilson:

> Your Excellency,
>
> With your letter of January 28, 1998, regarding the case of a priest accused of sexually abusing a minor, you asked whether the procedure of the *Instructio de modo Procendi in causis sollicitationis* should be followed, or whether these procedures only concern actions which are alleged to have occurred in the context of the Sacrament of Confession.
>
> This Congregation responds that in the above-mentioned case, the procedure of the *Instructio* should be followed as indicated in the fifth chapter of the document (De crimine pessimo).[53]

Archbishop Bertone stated clearly that *Crimen Sollicitationis* was not confined just to the confessional and was still in force for dealing with child sexual abuse matters. However, there seems to be no evidence of action on this information.

Many bishops around the world thought that the penal process was too difficult to implement; one reason was the lack of qualified, competent, and experienced priests. The procedural law of *Crimen Sollicitationis* remained unknown and confidential. Most bishops and religious superiors were ignorant of the law, and many did not act appropriately.

ROMAN CURIA DIVISIONS

During the pontificate of Pope Benedict XVI, reports of infighting among officials of the Roman Curia became increasingly public. *The Guardian* newspaper speculated that the butler Paolo Gabriele[54] was one of up to twenty whistleblowers trying to oust Benedict's powerful Secretary of State, Cardinal Tarcisio Bertone. The cardinal had previously been Cardinal Ratzinger's secretary at the Congregation for the Doctrine of the Faith.

Pope Francis (March 13, 2013–April 21, 2025) addressed these issues in his Christmas message to the Roman Curia officials on December 23, 2014, in which he stated that one of their problems was:

the disease of poor coordination. Once its members lose communion among themselves, the body loses its harmonious functioning and its equilibrium; it then becomes an orchestra that produces noise: its members do not work together and lose the spirit of fellowship and teamwork. When the foot says to the arm, "I don't need you," or the hand says to the head, "I'm in charge," they create discomfort and scandal.[55]

These issues were not new, and there is no doubt that poor coordination by Vatican officials very badly affected the handling of sexual abuse cases.

MODIFICATION OF PENAL LAW FOR THE UNITED STATES OF AMERICA

After another abuse scandal in 1992 in Fall River, bishops in the United States requested a quicker process than a penal trial to dismiss sexually abusive clergy. In 1993, Pope John Paul II convened a joint commission of American and Vatican canon lawyers to suggest improvements to the law.

The pope rejected a proposal from the joint commission to allow the bishops themselves to dismiss priests administratively without canonical trials. But the age for sexual abuse cases in the United States was raised from sixteen to eighteen years, and the statute of limitations was extended to ten years after the victim's eighteenth birthday.[56]

SACRAMENTORUM SANCTITATIS TUTELA

As the extent of the problem of sexual abuse became more obvious, Pope John Paul II issued the apostolic letter *motu proprio Sacramentorum Sanctitatis Tutela* for the universal Church on April 30, 2001.[57] The *delicta graviora* norms reiterated the jurisdiction of the Congregation for the Doctrine of the Faith for sexual abuse cases. Sexual abuse is specified as a very serious crime that causes grave damage to the normal development of the victim, as well as causing tremendous damage to the Church and its credibility and betraying the trust that people have in priests. This crime deserves the strictest punishments. As universal law, *Sacramentorum Sanctitatis Tutela* raised the age a person was considered a minor to eighteen and changed the time limit for laying a complaint until ten years after the minor had reached the age of eighteen. The Congregation for the Doctrine of the Faith was to supervise penal trials, investigations into credible offenses, and how they were dealt with.

Rev. Charles Scicluna, former Promoter of Justice at the Congregation for the Doctrine of the Faith, reported:

> Between 1975 and 1985 I do not believe that any cases of paedophilia committed by priests were brought to the attention of our Congregation. Moreover, following the promulgation of the 1983 Code of Canon Law, there was a period of uncertainty as to which of the *delicta graviora* were reserved to the competency of this dicastery.

> Only with the 2001 *motu proprio* did the crime of paedophilia again become our exclusive remit.[58]

SECRECY

The document *Crimen Sollicitationis* of 1922 was reissued in 1962 to ensure that religious priests were included in its procedures. Kieran Tapsell claims that *Crimen Sollicitationis* reflected the culture of secrecy that the Church adopted around the time of the 1917 Code of Canon Law, rather than its cause.[59] Tom Doyle acknowledges that the documents did not create the obsession with secrecy but are a result of it.[60]

The Church has not always had a culture of secrecy concerning the sexual misconduct of clergy. It appears that the obligation of secrecy for such cases was first imposed by Pope Pius IX in 1866. The official document that imposes the secrecy was published on February 20, 1866, by the Sacred Congregation of the Holy Office in the form of an instruction. This instruction provided clarification on certain aspects of the previous papal constitution, *Sacramentum Poenitentiae* (1741) of Pope Benedict XIV, which dealt with solicitation in the confessional.

Crimen Sollicitationis seems to have been sent to all the Superiors General of Religious Orders because religious priests were now encompassed by these procedures. This explains why Cardinal Francis George, OMI,[61] and religious in Australia at seminaries in 1962 heard of the existence of the document. The Sacred Congregation for the Propagation of the Faith did not appear to have sent it out to countries under its jurisdiction. The Congregation for the Doctrine of the Faith states:

> Copies of the 1962 re-print were meant to be given to the Bishops gathering for the Second Vatican Council (1962–1965). A few copies of this re-print were handed out to bishops who, in the meantime, needed to process cases reserved to the Holy Office but, most of the copies were never distributed.[62]

There was no copy at the Apostolic Nunciature in Wellington when I asked for a copy in 1994. There were no copies in diocesan archives in Australia, which in 1962 was still a missionary territory.[63]

Crimen Sollicitationis determined that the Church's legal process is covered by pontifical secrecy:

> Since, however, in dealing with these causes, more than usual care and concern must be shown that they be treated with the utmost confidentiality, and that, once decided and the decision executed, they are covered by permanent silence (Instruction of the Holy Office, 20 February 1867, No. 14), all those persons in any way associated with the tribunal, or knowledgeable of these matters by reason of their office, are bound to observe inviolably the strictest confidentiality, commonly known as the *secret of the Holy Office*, in all things and with all persons, under pain of incurring automatic excommunication, *ipso facto* and undeclared, reserved to the sole person of the Supreme Pontiff, excluding even

> the Sacred Penitentiary. Ordinaries are bound *by this same law,* that is, in virtue of their own office; other personnel are bound in virtue of *the oath* which they are always to swear before assuming their duties; and, finally, those delegated, questioned or informed [outside the tribunal], are bound in virtue of *the precept* to be imposed on them in the letters of delegation, inquiry or information, with express mention of the *secret of the Holy Office* and of the aforementioned censure. (no. 11)

Professor Gerardo Nunez from the University of Navarre explains:

> The secrecy requirement ended up being called the "secret of the Holy Office." A secret that did not end with the finalisation of the cases in the Congregation, as was the practice with the rest of the Roman Congregations. In effect the obligation to keep the secret over matters that it covered lasted forever. The persons who were bound by the secret were those that had anything to do with the Holy Office tribunal, and it applied equally to proceedings in the diocesan tribunal as the Roman one.[64]

According to the 1983 Code, each diocese is to have secret archives for confidential material such as penal trials and complaints of sexual abuse. Canon 489 states:

> §1. In the diocesan curia there is also to be a secret [*secretum*] archive, or at least in the common archive there is to be a safe or cabinet, completely closed and locked, which cannot be removed; in it documents to be kept secret are to be protected most securely. §2. Each year documents of criminal cases in matters of moral matters, in which the accused parties have died or ten years have elapsed from the condemnatory sentence, are to be destroyed. A brief summary of what occurred along with the text of the definitive sentence is to be retained.

"*Secretum*" can mean "separate" or "private." In this context "*secretum*" means "very confidential." Most organizations have archives to which the ordinary staff do not have access. The word *secretary* comes from *secretum*, because the person originally had access to the confidential information of a powerful person. Pontifical secrecy could be described as a greater than normal secrecy, like cabinet confidentiality or lawyer-client privilege. On the other hand, the secrecy of the confessional is absolute.[65]

The instruction *Secreta Continere*[66] addressed the secret of the Holy Office and applied to sexual abuse of children and all cases involving faith and morals. The document is headed "Concerning Pontifical Confidentiality." The pontifical secret bound members of the staff of the Holy Office and someone acting on their behalf. Since the crimes of sexual abuse of minors and solicitation were reserved to the Congregation, those investigating at a local level were obliged by the pontifical secrecy too. Article 1 §4 of *Secreta Continere* did provide for the accused to be told about the allegation "for his own defence."

Victims and witnesses were supposed to take the oath of secrecy about the questions they were asked and their answers. Since very few people in the Church or the world knew of *Crimen Sollicitationis*, it would have been very rare for people to know of pontifical secrecy. They were not prohibited from talking to police, but, according to John Beal, most would not realize they could talk to others.[67] The secrecy was to protect the privacy of the accuser, the good reputation of the accused, and to enable a fair trial. In fact, *Secreta Continere* abrogated the automatic excommunication reserved to the Roman Pontiff incurred for violating the pontifical secret, and a distinction was made between those who violated the secret in the service of the Roman Curia and other people.[68]

Both Pope John Paul II,[69] in 2001, and Pope Benedict XVI,[70] in 2010, provided that "cases of this kind [pedophilia] are subject to the pontifical secret," and their footnotes refer to Article 1 §4 of *Secreta Continere*. The 2010 revision extended the pontifical secret to cover cases involving clergy sexual abuse of intellectually disabled adults and the possession of child pornography. Those who are bound by the pontifical secret are obliged to keep it "forever."

Aurelio Yanguas argues that the real reason for the secrecy imposed by *Crimen Sollicitationis* was to enable "swift, decisive and secret action" before the crimes reached civil court and spare the Church the humiliation of priests in court as sex offenders.[71] *Crimen Sollicitationis* and its predecessor from 1922 are not part of a Vatican conspiracy to cover up sexual abuse crimes, but their relatively secret existence contributed a great deal to the crisis.

MANDATORY REPORTING

Associated with the secrecy of pedophilia cases is the subject of mandatory reporting in civil law to police. The Congregation for the Clergy deals with the interests of well over 400,000 priests in the Catholic Church.

In 1997, Cardinal Castrillón Hoyos, then the Prefect of that Dicastery, wrote to the Irish bishops through the papal nuncio, claiming that mandatory reporting of child sexual abuse conflicted with canon law and could invalidate any canonical process.[72]

Following that letter, on September 8, 2001, the cardinal congratulated French Bishop Pierre Pican for not reporting a sexually abusive priest to the police:

> I congratulate you for not denouncing a priest to the civil administration. You have acted well and I am pleased to have a colleague in the episcopate who, in the eyes of history and of all other bishops in the world, preferred prison to denouncing his son-priest.[73]

In the 1917 Code, canon 120 §1 stated the *privilegium fori*, which provided that all judicial proceedings, including criminal matters, against clerics must be brought before an ecclesiastical court, unless other provisions had been legitimately made for some countries, for example by concordat or custom. This privilege was abrogated when the revised

Code came into effect in November 1983. Thus, it is evident that the supreme legislator, Pope John Paul II, intended that any cleric whose behavior constitutes a crime in accordance with the norms of civil law cannot be shielded from the consequences of his actions. What punishment such actions deserve in canon law is another matter. Moreover, it is an obligation of bishops and other relevant church personnel to report crimes committed by clerics to the competent civil authority as required in accordance with the norms of civil law.

Accordingly, the content of the two letters of Cardinal Hoyos appears to reflect an attitude at odds with the law of the Church and of covering up crimes of pedophilia by clergy so that they are not held accountable for their actions before the civil law which they have also violated. Such attitudes have made the problem so much worse.

The Congregation for the Doctrine of the Faith has stated in its letter to bishops' conferences in 2011:

> The Guidelines prepared by the Episcopal Conference ought to provide guidance to Diocesan Bishops and Major Superiors in case they are informed of allegations of sexual abuse of minors by clerics present in the territory of their jurisdiction. Such Guidelines, moreover, should take account of the following observations: …g) the Guidelines are to make allowance for the legislation of the country where the Conference is located, in particular regarding what pertains to the obligation of notifying civil authorities.[74]

NEGLIGENCE OR COVER-UP BY BISHOPS

The Pontifical Commission for the Protection of Minors was established on March 22, 2014. Pope Francis promulgated the statutes of the Commission and authorized the establishment of a judicial section of the Congregation for the Doctrine of the Faith to punish and remove bishops who are negligent or cover up the sexual abuse of minors.[75]

The *motu proprio* "As a Loving Mother" (2016) contained the procedures to remove a bishop for negligence, and *Vos Estis Lux Mundi* (2019) informed bishops they could be removed for failing to deal with complaints of sexual abuse.

The judicial section of the Congregation for the Doctrine of the Faith judges the cases of bishops in the name of the pope.[76] Bishops can now be punished and removed by a judicial process rather than be asked to resign according to canon 401 §2.[77]

The most recent legislation concerning mandatory reporting is in *Vos Estis Lux Mundi* 2023:

> Art. 3 – Reporting. §1. Except for when a cleric learns of information during the exercise of ministry in the internal forum, whenever a cleric or a member of an Institute of Consecrated Life or of a Society of Apostolic Life learns, or has well-founded motives to believe, that one of the acts referred to in art.1 has been committed, that person is obliged to report it promptly to the local Ordinary where the events are said to have occurred or to another

> Ordinary among those referred to in canons 134CIC and 984 CCEO, except for what is established by §3 of the present article.

Vos Estis Lux Mundi (2023) includes the crime of religious leaders failing to act as required on information concerning sexual abuse:

> §3. When the report concerns one of the persons indicated in art. 6,[78] it is to be addressed to the Authority identified on the basis of articles 8 and 9. The report can always be sent to the competent Dicastery directly or through the Pontifical Representative. If the first option is chosen, the Dicastery will inform the Pontifical Representative about the matter.... §5. Information can also be acquired ex officio.

CONCLUSION

The moral teaching of the Catholic Church has always been that the sexual abuse of boys and girls is a grave or mortal sin. It has been regarded also as a crime in canon law from earliest times, and until the latter part of the twentieth century, offenders were severely punished. This underlies the realization that it has always been seen to have had serious effects on the victim and the Church in general. Both the cover-ups and the extent of the problem have been a huge scandal for the Catholic Church in recent years.

The secrecy surrounding *Crimen Sollicitationis* is a scandal. It has led to the inept handling of abuse cases in the upper levels of church administration. The secret procedures in *Crimen Sollicitationis* have caused confusion, inaction, and facilitated "geographical cures" of moving clergy from place to place.

Consequently, many bishops and religious superiors have not dealt with abusive clergy properly. Therefore, as Pope John Paul II stated on April 23, 2002, "People need to know that there is no place in the priesthood and religious life for those who would harm the young."[79] There is no doubt that the pope considered that one conviction of sexual abuse was sufficient to have a priest dismissed from the clerical state. Like many secular institutions, church leaders have failed to act and enabled abusers to continue to function and have access to more victims. Bishops around the world did not learn from the lessons of North America.

12

MAKING THE ABUSE OF MINORS AN IRREGULARITY

The Catholic Church has been under unprecedented attack. Sexual abuse of minors has been committed by priests and religious all over the world. In 2018, the *Pennsylvania Grand Jury Report into Child Sexual Abuse in Six Pennsylvania Roman Catholic Dioceses* detailed sexual abuse by over three hundred priests over seventy years that was often covered up.[1] The John Jay Study revealed that 4 percent of American priests serving over the last fifty years have been accused of sexual abuse.[2]

In 2017, the *Australian Royal Commission into Institutional Responses to Child Sexual Abuse* demonstrated that within the Catholic Church perpetrators of sexual abuse were just over 37 percent non-ordained religious (32 percent religious brothers and 5 percent religious sisters); 30 percent were priests; 29 percent were laypeople. In Australia, 7 percent of all Catholic priests who ministered between 1950 and 2010 were alleged perpetrators.[3]

Fewer applicants are entering seminaries in many countries, which results in lower standards for acceptance in some dioceses and some unsuitable people being ordained. Bishops are accepting seminarians without sufficient checks on their suitability. Some seminarians have "shopped around" dioceses to find a bishop who will ordain them, after they have been rejected for ordination by other bishops or having been asked to leave seminaries. The Holy See has attempted to curb this phenomenon by asserting the canon law on this matter to prevent unsuitable people from being ordained priests.[4] Bishops also accept priests to minister in their dioceses without sufficient checks on their suitability and formation.

Pope John Paul II told the American cardinals on April 23, 2002, that

> it must be absolutely clear to the Catholic faithful, and to the wider community, that Bishops and superiors are

concerned, above all else, with the spiritual good of souls. People need to know that there is no place in the priesthood and religious life for those who would harm the young.[5]

On March 17, 2010, Pope Benedict XVI wrote a pastoral letter to the Catholics of Ireland. In paragraph 11, he addresses his brother bishops stating:

> It cannot be denied that some of you and your predecessors failed, at times grievously, to apply the long-established norms of canon law to the crime of child abuse. Serious mistakes were made in responding to allegations. I recognize how difficult it was to grasp the extent and complexity of the problem, to obtain reliable information and to make the right decisions in the light of conflicting expert advice. Nevertheless, it must be admitted that grave errors of judgement were made and failures of leadership occurred. All this has seriously undermined your credibility and effectiveness. I appreciate the efforts you have made to remedy past mistakes and to guarantee that they do not happen again.

QUALITIES IN A PERSON TO BE ORDAINED

Those to be ordained are supposed to have integral faith, the right intention, requisite knowledge, a good reputation, integral morals and proven virtues, as well as the other physical and psychological qualities to be ordained. As the 1983 Code states:

> Only those are to be promoted to orders who, in the prudent judgment of their own bishop or of the competent major superior, all things considered, have integral faith, are moved by the right intention, have the requisite knowledge, possess a good reputation, and are endowed with integral morals and proven virtues and the other physical and psychic qualities in keeping with the order to be received. (Can. 1029)

The canon leaves the prudent judgment about a person's suitability for ordination to the discretion of the bishop or competent major superior. There is no mention of consultation with others as specified by the irregularity of insanity or "amentia" in canon 1041, no. 1 that requires consultation with experts. But the Congregation for Catholic Education has reminded all bishops and major superiors:

> The Bishop or major superior, before admitting the candidate to ordination, must arrive at a morally certain judgment on his qualities. In the case of a serious doubt in this regard, he must not admit him to ordination.[6]

Similarly, religious superiors, for seminarians and novitiates, are only to admit those who, besides the required age, have the health, suitable character, and sufficient qualities of maturity to embrace the proper life of the institute. This health, character, and maturity are to be verified by using experts, if necessary, without prejudice to the prescript of canon 220 and a person's right to privacy and informed consent about the release of information.

The Congregation for Divine Worship and the Discipline of the Sacraments has also stated that a doubtful candidate should not be ordained "for the good of the Church,"[7] and quoted scripture: "Do not be hasty in the laying on of hands" (1 Tim 5:22). The Congregation restated the law and its policy:

> Where a candidate comes from another diocese or from a Congregation or Institute of Consecrated Life or has received one of the stages of his formation in more than one house, the causes and motives for such an unusual occurrence should be studied. Of particular importance are those cases in which a candidate has been expelled from a formation house or has been invited to withdraw....It is not possible to admit a candidate to the Diaconate in the face of doubts concerning his suitability for the Priesthood.[8]

The Congregation for the Doctrine of the Faith has specified some qualities in relation to canon 1029 that make an applicant for ordination unsuitable for ordination. It was stated in 1995 that a person should not be ordained who suffers from a psychological infirmity such as alcoholism or a physical problem such as celiac disease:

> Given the centrality of the celebration of the Eucharist in the life of the priest, candidates for the priesthood who are affected by celiac disease or suffer from alcoholism or similar conditions may not be admitted to holy orders.[9]

Then in 2005, the Congregation for Catholic Education stated:

> The Church, while profoundly respecting the persons in question, cannot admit to the seminary or to holy orders those who practise homosexuality, present deep-seated homosexual tendencies or support the so-called "gay culture."[10]

Canon law is clear: "No one has a right to ordination."[11] Since there is a bias in the law for protecting the Church from unsuitable clergy, canon 1052 §1 reminds bishops that "positive arguments must prove the suitability of the candidate." This is much more demanding than saying that there is a lack of proof of the unsuitability of the person to be ordained. Canon 1052 §3, therefore, concludes, "If, all these notwithstanding, the bishop doubts for specific reasons whether a candidate is suitable to receive orders, he is not to promote him." With the other sacraments such as Eucharist, Penance, and Baptism, the opposite approach applies.[12] Therefore, when a person is doubtfully disposed to receive these sacraments, they have the benefit of the doubt and receive them.

HISTORY OF IRREGULARITIES

The Church has a long history of having irregularities or perpetual impediments to ordination to prevent unsuitable people being ordained. Saint Paul forbade the ordination of anyone who had been married twice. He told Timothy,

"Let deacons be married only once" (1 Tim 3:12), while "a bishop must be... married only once" (1 Tim 3:2), and instituted the equivalent of an impediment because a bishop must "not be a recent convert (Neophyte)" (1 Tim 3:6).

Cappello defines an irregularity as

> a perpetual impediment, established by ecclesiastical law out of reverence of the divine ministry, prohibiting primarily the reception of order, and secondarily the exercise of orders received.[13]

All irregularities are ecclesiastical laws. They might, as with abortion, relate to divine law and the fifth commandment, but they are still ecclesiastical laws.[14] Sexual abuse of minors contravenes natural law and the sixth commandment, so its effect as an irregularity would be similar.

The word *irregularity* was first used by Saint Augustine [354–430].[15] Pope Innocent III [1198–1216] outlined circumstances that barred a person from being ordained and irregularities that prevented a priest from functioning.[16]

The 1917 Code used "irregularity" to mean a perpetual obstacle to someone being ordained or exercising the power of orders. Irregularities may be the result of a defect that disqualifies them from ordination or a crime. The irregularity was not received as a penalty or a punishment but existed to uphold the dignity and reverence for ordained clerics. It helped ensure that the ordained ministers had the necessary qualities to be ordained.

An irregularity must be interpreted in the light of canons 14 and 18. Laws restricting people's rights are subject to a strict interpretation.[17] When there is doubt whether a fact is present, canon 14 states that the Ordinary can dispense from it if it is something the dispensing authority usually grants.[18] The Holy See regularly refuses to grant dispensations from irregularities.

While impediments are qualities that prevent ordination temporarily while they exist, irregularities are permanent impediments. Impediments are based on factual circumstances that are of a temporary nature. The sources of irregularities are crimes or other noncriminal things that can be physical or psychological.

Even if the one to be ordained is unaware that he has an irregularity, he is still bound by the irregularity when he learns he has become subject to it. An example is a non-Catholic being involved in an abortion. Canon 1041 states:

> The following are irregular for receiving orders: 4/ a person who has committed voluntary homicide or procured a completed abortion and all those who positively cooperated in either.

Amy Strickland notes that even if a candidate for ordination was not a Catholic,

> when the abortion took place does not exempt him from the irregularity, since abortion is a grave offence against divine law. Therefore, it has juridical effects for a non-Catholic who later becomes Catholic, in much the same way that

a valid natural marriage constitutes an impediment to a future union.[19]

The involvement of the person to be ordained in the abortion must have been a deliberate, sinful action to become subject to the irregularity. The irregularity could have arisen from being an accomplice in an abortion as a doctor or nurse or boyfriend of the woman. Canon 1329 §2 states:

> Accomplices who are not named in a law or precept incur a *latae sententiae* penalty attached to a delict if without their assistance the delict would not have been committed, and the penalty is of such a nature that it can affect them; otherwise, they can be punished by *ferendae sententiae* penalties.

To become subject to the irregularity, the person to be ordained must have supported or encouraged the abortion. Therefore, if a priest had an affair with a woman who became pregnant, and he encouraged her to have an abortion, he would become subject to the irregularity for the exercise of orders.[20]

IRREGULARITIES IN THE 1983 CODE

The 1983 Code contains a list of irregularities in Canon 1041:

> The following persons are irregular for the reception of orders: 1/ one who suffers from any form of insanity, or from any other psychological infirmity, because of which he is, after experts have been consulted, judged incapable of properly fulfilling the ministry; 2/ one who has committed the offence of apostasy, heresy or schism; 3/ one who has attempted marriage, even a civil marriage, either while himself prevented from entering marriage whether by an existing marriage bond or by a sacred order or by a public and perpetual vow of chastity, or with a woman who is validly married or is obliged by the same vow; 4/ one who has committed willful homicide, or one who has actually procured an abortion, and all who have positively cooperated; 5/ one who has gravely and maliciously mutilated himself or another, or who has attempted suicide; 6/ one who has carried out an act of order which is reserved to those in the order of the episcopate or priesthood, while himself either not possessing that order or being barred from its exercise by some canonical penalty, declared or imposed.

An irregularity can occur without any fault of the person to be ordained, for example, due to, insanity or amentia. The other irregularities, however, are the result of a crime or a wrongful action and are governed by penal law. For a person to incur an irregularity, they must be responsible for their action.[21]

Canon 1321 states:

> §1. No one can be punished for the commission of an external violation of a law or precept unless it is gravely imputable by reason of malice or of culpability. §2. A person who deliberately violated a law or precept is bound by the penalty prescribed in the law or precept. If, however, the violation was

> due to the omission of due diligence, the person is not punished unless the law or precept provides otherwise. §3. When there has been an external violation, imputability is presumed, unless it appears otherwise.

A crime is "an external and morally imputable violation of a law to which a canonical sanction is attached."[22] In other words, to receive a penalty, a person must have gravely sinned. Not all grave sins are crimes, but grave sins that seriously affect the individual or the church community are sometimes classified by the Church also to be crimes. Crimes are opposed to everything the Church stands for. The Ten Commandments guide the faithful about the content of grave matter.

When a person does something gravely wrong, it is a mortal sin. Some of the worst sins are also classified as crimes. However, factors such as ignorance of a sin being a crime result in the offender not receiving the penalty for the crime.[23] When a grave sinner receives forgiveness for the crime, he is also usually released from the penalty that is a consequence of the crime.

Crimes can also be classified as irregularities. However, irregularities are very different from crimes. Even someone who is not a Catholic can incur an irregularity. An offender becomes subject to the irregularity even if at the time of the commission of the offense they were ignorant of the existence of the irregularity. Even though the sin has been forgiven and the penalty has been removed in the sacrament of Penance, the irregularity remains to prevent ordination or the exercise of ministry such as celebrating the sacraments.

IRREGULAR FOR THE EXERCISE OF MINISTRY

Besides preventing an ordination, an irregularity also prevents an ordained priest from exercising ministry. Canon 1044 outlines the effects of an irregularity that a priest may become subject to after ordination. Some of the irregularities, such as abortion, prevent the priest from celebrating sacraments or any ministry:

> §1. The following are irregular for the exercise of orders already received: 1/ one who, while bound by an irregularity for the reception of orders, unlawfully received orders; 2/ one who committed the offence mentioned in Canon 1041, 2/, if the offence is public; 3/ one who committed any of the offences mentioned in Canon 1041 numbers 3, 4, 5, 6. §2. The following are impeded from the exercise of orders: 1/ one who, while bound by an impediment to the reception of orders, unlawfully received orders; 2/ one who suffers from insanity or from some other psychological infirmity mentioned in Canon 1041 no. 1, until such time as the Ordinary, having consulted an expert, has allowed the exercise of the order in question.

A cleric who is ordained with an irregularity and a cleric who becomes subject to an irregularity are irregular for the exercise of orders. This means that, if sexual abuse of a minor is an irregularity, the priest who abused a minor could not exercise ministry. He is like a suspended priest.

EFFECTS OF AN IRREGULARITY

When a man is ordained with an irregularity, the ordination is valid but illegitimate. When such a cleric attempts to exercise the orders received, his celebrations of the sacraments are valid but illegitimate. This means that the effect of the irregularity is like that of a priest being suspended as far as the celebration of the Eucharist and the other sacraments is concerned.

ADVANTAGES OF IRREGULARITIES

Some bishops have played down the seriousness of sexual abuse cases. If sexual abuse of minors were classified as an irregularity, it would be more difficult to overlook it. For example, there are priests who have had affairs, and the woman has had an abortion. If the priest opposed her having the abortion, he does not incur the irregularity in canon 1041, no. 4. However, if he encouraged or pressured the woman to have the abortion, he becomes subject to the irregularity. Therefore, even if the bishop is prepared to let him continue in ministry, the fact of the irregularity remains, and a dispensation is required from the Holy See.

The same would apply to an abusive cleric, if abuse of minors was an irregularity. It would not matter if the cause of the sexual abuse were a severe psychological problem. The fact that sexual abuse occurred would mean that the man could not be ordained and could not function as a priest.

Law has an educational role. It also sets minimum standards for a variety of matters. These include the capacity to act. It is important that the Church delivers the message that it is doing everything it can to prevent and stop sexual abuse of minors. Irregularities are not silver bullets solving all the problems and issues in relation to unsuitable people being ordained or exercising ministry. Irregularities represent minimum standards concerning the qualities of those to be ordained or exercising ministry. Since an irregularity prevents someone from being ordained and prevents someone already ordained from functioning as a priest, making "sexual abuse of a minor" an irregularity would be a significant step forward. It would state very clearly that anyone who sexually abuses someone under eighteen years of age is not fit to be a priest.

Even if the person to be ordained were unaware at the time of the offense that he has incurred an irregularity, the person to be ordained would still be bound by the irregularity when he learns he has incurred it. Impediments and irregularities are, in that sense, very different from crimes. Ignorance of a crime results in one not receiving the penalty.[24] Impediments and irregularities forbid the exercise of orders in celebrating sacraments, but they do not stop a cleric from engaging in other pastoral work such as visiting the sick.[25]

DISPENSATION FROM AN IRREGULARITY

The Holy See does grant a dispensation from the irregularity for the reception of orders if the circumstances of the case warrant it.

Canon 1047 outlines who can dispense from impediments and irregularities:

> §1. If the fact on which they are based has been brought to the judicial forum, dispensation from all irregularities is reserved to the Apostolic See alone. §2. Dispensation from the following irregularities and impediments to the reception of orders is also reserved to the Apostolic See: 1/ irregularities arising from the offences mentioned in Canon 1041 numbers 2 and 3, if they are public; 2/ an irregularity arising from the offence, whether public or occult, mentioned in Canon 1041, no. 4; 3/ the impediment mentioned in Canon 1042, no. 1. §3. To the Apostolic See is also reserved the dispensation from the irregularities for the exercise of an order received mentioned in Canon 1041, no. 3 but only in public cases, and in number 4 of the same canon even in occult cases. §4. The Ordinary can dispense from irregularities and impediments not reserved to the Holy See.

Whenever the fact of the irregularity has been established in the judicial forum, canonical or secular,[26] either in a marriage nullity or criminal case, then the dispensation is reserved to the Holy See.

Once a dispensation is granted for an ordination to diaconate, there is no need for another dispensation for ordination to priesthood.[27] The Apostolic Penitentiary is competent for all occult cases of abortion. For example, if a priest was involved in supporting an abortion and it is not known by the bishop or many people. The priest could on his own initiative apply for the dispensation in the internal forum.

An actual example is a case where a non-Catholic man assisted in the procurement of an abortion of his child. Then, fourteen years later, he became a Catholic and entered a seminary. The diocesan bishop requested a dispensation from the irregularity. The Apostolic Penitentiary granted the faculty "to dispense the Petitioner from the irregularity incurred. This is to be done in the internal forum, sacramental or nonsacramental, whichever you deem more appropriate."[28]

If the woman complained about what happened or the matter came to the attention of the bishop, then the case would come to the Dicastery for Clergy, who are competent according to article 116 of *Praedicate Evangelium*:

> Article 116 §1. The Dicastery is responsible for handling, in conformity with the canonical norms, matters having to do with the clerical state as such, for all clergy, including members of Institutes of Consecrated Life and Societies of Apostolic Life, and for permanent deacons, in cooperation with the competent Dicasteries whenever circumstances so demand.[29]

The Dicastery is competent for all nonoccult cases of clergy.

Canon 1048 does allow a cleric to exercise orders when it is an urgent, occult case and the Ordinary is inaccessible; or if it is a case of attempted marriage, voluntary homicide, or abortion and access to the Sacred Penitentiary cannot be had:

> In the more urgent occult cases, if the Ordinary or, in the case of the irregularities mentioned in Canon 1041 numbers 3 and 4, the Penitentiary cannot be approached, and if there is imminent danger of serious harm or loss of reputation, the person who is irregular for the exercise of an order may exercise it. There remains, however, the obligation of his having recourse as soon as possible to the Ordinary or the Penitentiary, without revealing his name, and through a confessor. (Can. 1048.)

However, the impeded or irregular cleric is obliged to make recourse to the ordinary or Sacred Penitentiary anonymously through a confessor as soon as possible.[30] There is the requirement that when a dispensation from irregularities is sought, the number of irregularities as well as the number of delicts for abortion or attempted suicide must be stated for the validity of the dispensation. Any omitted in good faith are covered by the dispensation, but those omitted in bad faith are not covered.[31]

PEDOPHILIA

During the 1990s, there was discussion among North American canon lawyers about the possibility of declaring a pedophile priest irregular based on canon 1041, no. 1. This discussion is reflected in two articles in *Monitor Ecclesiasticus* by William Woestman and John Beal.[32]

Canon 1041 of the 1983 Code states:

> The following persons are irregular for the reception of orders: 1/ one who suffers from any form of insanity, or from any other psychological infirmity, because of which he is, after experts have been consulted, judged incapable of properly fulfilling the ministry.

William Woestman argued that a priest who was irregular because of canon 1041, no. 1 could not celebrate the Eucharist or any of the other sacraments because of his sexual inclination to sexually abuse children. Ronny Jenkins believes that Woestman is interpreting "moral fitness" to exercise ministry as "could not" or "incapable" of ministry.[33] John Beal believes that the Church's understanding of ministry has been broadened from Vatican II, so more emphasis is placed on nonsacramental activities such as preaching and leading the Christian community.

Regardless, there is a fundamental problem proving insanity or psychological infirmity to establish the irregularity. Experts such as psychiatrists or psychologists must be involved. In most countries there must be personal interviews by the psychologist or psychiatrist with the person concerned before any diagnosis is asserted, and offending priests are not likely to agree to this.

Consequently, adequate proof cannot be obtained and there would be insufficient proof to have moral certainty of the psychological or psychiatric condition without the involvement of experts.

SEXUAL ABUSE

As noted earlier, in 2021, Pope Francis revised the penal law of the Catholic Church with a new canon 1398 concerning sexual abuse in the section of the Code appropriately entitled "Offenses against Human Life, Dignity and Liberty."

This canon uses the traditional term "offense against the sixth commandment" when defining sexual abuse. This term is also used by the *Catechism of the Catholic Church* (§§2351–56), where it is made clear that these offenses include adultery, rape, and the accessing of pornography.

There has been discussion about whether pedophilia can be used as an irregularity under current legislation.[34] Ronny Jenkins has considered the advisability of having an additional irregularity of pedophilia.[35] He made a strong case for changing the Code of Canon Law and adding number "7" to canon 1041:

> A person who has sexually abused under age 18 years in any way, including acquisition, possession or distribution of pornographic images of minors under the age of 18 for purposes of sexual gratification, by whatever means or using whatever technology.

This could be added to canon 1044:

> §1, no. 3 one who committed any of the offences mentioned in Canon 1041 numbers 3, 4, 5, 6, and 7.

John Renken also argues for sexual abuse to be a permanent impediment (irregularity):

> If someone has committed acts of sexual abuse, the perpetrator certainly ought not be admitted to formation for leadership-service in the Church, nor should he or she be permitted to continue the same. *De facto*, sexual abuse constitutes a disqualification for ordained and lay ministry, ecclesiastical office and functions (whether paid or volunteer), consecrated life, etc.
>
> In the future given the scope of sexual abuse and its lasting harmful effects in its victims, and given the desire of the Church to eradicate the threat and trauma of sexual abuse, should not sexual abuse be established formally, *de iure*, as a "perpetual impediment" (see c. 1040) to various roles of ecclesiastical leadership-service—e.g., the irregularity to receive orders (c. 1041); to exercise orders received (c. 1044 no. 1); to enter a major seminary (c. 241); to enter formation in a religious institute (c. 643); a secular institute (c. 721), or a society of apostolic life (c. 753 no. 2)? Why would the Church, which can create such disqualifications, not establish them *pro bono et tutela Ecclesiae*?[36]

Since, as Pope John Paul II told the American cardinals on April 23, 2002, "there is no place in the priesthood and religious life for those who would harm the young,"[37] there is good reason to make a modification to the Code of Canon Law so that the crime of sexual abuse of minors is added to the list of irregularities. In many countries, prospective seminarians must have a police check to prove that they have no criminal convictions including sexual abuse. Some countries require that those who intend to work with children as sport coaches, teachers, and clergy have a license to work with children from a child protection agency. However, numerous priests have been ordained who have sexually abused minors before ordination. Making sexual abuse of a minor an irregularity would assist in dealing with these situations, especially with the changed canon 1388.[38] It is important that the Church delivers the message that it is doing everything possible to prevent and stop sexual abuse of minors by clergy and religious.

CONCLUSION

Irregularities have a long history in relation to the sacrament of Holy Orders. They represent necessary and significant minimum standards concerning the qualities of those to be ordained or exercising ministry.

Irregularities are not silver bullets solving all the problems and issues in relation to unsuitable people being ordained or exercising sacramental ministry. Some irregularities require the use of experts, and their expertise and interpretations of symptoms can vary. Occasionally, there are complications with interpretations of what "public" and "proven" mean. Making the sexual abuse of a person under the age of eighteen years an irregularity would not require the use of an expert such as a psychologist or a psychiatrist. It would be like the application of the law concerning abortion as an irregularity.

There are many cases of seminarians around the world who have abused minors before they entered the seminary, or while they were seminarians. If sexual abuse of a minor was an irregularity, any of these ordinands ordained while concealing the irregularity would be suspended.[39]

If someone ordained had abused a minor, that cleric would then be irregular for the exercise of ministry, even if knowledge of the sexual abuse was obtained after the ordination. This would have the advantage that because a bishop could not dispense from the irregularity, the bishop or the priest himself would have to approach the Holy See to seek a dispensation. This would help to prevent bishops from allowing pedophiles to continue in ministry.

The Church has a long history going back to New Testament times of legislating for irregularities. Making the sexual abuse of a person under the age of eighteen years an irregularity would be a most effective way to deal with offenders. It would stop offenders from continuing to function as priests. It would also stop the rare cases of a pedophile priest granting absolution to another pedophile priest.

The Church cannot unordain someone in the way a person can be struck off the register of accredited teachers. Proving the nullity of an ordination can be very difficult, especially if the offending priest does not cooperate with Church authorities.

The irregularity would be incurred automatically upon the commission of one act of sexual abuse of a minor under the age of eighteen years. The diocesan bishop or Major Superior does not have to do anything. The priest is unable to function. Even if the diocesan bishop or the Major Superior wanted to allow the priest to function, the irregularity could only be dispensed by the Holy See.

Appendix

SAMPLE DIOCESAN LETTERS

DECREE OPENING A PRELIMINARY INVESTIGATION (CAN. 1717)

I have received information *notitia de delicto* regarding sexual abuse and/or sexual misconduct which may be a crime committed by [name of respondent.]
Therefore, I decree the opening of a preliminary investigation concerning this alleged crime.
Given at the Diocesan Offices [city] on this […] day of [month], [year].

Signed
Bishop
Bishop of

Signed
Chancellor

APPOINTMENT OF A PERSON CARRYING OUT THE INVESTIGATION (CAN. 1717)

I have received information *notitia de delicto* of sexual abuse/sexual misconduct which may be a crime.
I hereby appoint .... to investigate the complaint and I give him/her delegated authority to enlist the services of whomever he/she needs to assist him/her in carrying out this investigation.
The investigation is to be carried out according to the canon law of the Catholic Church.
All documentation and evidence are to be held by the National Office for Professional Standards.
I appoint as notary [name].
Once the investigation has been completed, the person carrying out the investigation shall send a report of the investigation with a copy of the evidence to me as soon as possible.
Given at the Diocesan Offices [city] on this [...] day of [month], [year].

Signed
Bishop
Bishop of

Signed
Chancellor

DECREE CLOSING A PRELIMINARY INVESTIGATION

I have received the report of the person carrying out the investigation and the evidence from the preliminary investigation of the complaint received from [name].

Therefore, I decree the closing of the preliminary investigation concerning this alleged crime.

Given at the Diocesan Offices [city] on this […] day of [month], [year].

Signed
Bishop
Bishop of

Signed
Chancellor

DECREE FOR ADMINISTRATIVE PROCESS

Month/Day/Year

Case

Having received the mandate from the Dicastery for………. (Prot. N.:) authorizing me to initiate an Extrajudicial Penal Process observing canon 1720 and the norms of canon law, I hereby decree the opening of the extrajudicial or administrative penal process to ascertain with moral certainty whether Rev. Fr. [name] committed the delict of canon 1395 par. 2 with violence.
I will exercise this authority through a person carrying out the investigation.
This act is to be notified to Rev. Fr. [name].

Signed
Bishop
Bishop of

Signed
Chancellor

Precept

Precept penal:
Date:

Priest: [name]
Address:

Dear [name]:

I, Bishop [name], have decided it is necessary to issue you with this penal precept to foster the spiritual good of the Diocese of [name] and to lessen any scandal which has been associated with certain actions of yours that have been under canonical investigation.

The reasons motivating this precept are most serious and compelling because they involve offences against the sixth commandment with a young man/woman.

In light of this and to respond to the spiritual and pastoral needs of the Church community and for your own good and the good the Church, in accord with the provisions of canons 49 and 1339 § 1, I, Bishop [name], do hereby admonish and warn you concerning the following:

1. To avoid any contact whatsoever and in any other manner, either at your initiative or from their own initiative, with persons under the age of 18 years unless in the presence of an adult.
2. To avoid any contact whatsoever and in any manner, either from your own initiative or from their own initiative, with the person who has lodged the above referenced complaint against you.
3. To avoid any contact whatsoever and in any manner, either on your own initiative or on their own initiative, with the family members or friends of the person who has lodged the above-referenced complaint against you.
4. To avoid physical presence in the parish of [name] and town of [name], which is where the allegation arose.
5. To avoid persons or situations that could endanger your continence or any conduct that might cause scandal to the faithful or that would receive publicity in the media.

I, Bishop [name], require you to live at [name]. You require my prior written permission to stay overnight anywhere else.

The provisions of this precept are necessary and prudent precautions as a pastoral measure to protect the rights and reputations of all involved and to safeguard the salvation of souls.

The gravity of this matter requires me to state further that failing to observe the provisions of this precept shall be deemed a violation of canon 1371 §1, which can result in further disciplinary action against you, and which may render you liable to additional canonical penalties. Accordingly, this precept itself stands as a canonical warning concerning these matters.

This precept is effective immediately upon its notification to you. It shall remain in effect until specifically revoked by me or by my successors.

NOTES

FOREWORD

1. Dereck Farrell, "Sexual Abuse Perpetrated by Roman Catholic Priests and Religious," *Mental Health Religion & Culture* 12, no. 1 (2009): 41; "Those who sexually abuse children (Canon LXXI, cited in Laeuchli, 1972, p. 47) are threatened with irrevocable exclusion, meaning they could not receive communion, not even at the moment of death."

2. F. G. Cuéllar, *I. Ortiz de Urbina, Nicea y Constantinopla*, Historia de los Concilios Ecuménicos, vol. 1 (Vitoria: Editorial Eset, 1969), 108.

3. Gil José Sáez Martínez, "Aproximación Histórica a los Abusos Sexuales de Menores," *Eguzkilore* 29 (2015): 156.

4. Sáez Martínez, "Aproximación Histórica a los Abusos Sexuales de Menores."

5. For example, the Royal Commission in Australia 2017 or the Independent Inquiry into Child Sexual Abuse (ICSA) in England and Wales, 2022. There are other reports funded by the Catholic Church and the episcopal conferences such as the John Jay Report in the United States (2004) and the Independent Commission on Sexual Abuse in the Church (CIASE) in France, 2021.

CHAPTER 1

1. See Canon 1717 §1. Translations of the CIC 1983 from the translation of the Canon Law Society of America 2001 (hereinafter CIC 17).

2. Dicastery for the Doctrine of the Faith, *Vademecum: On Certain Points of Procedure in Treating Cases of Sexual Abuse of Minors Committed by Clerics*, Ver. 2.0 (June 5, 2022) (vatican.va) (*Vademecum*) 9.

3. *Vademecum* 37.

4. Pope Francis, moto proprio, *Vos Estis Lux Mundi*, May 7, 2019 (revised on March 25, 2023), https://www.vatican.va/content/francesco/en/motu_proprio/documents/papa-francesco-motu-proprio-20190507_vos-estis-lux-mundi.html.

5. "*The present norms are approved* ad experimentum *for three years. I establish that the present Apostolic Letter in the form of* Motu Proprio *be promulgated by means of publication in the* Osservatore Romano, *entering into force on 1 June 2019, and then published in the* Acta Apostolicae Sedis," VELM.

6. See https://www.vatican.va/content/francesco/it/motu_proprio/documents/20230325-motu-proprio-vos-estis-lux-mundi-aggiornato.html.

7. VELM, art. 1. §1.

8. VELM, art. 1. §1 a).

9. VELM 3 §1.

10. VELM 3 §2.

11. VELM 6.

12. VELM 15 §1.

13. Pope Francis, "New Book VI of the Code of Canon Law, 2021," hereinafter all translations of the changed Book VI from this source; https://www.vatican.va/archive/cod-iuris-canonici/cic_index_en.html.

14. Luis Figari, born July 8, 1947, is a Peruvian Catholic layman, the founder and former superior general of Sodalitium Christianae Vitae (SCV).

15. See Bernard Granger, Nicole Jeammet, Florian Michel, Antoine Mourges, Gwennola Rimbaut, and Claire Vincent-Mory, *Control and Abuse: Investigation on Thomas Philippe, Jean Vanier and L'Arche (1950–2019)* (Châteauneuf-sur-Charente: Frémur Publications, 2023), 569, https://commissiondetudejeanvanier.org/commissiondetudeindependante2023-empriseetabus/wp-content/uploads/2023/01/Report_Control-and-Abuse_EN.pdf.

16. *Vademecum* 5.

17. Archbishop Scicluna to the American bishops; https://www.pillarcatholic.com/p/local-bishops-must-prosecute-abuse.

18. *Vademecum* 22, 31; VELM (2019) 2 §3.

19. Canon 1428 §3; VELM 14; *Vademecum* 38.

20. *Vademecum* 40; c. 1719, CCEO c. 1470.

21. Canon 1428 §3. It is for the auditor, according to the mandate of the judge, only to collect the proofs and hand those collected over to the judge. Unless the mandate of the judge prevents it, however, the auditor can in the meantime decide what proofs are to be collected and in what manner if a question may arise about this while the auditor exercises his or her function.

22. Dicastery for Legislative Texts, *Penal Sanctions in the Church: User Guide for Book VI of the Code of Canon Law*, 3, May 31, 2023.

23. Canon 383.

24. Canon 384.

25. CIC c. 483 §2; CCEO c. 253 §2.

26. Pontifical Commission for the Protection of Minors, *Universal Guidelines Framework*, 4.2.8, March 2024; https://acrobat.adobe.com/id/urn:aaid:sc:AP:1ed671aa-794e-468b-b48e-3ddcbd32c38a?comment_id=a54f1bf5-2d22-49a5-bc78-04f75524ecce&showComments=true (hereinafter *UGF*).

27. Canon 1428 §2.

28. *Vademecum* 38–39.

29. Cf. USCCB, "Directives for the Implementation of the Provisions of *Vos Estis Lux Mundi* Concerning Bishops and their Equivalents," https://www.usccb.org/sites/default/files/about/leadership/usccb-general-assembly/2019-june-meeting/upload/usccb-modified-amended-directives-2019-06.pdf.

30. CIC 83, c. 1717 §2.; CCEO 23; *Vademecum* 44.

31. *Vademecum* 12, 13, 16, 18, 19, 37.

32. John D. Faris and Jobe Abbass, OFM Conv, *A Practical Commentary to the Code of Canons of the Eastern Churches*, vol. 2 (Montreal: Wilson & Lafleur. 2019), 2616.

33. Faris and Abbass, *A Practical Commentary*, 2616.

34. Canon 1505 §2. A libellus can be rejected only: 4/ if it is certainly clear from the libellus itself that the petition lacks any basis and that there is no possibility that any such basis will appear through a process.

35. See https://www.justice.govt.nz/about/learn-about-the-justice-system/explore-the-criminal-justice-system/the-crime/.

36. Henry Campbell Black, Joseph R. Nolan, and Michael J. Connolly, eds., *Black's*

Law Dictionary: Definitions of the Terms and Phrases of American and English Jurisprudence, Ancient and Modern (St. Paul, MN: West Publishing Co., 1983), 614.

37. See https://www.justice.govt.nz/assets/Documents/Publications/MOJ0100.3C-At-a-glance-factsheet-AUG19-WEB.pdf.

38. CIC 83, c. 1717 §1.

39. CIC 83, c. 1718 §1.

40. CIC 83, c. 1718 §3.

41. CIC 83, c. 1717 §1; *Vademecum* 34.

42. *Vademecum* 34, 51.

43. *Vademecum* 34.

44. *Vademecum* 102; SST art. 4 §2.

45. *Vademecum* 34, 35, 66.

46. *Vademecum* 58–65.

47. SST, art. 19.

48. Canon 1722.

49. See cc. 220; 1321 §3; 1728 §2; cf. Kenneth Pennington, "Innocent until Proven Guilty: The Origins of a Legal Maxim," *The Jurist* 63 (2003): 106–24.

50. See Canon 1717 §1.

51. P. Dugan and P. Gargaro, *A Simple Dictionary of Canon Law* (Philadelphia: Canon Law Books, 2012), 29.

52. Canon 1321 §3 states: "When there has been an external violation, imputability is presumed, unless it appears otherwise."

53. CIC 83, c. 1326.

54. CIC 83, cc. 1323–1325.

55. CIC 83, c. 1717 §2; c. 220; *Vademecum* 44–46.

56. See Jason Horowitz, "Pope Issues First Rules for Catholic Church Worldwide to Report Sex Abuse," *New York Times*, May 9, 2019. https://www.nytimes.com/2019/05/09/world/europe/pope-francis-abuse-catholic-church.html.

57. VELM 4.

58. *Vademecum* 52. During the investigative process, a particularly sensitive task falling to the Ordinary or Hierarch is to decide if and when to inform the person being accused. 53. In this regard, there is no uniform criterion or explicit provision in law. An assessment must be made of all the goods at stake: in addition to the protection of the good name of the persons involved, consideration must also be given, for example, to the risk of compromising the preliminary investigation or giving scandal to the faithful, and the advantage of collecting beforehand all evidence that could prove useful or necessary. 54. Should a decision be made to question the accused person, since this is a preliminary phase prior to a possible process, it is not obligatory to name an official advocate for him. If he considers it helpful, however, he can be assisted by a patron of his choice. An oath cannot be imposed on the accused person (cf. *ex analogia*, canons 1728 §2 CIC and 1471 §2 CCEO).

59. VELM 5; *Vademecum* 55.

60. CIC 83, c. 383 §1. In exercising the function of a pastor, a diocesan bishop is to show himself concerned for all the Christian faithful entrusted to his care, of whatever age, condition, or nationality they are, whether living in the territory or staying there temporarily; he is also to extend an apostolic spirit to those who are not able to make sufficient use of ordinary pastoral care because of the condition of their life and to those who no longer practice their religion.

61. See Canon 1718 §1.

62. *Vademecum* 68; CIC 83, c. 1719 and CCEO 1470.

63. CIC 83, c. 1718.

64. *Vademecum* 49–50.

65. CIC 83, c. 1717ff.

66. CIC 83, c. 1378 formerly c. 1389.

67. CIC 83, c. 1341 states that "an ordinary is to take care to initiate a judicial or administrative process to impose or declare penalties only after he has ascertained that

fraternal correction or rebuke or other means of pastoral solicitude cannot sufficiently repair the scandal, restore justice, reform the offender."

68. Kevin McKenna, "We Can Have Both: Due Process for Accused Priests and Justice for Sex Abuse Survivors," *America*, June 2, 2023, https://www.americamagazine.org/faith/2023/06/02/due-process-clergy-sexual-abuse-accusation-245117.

69. See https://www.vatican.va/roman_curia/congregations/cfaith/ddf/ddf-tabella-vademecum2.0_en.doc. In regions where there is no surname, please indicate the name of the cleric's father. Note that this tabular summary is intended to summarize the case and does not replace the acts of the preliminary investigation. It is important to include the acts of the investigation along with the summary, and if possible, send the summary in Word format to: disciplinaryoffice@cfaith.va.

70. See Appendix for diocesan sample letters for (1) a decree opening and closing a preliminary investigation; (2) appointing a person to carry out the investigation; and (3) a decree for administrative process.

CHAPTER 2

1. Dicastery for the Doctrine of the Faith, *Vademecum* 91, June 5, 2022, https://www.vatican.va/roman_curia/congregations/cfaith/ddf/rc_ddf_doc_20220605_vademecum-casi-abuso-2.0_en.html; hereinafter *Vademecum*. Translations of canons by Canon Law Society of America on the Vatican website.

2. CIC 83, c. 221 §1. The Christian faithful can legitimately vindicate and defend the rights which they possess in the Church in the competent ecclesiastical forum according to the norm of law. §2. If they are summoned to a trial by a competent authority, the Christian faithful also have the right to be judged according to the prescripts of the law applied with equity. All translations from the Vatican website using the Canon Law Society of America translation.

3. Juan Ignacio Arrieta, *Code of Canon Law Annotated,* 4th ed. (Montreal: Wilson & Lafleur, 2022), 1052.

4. Congregation for the Doctrine of the Faith, *Sacramentorum Sanctitatis Tutela,* October 11, 2021, https://www.vatican.va/roman_curia/congregations/cfaith/documents/rc_con_cfaith_doc_20211011_norme-delittiriservati-cfaith_en.html; hereinafter SST.

5. Judith Hahn, "What Does It Mean to be 'Morally Certain'? How Secular Standards of Proof Help to Understand Canonical Decision Making," *The Canonist* 11, no. 2 (2020): 242, and Judith Hahn, "Moral Certitude: Merits and Demerits of the Standard of Proof Applied in Roman Catholic Jurisprudence," *Oxford Journal of Law and Religion* 8 (2019): 324.

6. CIC 83, c. 1717 §1. Whenever the Ordinary receives information, which has at least the semblance of truth, about an offence, he is to enquire carefully, either personally or through some suitable person, about the facts and circumstances, and about the imputability of the offence, unless this enquiry would appear to be entirely superfluous.

7. VELM 2.

8. CIC 83, c. 384. With special solicitude, a diocesan bishop is to attend to presbyters and listen to them as assistants and counselors. He is to protect their rights and take care that they correctly fulfill the obligations proper to their state and that the means and institutions which they need to foster spiritual and intellectual life are available to them. He also is to take care that provision

is made for their decent support and social assistance, according to the norm of law.

9. CIC 83, c. 1717 §1. Whenever an ordinary has knowledge, which at least seems true, of a delict, he is carefully to inquire personally or through another suitable person about the facts, circumstances, and imputability, unless such an inquiry seems entirely superfluous. §2. Care must be taken so that the good name of anyone is not endangered from this investigation. CIC 83, c. 383 §1. In exercising the function of a pastor, a diocesan bishop is to show himself concerned for all the Christian faithful entrusted to his care, of whatever age, condition, or nationality they are, whether living in the territory or staying there temporarily; he is also to extend an apostolic spirit to those who are not able to make sufficient use of ordinary pastoral care because of the condition of their life and to those who no longer practice their religion.

10. CIC 83, c. 1728 §2. The accused is not bound to confess the delict, nor can an oath be administered to the accused.

11. *Vademecum* 60; cc. 391, 392, 1722.

12. See *Vademecum* 91.

13. The 1983 code had previously stated in Canon 1341 that "only after he has ascertained that scandal cannot sufficiently be repaired, that justice cannot sufficiently be restored and that the accused cannot sufficiently be reformed by fraternal correction, rebuke and other ways of pastoral care is the Ordinary then to provide for a judicial or administrative procedure to impose or to declare penalties."

14. CIC 83, cc. 1311 §2 and 1342.

15. CIC 83, c. 1326 §1. "A judge must [*debet*] inflict a more serious punishment than that prescribed in the law or precept when: 2° a person who is established in some position of dignity, or who, in order to commit a crime, has abused a position of authority or an office; § 3. In the same cases, if the penalty constituted is discretionary, it becomes obligatory."

16. Arrieta, *Code of Canon Law Annotated*, 1051.

17. Canon 1311.

18. *Vademecum* 95.

19. *Vademecum* 93.

20. *Vademecum* 96.

21. CIC 83, c. 1728 §1. Without prejudice to the prescripts of the canons of this title and unless the nature of the matter precludes it, the canons on trials in general and on the ordinary contentious trial must be applied in a penal trial; the special norms for cases which pertain to the public good are also to be observed. §2. The accused is not bound to confess the delict, nor can an oath be administered to the accused.

22. CIC 83, c. 1448 §1. A judge is not to undertake the adjudication of a case in which the judge is involved by reason of consanguinity or affinity in any degree of the direct line and up to the fourth degree of the collateral line or by reason of trusteeship, guardianship, close acquaintance, great animosity, the making of a profit, or the avoidance of a loss. §2. In these circumstances the promoter of justice, the defender of the bond, the assessor, and the auditor must abstain from their office.

23. SST 4 §2.

24. CIC 83, c. 1720 no. 3 states that if the delict is certainly established and a criminal action is not extinguished, he is to issue a decree according to the norm of cc. 1342–50, setting forth the reasons in law and in fact at least briefly.

25. CIC 83, c. 1734.

26. *Vademecum* 94.

27. *Codex Iuris Canonici*, the Code of Canon Law for the Latin Church.

28. *Code of Canons of the Eastern Churches*, the Code of Canon Law for the twenty-three Eastern Churches in the Catholic Church.

29. CIC 83, c. 1487 §1. Recourse against the decree by which a penalty is imposed can be made to the competent higher authority within ten available days (tempus utile) after it has been communicated. §2. This recourse suspends the force of the decree. §3. There is no further recourse against the decision of the higher authority.

30. *User Guide* 135.

31. *User Guide* 136.

32. *User Guide* 137.

33. CCEO c. 1520 §1. A decree has legal force when it is communicated to the one to whom it is destined, according to the laws and the most secure ways of the place. §2. If there is danger of a public or private harm so that the text of the decree cannot be given in writing, the ecclesiastical authority can issue it by reading it before an ecclesiastical notary or two witnesses to the person for whom it is destined and by having all present sign an instrument stating that this was done; the decree is then considered to have been communicated. §3. If a person for whom a decree is destined refuses to accept the communication or, summoned according to the law to a meeting in order to receive or hear the decree, refuses, without a just cause to be evaluated by the author of the decree, to come to the meeting or to sign the instrument mentioned in 2, the decree is considered to have been communicated.

34. *User Guide* 138.

35 *Vademecum* 143. If it was the procedure mentioned in article 26 SST, inasmuch as it concerns an act of the Roman Pontiff, no appeal or recourse is admitted (cf. canons 333 § 3 CIC and 45 § 3 CCEO).

36. Restitution to the original position, e.g., as if there was no contract.

37. *Vademecum* 144.

38. *Vademecum* 146.

39. *Vademecum* 147; the Dicastery for Legislative Texts explains this in article 223 of *Penal Sanctions in the Church User Guide for Book VI of the Code of Canon Law.*

40. *Vademecum* 148.

41. *Vademecum* 149.

42. *Vademecum* 151.

43. *Vademecum* 152.

44. *Vademecum* 153.

CHAPTER 3

1. Henry C. Black, *Black's Law Dictionary* (St. Paul, MN: West Publishing Co., 1983), 634.

2. Zenon Grocholewski, "Art. 1. The Judge," in Ángel Marzoa, Jorge Miras, and Rafael Rodríguez-Ocaña, eds., *Exegetical Commentary on the Code of Canon Law* 4, no. 1 (Chicago: Midwest Theological Forum, 2004), 761.

3. William H. Woestman, OMI, *Ecclesiastical Sanctions and the Penal Process* (University of St. Paul, 2000), 168.

4. Peter Akpoghiran, *Delicta Graviora Manual*, vol. 1, *A Commentary on the Normae de Gravioribus Delictis Congregationi pro Doctrina Fidei Reservatis* (New Orleans: Transfiguration Press, 2019), 260.

5. Thomas Brundage, "The Office for Promoter of Justice: Once Thought Nearly Irrelevant Again Becomes Relevant," in *CLSA Proceedings* 76 (2014): 160.

6. Angelo Urru, "Considerations on Imposing Penalties in Specific Cases," in *The Penal Process and the Protection of Rights in Canon Law,* 301 (according to the norm of law, according to the truth and not misusing the law).

7. *Unofficial Translation of Crimen Sollicitationis (1962)*, http://www.vatican.va/resources/index_en.htm.

8. Pope John Paul II, apostolic constitution *Divinus Perfectionis Magister*, January 25, 1983, in *AAS* 75 (1983): 349–55; Jason Gray, *The Evolution of the Promoter of the Faith in Causes of Beatification and Canonization: A Study of the Law of 1917 and 1983* (Rome: Lateran University, 2015.

9. A. Stitt, *De Promotere Justitiae: Ejusque Munere in Curia Diocesana* (Rome: Pontifical Universitas Lateran, 1939), 13; Gray, *The Evolution of the Promoter of the Faith,* 35.

10. C. 2 q. 1 c. 4; C. 2 q. 1 c. 17 in Gray, *The Evolution of the Promoter of the Faith*, 36.

11. C. 2 q. 1 c. 17 in Gray, *The Evolution of the Promoter of the Faith*, 36–37.

12. John C. Glynn, *The Promoter of Justice: His Rights and Duties*, Canon Law Studies 101 (Washington, DC: The Catholic University of America, 1936), 15.

13. *Concilium Lateranense* IV (1215), in J. D. Mansi, ed., *Sacrorum Conciliorum*, XXII, 1994; in Gray, *The Evolution of the Promoter of the Faith,* 39.

14. *Concilium Lateranense* IV (1215), in J. D. Mansi, ed., *Sacrorum Conciliorum*, XXII, 1994: 995; in Gray, *The Evolution of the Promoter of the Faith*, 40.

15. Glynn, *The Promoter of Justice*, 5.

16. Gray, *The Evolution of the Promoter of the Faith*, 44.

17. Gray, *The Evolution of the Promoter of the Faith*, 29.

18. Concilium Provinciale Magdeburgense (1370), Caput 21, *De institutionibus*, in J. D. Mansi, ed., Sacrorum Conciliorum, XXVI, 567–89; Gray, *The Evolution of the Promoter of the Faith,* 45; Grocholewski, in *Exegetical Commentary,* IV/I, 762.

19. *Historia Procuratoris Fiscalis tenebris obvolvitur remotioris antiquitatis et certe in jure canonico initium habet*, in Lega, *De Judiciis Eccl.* I, 171, note 1, quoted in John Glynn, *The Promoter of Justice*, 8. This was accepted by Noval in *De Processibus*, I, 78, 79.

20. See P. Francisco Wernz and P. Petri Vidal, *Ius Canonicum* VI (Vatican City: Apud Custodiam Librariam Pontificii Instituti Utriusque Iuris, 1928VI, 97, 98.

21. Glynn, *The Promoter of Justice*, 337

22. Benedict XIV, *De Servorum Dei Beatificatione et Beatorum Canonizatione*, lib. I, cap. XVIII, in John Glynn, *The Evolution of the Promoter of the Faith*, 31–33.

23. Instr. S.C. EE. Et RR., 11 Junii, 1880 – *AAS* XIII (1880-) 325, in John Glynn, *The Evolution of the Promoter of the Faith*, 53.

24. *Collectanea de S.C. de Prop. Fide*, n. 1586, 169.

25. *Lex Propria Sanctae Romana Rotae et Signatura Apostolicae*, June 29, 1908*, AAS* I, 1909, 20, and in the *Regulae Servandae apud Sanctam Romanam Totam*, August 4, 1910, *AAS* II, 1910, 783, in John Glynn, *The Evolution of the Promoter of the Faith*, 54.

26. CIC 17, c. 1586. There shall be constituted in a diocese a promoter of justice and a defender of the bond; the former [acts] in cases, whether contentious in which the public good, in the judgment of the Ordinary, can be called into question, or in criminal cases; the latter [acts] in cases in which the bond of sacred ordination or matrimony is concerned.

27. CIC 17, c. 1587 §1. In cases in which his presence is required, [if] the promoter of justice or the defender of the bond is not cited, the acts are invalid unless he, even though cited, participated.

28. CIC 17, c. 1588 §1. The same person can hold the office of promoter of justice and

defender of the bond unless from a multiplicity of affairs and cases this is prohibited.

29. CIC 17, c. 189 §1. It is for the Ordinary to select the promoter of justice and defender of the bond; [these] shall be priests of intact reputation, doctors of canon law or otherwise expert, and proven for prudence and zeal for justice.

30. CIC 17, c 1589 §2. In the tribunal of a religious institute, the promoter of justice must also be a member of the religious institute.

31. CIC 17, c. 655 §2. The president will appoint a promoter of justice with the consent of the others according to the norm of canon 1689 §2.

32. CIC 17, c. 1590 §1. The promoter of justice and the defender of the bond appointed for a universe of cases do not cease from responsibility upon the vacancy of the see, nor can they be removed by the Vicar Capitulary; the new Prelate arriving, however, they need confirmation. §2. A just cause interceding, however, the bishop can remove them.

33. CIC 17, c. 1613 §1. A judge should not take up hearing a case in which, by reason of consanguinity or affinity in any degree of the direct line and if the first or second degree of the collateral line, or in which, by reason of guardianship or care or intimate custom of life, or great animosity, or the possibility of making a profit or of avoiding damages, or anything else, he has an interest, or in which in any way he [earlier] acted as an advocate or procurator. §2. Under the same circumstances of things, the promoter of justice and defender of the bond must abstain from their office.

34. CIC 17, c. 1646. Anyone can act in a trial, unless he is prohibited by the sacred canons; a respondent legitimately convened must respond.

35. CIC 17, c. 1971 §1. [The following] are capable of accusing [marriage]: 1. The spouses in all cases of separation and nullity unless they themselves were the cause of the impediment; 2. The promoter of justice in [cases involving] impediments [that are] public by their nature.

36. See Wernz-Vidal, *Ius Canonicum* V, 147.

37. Sacred Congregation for the Discipline of the Sacraments, Instruction, *Provida Mater Ecclesiae*, August 15, 1936, *AAS* 28 (1936): 313–72, English trans. from *Canon Law Digest*, vol. 2, ed. T. Lincoln Bouscaren SJ, 471– 529 (hereinafter cited as *Provida Mater* and *CLD*), Art. 40. The Ordinary himself, even though the marriage has been denounced to him for nullity, should never make the formal accusation, but should refer the matter to the promoter of justice of his tribunal, who shall proceed according to the directions given above.

38. *Provida Mater*, Article 16 §1. The promoter of justice must intervene when he himself attacks the marriage, and whenever there is a question of safeguarding the procedural law. In this latter case the intervention of the promoter of justice is decreed by the Bishop or by the collegiate tribunal either *ex officio* or at the instance of the promoter of justice himself, or of the defender of the bond, or of the parties.

39. *Provida Mater*, Article 35 §1. The following are capable of accusing the marriage: 1. The parties to it, unless they were the cause of the impediment. 2. The promoter of justice, in the case of impediments which are of their nature public, in his own right (Cod. Com., July 17, 1933, ad IV) and without any previous denunciation; and in the case of other impediments, where a previous denunciation of the marriage has been made, if the person making it has not the right to bring

suit to obtain a declaration of nullity of his or her marriage, but without prejudice to the provisions of articles 38 and 39. §2. All other persons, even though they be blood relatives of the parties to the marriage, have not the right to attack it, but only to denounce the nullity of the marriage to the Ordinary or to the promoter of justice (cf. canon 1971). 1. Likewise, non-Catholics, whether baptized or unbaptized, cannot be plaintiffs in matrimonial cases; but if special reasons arise in favor of admitting them as such, recourse must be had in each case to the Holy Office (cf. reply of the Holy Office, of 27 Jan. 1928).

40. CIC 83, c. 87. By baptism a man is constituted a person in the Church of Christ with all the rights and duties of Christians unless, in what applies to rights, some bar obstructs, impeding the bond of ecclesiastical communion, or there is a censure laid down by the Church. This was clarified and re-iterated by a Reply of the S.C.S. Holy Office, 17 January 1928, *AAS* 20–75, *CLD*, vol. 1, 762–63. The *motu proprio* of Pope Paul VI, *Causas Matrimoniales*, 28 March, 1971, in *CLD,* vol. 7, 969–74, changed this provision.

41. *Provida Mater*, Art. 38 §1. Where there is a question of a denunciation of nullity made by the party or both parties to the marriage, on the ground that the party or both parties: (a) by a positive act of the will excluded the marriage itself, or all right to the conjugal act, or some essential property of marriage; or, (b) placed a condition contrary to the substance of marriage; the promoter of justice shall not accuse the marriage, but shall to the best of his ability warn the parties to have regard for their consciences, and if possible to remove the cause of the impediment, for example by duly making a new act of consent.

42. *Provida Mater*, Art. 39. But if the marriage is denounced as null by one or both parties to it, who were culpable cause either of the impediment or of the nullity of the marriage, in any other cases than those dealt with in the preceding article, the promoter of justice shall make the accusation of the marriage unless the three following circumstances concur: (a) the impediment is one which has become public, and which rests on evidence so certain and valid either in fact or in law that there can be no serious doubt of the existence of the impediment; (b) the public welfare; namely, the removal of scandal, in the judgment of the Ordinary, really demands it; (c) even after the impediment has ceased it is impossible that the marriage be duly contracted.

43. *Provida Mater*, Art. 38 §2. However, if the alleged nullity of the marriage has become public, and scandal really exists, but the person who denounced the marriage has in the opinion of the Ordinary, truly given signs of repentance, and at the same time the alleged ground of nullity is supported by evidence so certain and valid either in fact or in law that the nullity of the marriage is altogether probable, then the promoter of justice has the right and duty to make due accusation of the marriage which has been denounced.

44. *Provida Mater*, Art. 41 §3. If any denunciation made by other persons contains proofs from which the nullity of the marriage appears probable, the Ordinary or the promoter of justice should investigate, by cautiously and secretly questioning the persons who made the denunciation, whether the case is a proper one for an accusation *ex officio* according to articles 38 and 39, or for a dispensation to revalidate the marriage. §4. It is the part of the promoter of justice to withdraw the accusation if he afterward

learns for certain that the accusation cannot be sustained either in law or in fact.

45. *Provida Mater*, Art. 91 §2. The promoter of justice, however, is allowed to make the proceeding his own, and to prosecute the action, whenever, in the judgment of the Bishop, the public good, that is, the removal of scandal, seems to require it (cf. c. 1850 §2).

46. *Provida Mater*, Art. 69.

47. An example of an incidental question being judged is in the case concerning a Priest's remuneration fund, on 7 October 1999, and whether the tribunal is competent, in Canon Law Society of Australia and New Zealand, *Newsletter*, 2000, no. 2, 35–40.

48. CIC 17, c. 1675.

49. CIC 17, c. 1663.

50. Grocholewski, in *Exegetical Commentary,* IV/I, 764.

51. Grocholewski, *Exegetical Commentary,* IV/I, 764.

52. CIC 83, cc. 1454–57.

53. CIC 83, c. 1435. It is the Bishop's responsibility to appoint the promoter of justice and defender of the bond. They are to be clerics or laypersons of good repute, with a doctorate or a licentiate in canon law, and of proven prudence and zeal for justice.

54. CIC 83, c 483 §2. The chancellor and notaries must be of unblemished reputation and above suspicion. In cases which could involve the reputation of a priest, the notary must be a priest. Cf. *Canon Law Society of America Proceedings* 49 (1987): 237–38.

55. E. Caparros, M. Thériault, and J. Thorn, eds., *Code of Canon Law Annotated,* 2nd ed. (Montreal: Wilson & LaFleur, 2004), 890.

56. Second Vatican Council, *Gaudium et Spes*, no. 26, http://www.vatican.va/archive/hist_councils/ii_vatican_council/documents/vat-ii_const_19651207_gaudium-et-spes_lt.html.

57. CIC 83, c. 1696. Cases of separation of spouses also concern the public good; the promoter of justice must, therefore, always intervene, in accordance with canon 1433. Canon 1691 also indicates this.

58. CIC 83, c. 1431 §1. In contentious cases it is for the diocesan Bishop to decide whether the public good is at stake or not, unless the law prescribes the intervention of the promoter of justice, or this is clearly necessary from the nature of things. §2. If the promoter of justice has intervened at an earlier instance of a trial, this intervention is presumed to be necessary at a subsequent instance.

59. Joseph Noval, *Commentarium in Codicem Juris Canonici, IV, De Processibus* (Rome: Augustae Taurinorum, 1920), 569.

60. CIC 83, c. 1431 §2. If the promoter of justice has intervened at an earlier instance of a trial, this intervention is presumed to be necessary at a subsequent instance.

61. This tribunal was established by decree of the New Zealand Catholic Bishops Conference on March 5, 1987, after approval for this was obtained from the Apostolic Signatura on December 16, 1986.

62. Apostolic Signatura, Norms for Interdiocesan, Regional or Interregional Tribunals, December 28, 1970, Article 5, in L. Wrenn, *Procedures* (Washington, DC: Canon Law Society of America, 1987), 103, or in *CLD,* 7, 920–26.

63. Apostolic Signatura, Norms for Interdiocesan, Regional or Interregional Tribunals, Art. 6, 104.

64. Apostolic Signatura, Norms for Interdiocesan, Regional or Interregional Tribunals, Art. 8, 104.

65. Apostolic Signatura, Norms for Interdiocesan, Regional or Interregional Tribunals, Art. 9, 104.

66. CIC 83, c. 1448 §1. The judge is not to undertake the hearing of a case in which any personal interest may be involved by reason of consanguinity or affinity in any degree of the direct line and up to the fourth degree of the collateral line, or by reason of guardianship or tutelage, or of close acquaintanceship or marked hostility or possible financial profit or loss. §2. The promoter of justice, the defender of the bond, the assessor and the auditor must likewise refrain from exercising their offices in these circumstances.

67. CIC 83, c. 1449 §4. If the objection is directed against the promoter of justice, the defender of the bond, or any other officer of the tribunal, it is to be dealt with by the presiding judge of a collegiate tribunal, or by the sole judge if there is only one.

68. CIC 83, c. 1436 §1 The same person can hold the office of promoter of justice and defender of the bond, although not in the same case.

69. CIC 83, c. 1693 §1. The oral contentious process is to be used, unless either party or the promoter of justice requests the ordinary contentious process.

70. CIC 83, c. 1674. The following are capable of impugning the validity of a marriage: 1. the spouses themselves; 2. the promoter of justice, when the nullity of the marriage has already been made public, and the marriage cannot be validated, or it is not expedient to do so. See *Dignitas Connubii: Norms and Commentary,* 167: art. 92 §1. The following have the ability to challenge a marriage: 1. The spouses, whether Catholics or non-Catholics (cf. canons 1674, no. 1; 1476; art. 3, §2); 2. The promoter of justice, when the nullity of the marriage has been revealed and the marriage cannot be convalidated or this would not be expedient (cf. canon 1674, no. 2).

71. CIC 83, c. 1721 §1. If the ordinary has decreed that a judicial penal process must be initiated, he is to hand over the acts of the investigation to the promoter of justice who is to present a libellus of accusation to the judge according to the norm of canons 1502 and 1504. §2. The promoter of justice appointed to the higher tribunal acts as the petitioner before that tribunal.

72. See Kalus Ludicke and Ronny Jenkins, *Dignitas Connubii: Norms and Commentary* (Washington, DC: Catholic University of America, 2006), 113.

73. Ludicke and Jenkins, *Dignitas Connubii: Norms and Commentary*, 115–16.

74. Ludicke and Jenkins, *Dignitas Connubii: Norms and Commentary*, 223.

75. CIC 83, c. 1678 §1. The defender of the bond, the legal representatives of the parties, and, if involved in the trial, the promoter of justice, also have the right: 1/ to be present at the examination of the parties, the witnesses and the experts, without prejudice to Can. 1559; 2/ to inspect the judicial acts, even if they are not yet published, and to examine documents produced by the parties. §2 The parties cannot assist at the examination mentioned in §1 no. 1.

76. Apostolic Signatura, letter 18 June 1987, in *Roman Replies 1987*, 60–61.

77. Thomas Brundage, "The Promoter of Justice in the 1983 Code of Canon Law," Catholic University of America JCL Diss. 1991, 34.

78. CIC 83, c. 1430. A promoter of justice is to be appointed in the diocese for penal cases, and for contentious cases in which the public good may be at stake. The promoter is bound by office to safeguard the public good.

79. CIC 83, c. 1721 §1. If the Ordinary decrees that a penal judicial process is to be initiated, he is to pass the acts of the investigation to the promoter of justice, who is to

present to the judge a petition of accusation in accordance with Canons 1502 and 1504. §2. Before a higher tribunal, the promoter of justice constituted for that tribunal adopts the role of plaintiff.

80. CIC 83, c. 1717 §1. Whenever the Ordinary receives information, which has at least the semblance of truth, about an offence, he is to enquire carefully, either personally or through some suitable person, about the facts and circumstances, and about the imputability of the offence, unless this enquiry would appear to be entirely superfluous.

81. See John Beal, Administrative Leave: Canon 1722 revisited, in *Studia Canonica* 27 (1993): 293–320.

82. Akpoghiran, *Delicta Graviora Manual*, vol. 1, 261.

83. Victoria Vondenberger, RSM, "The Promoter of Justice," in P. Dugan, P. Gargaro, and V. Vondenberger, *Canon Law 101, Penal Law, Priest Problems and Legal Issues* (Philadelphia: Canon Law Books, 2017), 39.

84. *Guide to the Implementation of the U.S. Bishop's Essential Norms for Diocesan/Eparchial Policies Dealing with Allegations of Sexual Abuse of Minors by Priests or Deacons* (Washington, DC: Canon Law Society of America, 2003), 35.

85. DDF, *Norms,* art. 4. §2. In the cases concerning the delicts mentioned in §1, it is not permitted for anyone to indicate the name of the accuser or the penitent either to the accused or to his or her patron, unless the one making the accusation or the penitent has expressly consented; the question of the credibility of the accuser is to be considered attentively; and any danger of violating the sacramental seal is to be altogether avoided, taking care, however, that the right of defense of the accused remains intact; https://www.vatican.va/roman_curia/congregations/cfaith/documents/rc_con_cfaith_doc_20211011_norme-delittiriservati-cfaith_en.html; *Communicationes* 12 (1980): 194.

86. CIC 83, c. 221 §3. Christ's faithful have the right that no canonical penalties be inflicted upon them except in accordance with the law.

87. Dicastery for Legislative Texts, *Penal Sanctions: User Guide for Book VI of the Code of Canon Law*, 2023, 191.

88. United States Conference of Catholic Bishops, *Charter for the Protection of Children and Young People*, June 2011, http://www.usccb.org/issues-and-action/child-and-youth-protection/upload/Charter-for-the-Protection-of-Children-and-Young-People-revised-2011.pdf.

89. DDF, *Normae de Gravioribus Delictis*, October 11, 2021; https://www.vatican.va/roman_curia/congregations/cfaith/documents/rc_con_cfaith_doc_20211011_norme-delittiriservati-cfaith_en.html.

90. DDF, *Normae de Gravioribus Delictis*, October 11, 2021.

91. CIC 83, c. 1502. A person who wishes to bring another to trial must present to a competent judge a libellus which sets forth the object of the controversy and requests the services of the judge. Can. 1504. The libellus, which introduces litigation, must: 1/ express the judge before whom the case is introduced, what is being sought and by whom it is being sought; 2/ indicate the right upon which the petitioner bases the case and, at least generally, the facts and proofs which will prove the allegations; 3/ be signed by the petitioner or the petitioner's procurator, indicating the day, month, and year, and the address where the petitioner or procurator lives or where they say they reside for the purpose of receiving the acts; 4/ indicate the domicile or quasi-domicile of the respondent.

92. John Renken, *The Penal Law of the Roman Catholic Church* (Ottawa: St. Paul University, 2015), 419.

93. CIC 83, c. 1412 In penal cases the accused, even if absent, can be brought to trial before the tribunal of the place where the delict was committed.

94. CIC 83, c. 1415 By reason of prevention, if two or more tribunals are equally competent, the right of adjudicating the case belongs to the one which legitimately cited the respondent first.

95. CIC 83, c. 1608 §1. For the pronouncement of any sentence, the judge must have moral certitude about the matter to be decided by the sentence. §2. The judge must derive this certitude from the acts and the proofs. §3. The judge, however, must appraise the proofs according to the judge's own conscience, without prejudice to the prescripts of law concerning the efficacy of certain proofs. §4. A judge who was not able to arrive at this certitude is to pronounce that the right of the petitioner is not established and is to dismiss the respondent as absolved, unless it concerns a case which has the favour of law, in which case the judge must pronounce for that.

96. CIC 83, c. 1453. Without prejudice to justice, judges and tribunals are to take care that all cases are completed as soon as possible and that in a tribunal of first instance they are not prolonged beyond a year and in a tribunal of second instance beyond six months.

97. CIC 83, c. 1407 §1. No one can be brought to trial in first instance except before a judge who is competent on the basis of one of the titles determined in Canons 1408–14. CIC 83, c. 1408. Anyone can be brought to trial before the tribunal of domicile or quasi-domicile.

98. CIC 83, c. 1412. A person accused in a penal case can, even though absent, be brought to trial before the tribunal of the place in which the offence was committed.

99. William Woestman, "Schematic Outline of Penal Procedures," unpublished.

100. CIC 83, cc. 1502, 1504.

101. CIC 83, c. 1321 §4. When there has been an external violation, imputability is presumed, unless it appears otherwise.

102. CIC 83, c. 1730 §2. When the judge does this he must, after giving judgement in the penal trial, hear the case concerning damages, even though the penal trial is still pending because of a proposed challenge to it, or even though the accused has been acquitted, when the reason for the acquittal does not take away the obligation to make good the damages. Cf. Frank Morrisey OMI, Lecture, *Penal Law Today*, Biloxi, December 4, 2002.

103. CIC 83, c. 1507 §2. If the libellus is considered as accepted according to the norm of canon 1506, the decree of citation to the trial must be issued within twenty days from the request mentioned in that canon.

104. CIC 83, c. 1513.

105. CIC 83, c. 1516. These can be extended under canon 1465.

106. Vondenberger, "The Promoter of Justice," 43.

107. Vondenberger, "The Promoter of Justice," 41.

108. CIC 83, c. 1553 It is for the judge to curb an excessive number of witnesses. CIC 83, c. 1552 §1. When proof by means of witnesses is sought, the names and domicile of the witnesses are to be communicated to the tribunal. §2. The propositions on which the interrogation of the witnesses is requested, are to be submitted within the time-limit determined by the judge; otherwise, the request is to be deemed abandoned.

109. CIC 83, c. 1434. Unless otherwise expressly provided: 1. whenever the law

directs that the judge is to hear the parties or either of them, the promoter of justice and the defender of the bond, if they are engaged in the trial, are also to be heard; CIC 83, c. 1561. The examination of a witness is conducted by the judge, or by his delegate or an auditor, who is to be attended by a notary. Accordingly, unless particular law provides otherwise, if the parties or the promoter of justice or the defender of the bond or the advocates who are present at the hearing have additional questions to put to the witness, they are to propose these not to the witness, but to the judge, or to the one who is taking the judge's place, so that he or she may put them.

110. CIC 83, c. 1561. The examination of a witness is conducted by the judge, or by his delegate or an auditor, who is to be attended by a notary. Accordingly, unless particular law provides otherwise, if the parties or the promoter of justice or the defender of the bond or the advocates who are present at the hearing have additional questions to put to the witness, they are to propose these not to the witness, but to the judge, or to the one who is taking the judge's place, so that he or she may put them.

111. CIC 83, c. 220.

112. The Congregation for the Doctrine of the Faith, contrary to the Congregation for Clergy (9 June 1988), wants psychological and medical records used in SST cases.

113. CIC 83, cc. 1574–81.

114. Vondenberger, "The Promoter of Justice," 30.

115. CIC 83, c. 1603 §3. The promoter of justice and the defender of the bond have the right to respond to every reply of the parties.

116. CIC 83, c. 1678 §1. In cases of the nullity of marriage, a judicial confession and the declarations of the parties, possibly supported by witnesses to the credibility of the parties, can have the force of full proof, to be evaluated by the judge after he has considered all the indications and supporting factors, unless other elements are present which weaken them. §2. In the same cases, the testimony of one witness can produce full proof, if it concerns a qualified witness making a deposition concerning matters *ex officio*, or unless the circumstances of things and persons suggest otherwise. §3. In cases of impotence or defect of consent because of mental illness or an anomaly of a psychic nature, the judge is to use the services of one or more experts unless it is clear from the circumstances that it would be useless to do so; in other cases the prescript of can. 1574 is to be observed. §4. Whenever, during the instruction of a case, a very probable doubt emerges that consummation of the marriage did not occur, having heard the parties, the tribunal can suspend the case of nullity, complete the instruction for a dispensation *super rato*, and then transmit the acts to the Apostolic See together with a petition for a dispensation from either one or both of the spouses and the *votum* of the tribunal and the bishop.

117. CIC 83, c. 1598 and c. 1434.

118. CIC 83, c. 1678 §1. The defender of the bond, the legal representatives of the parties, and also the promoter of justice, if involved in the trial, have the following rights: 1/ to be present at the examination of the parties, the witnesses, and the experts, without prejudice to the prescript of canon 1559; 2/ to inspect the judicial acts, even those not yet published, and to review the documents presented by the parties. §2. The parties cannot be present at the examination mentioned in §1, no. 1.

119. CIC 83, c. 1598.

120. CIC 83, c. 1603. The promoter of justice and the defender of the bond have the right to respond to every reply of the parties.

121. CIC 83, c. 1725.

122. CIC 83, cc. 1599, 1601–3.

123. CIC 83, c. 1626 §1. Not only the parties who consider themselves aggrieved can introduce a complaint of nullity but also the promoter of justice and the defender of the bond whenever they have the right to intervene.

124. Z. Grocholewski, in *Exegetical Commentary*, IV/I, 781.

125. CIC 83, c. 1724 §1. At the direction or with the consent of the Ordinary who decided that the process should be initiated, the promoter of justice in any grade of the trial can renounce the instance. §2. For validity, the renunciation must be accepted by the accused person, unless he or she has been declared absent from the trial. N.B. the accused cannot request a trial to clear his name. The person is presumed to have a good reputation. See *Communicationes* 12 (1980): 191.

126. Renken, *The Penal Law of the Roman Catholic Church*, 430.

127. CIC 83, c. 1724.

128. CIC 83, c. 1726. If in any grade or at any stage of a penal trial, it becomes quite evident that the offence has not been committed by the accused, the judge must declare this in a judgement and acquit the accused, even if it is at the same time clear that the period for criminal proceedings has elapsed.

129. Congregation for the Evangelisation of Peoples, *Circular Letter*, Prot. No. 0579/09, in Renken, *The Penal Law*, 485. Similar faculties were granted to the Congregation for the Clergy on January 30, 2009. Canon 1392; Congregation for the Clergy, circular letter, Prot. No. 2009 0556, in Renken, *The Penal Law*, 496.

130. Renken, *The Penal Law of the Roman Catholic Church*, 419.

131. CIC 83, c. 1598 and c. 1434.

132. CIC 83, c. 1678 §1. The defender of the bond, the legal representatives of the parties, and also the promoter of justice, if involved in the trial, have the following rights: 1/ to be present at the examination of the parties, the witnesses, and the experts, without prejudice to the prescript of canon 1559; 2/ to inspect the judicial acts, even those not yet published, and to review the documents presented by the parties. §2. The parties cannot be present at the examination mentioned in §1, no. 1.

133. CIC 83, c. 1724 §1 At the direction or with the consent of the Ordinary who decided that the process should be initiated, the promoter of justice in any grade of the trial can renounce the instance. §2 For validity, the renunciation must be accepted by the accused person, unless he or she has been declared absent from the trial.

134. CIC 83, c. 1725.

135. Grocholewski, in *Exegetical Commentary*, IV/I, 782; cc. 1436 §2 and 1457.

136. Grocholewski, in *Exegetical Commentary*, IV/I, 781; using the parallel of A. Corbi Copovi, *El Defensor del vincula matrimonial* (Pamplona: University of Navarre, 1994), 243–46.

137. CIC 83, c. 221.

138. DDF, *Norms*, October 11, 2021, Art. 17. If, in the appellate stage, the Promoter of Justice brings forth a specifically different accusation, this Supreme Tribunal may admit and judge it, as if it were in the first instance; https://www.vatican.va/roman_curia/congregations/cfaith/documents/rc_con_cfaith_doc_20211011_norme-delittiriservati-cfaith_en.html.

139. F. Loza, "The Penal Process," in *Code of Canon Law Annotated*, 1065.

140. CIC 83, c. 1727 §1. The accused can propose an appeal even if the sentence dismissed the accused only because the penalty was facultative or because the judge used the power mentioned in canons 1344 and 1345. §2. The promoter of justice can appeal whenever the promoter judges that the repair of scandal or the restoration of justice has not been provided for sufficiently.

141. CIC 83, c. 1626 §1. A plaint of nullity can be made not only by parties who regard themselves as injured, but also by the promoter of justice and the defender of the bond, whenever they have a right to intervene.

142. David Price, "Elements of a Sentence and Its Publication," in *Proceedings of the Annual Conference of the Canon Law Society of Australia and New Zealand*, 2002, 61–75.

143. CIC 83, cc. 1645–1648. *Restitutio in integrum* is a legal remedy whereby a person injured by an unjust judgment can have their status restored to the state before the unjust sentence. It is sometimes called "total reinstatement."

144. CIC 83, c. 1628. A party who considers himself or herself aggrieved by any sentence as well as the promoter of justice and the defender of the bond in cases which require their presence have the right to appeal the sentence to a higher judge, without prejudice to the prescript of canon 1629. CIC 83, c. 1341. The Ordinary must start a judicial or an administrative procedure for the imposition or the declaration of penalties when he perceives that neither by the methods of pastoral care, especially fraternal correction, nor by a warning or correction, can justice be sufficiently restored, the offender reformed, and the scandal repaired.

145. CIC 83, c. 1628. Without prejudice to the provisions of Can. 1629, a party who considers himself or herself to be injured by a judgement has a right to appeal from the judgement to a higher judge; in cases in which their presence is required, the promoter of justice and the defender of the bond have likewise the right to appeal.

146. CIC 83, c. 1629. No appeal is possible against: 1/ a judgement of the Supreme Pontiff himself, or a judgement of the Apostolic Signatura; 2/ a judgement which is null, unless the appeal is lodged together with a plaint of nullity, in accordance with Can. 1625; 3/ a judgement which has become an adjudged matter; 4/ a decree of the judge or an interlocutory judgement, which does not have the force of a definitive judgement, unless the appeal is lodged together with an appeal against the definitive judgement; 5/ a judgement or a decree in a case in which the law requires that the matter be settled with maximum expedition.

147. CIC 83, c. 1636 §2. Unless the law provides otherwise, an appeal made by the defender of the bond or the promoter of justice can be renounced by the defender of the bond or the promoter of justice of the appeal tribunal.

148. CIC 83, c. 1441 The tribunal of second instance is to be constituted in the same way as the tribunal of first instance. However, if a sole judge has given a judgement in first instance in accordance with canon 1425 §4, the second instance tribunal is to act collegially.

149. CIC 83, c. 1501. A judge cannot investigate any case unless a plea, drawn up in accordance with canon law, is submitted either by a person whose interest is involved, or by the promoter of justice. Minors or those lacking the use of reason can only stand in court through other people such as guardians, parents or a curator according to canon 1478.

150. CIC 83, c. 1431 §1. In contentious cases it is for the diocesan Bishop to decide whether the public good is at stake or not, unless the law prescribes the intervention of the promoter of justice, or this is clearly necessary from the nature of things.

151. Canon Law Society of Great Britain and Ireland, *Newsletter*, December 2002, 8.

152. Canon CIC 17, c. 2010 §1. A promoter of faith must take part by a protected right in any process [and] must always be cited according to the norm of canon 1587. §2. The promoter of faith before the Sacred Congregation is called the *Promoter General of Faith*, and the Assessor of the Sacred Congregation who assists him is called the sub-promoter general of faith.

153. CIC 17, c. 2011 §1. A promoter of faith outside the Sacred Congregation can be constituted either for all causes or for a certain particular cause.

154. Code of Canon Law Annotated, *Divinus perfectionis Magister*, 1142–55, *Promotere fidei* is referred to in numbers 10 and 13. The norms are in *AAS* 75 (1983), 396–403. For a full explanation of the process, there is William H. Woestman, *Canonization: Theology, History, Process* (Ottawa: St. Paul University, 2014), 153.

155. See Congregatio De Causis Sanctorum, instructio: Sanctorum Mater, May 17, 2007, in *AAS* 99 (2007): 465–510.

156. Gray, *The Evolution of the Promoter of the Faith*, 284.

CHAPTER 4

1. F. Salvioli, "The Rights of the Victims: International Standards and the Need of a Holistic Approach," in C. Scicluna and M. Wijlens, *Rights of Alleged Victims in Penal Proceedings Provisions in Canon Law and the Criminal Law of Different Legal Systems* (Baden-Baden: Nomos Verlagsgesellschaft, 2023), 39.

2. Maria Ines Franck, "Rights of Alleged Victims in Penal Procedures in Argentina and Current Approach to Victims' Rights in Canon Law," in Scicluna and Wijlens, *Rights of Alleged Victims in Penal Proceedings*, 206.

3. Kevin McKenna, "We Can Do Both: Due Process for Accused Priests and Justice for Sex Abuse Survivors," *America,* June 2, 2023, https://www.americamagazine.org/faith/2023/06/02/due-process-clergy-sexual-abuse-accusation-245117.

4. See European Court of Human Rights, "Convention for the Protection of Human Rights and Fundamental Freedoms," https://www.echr.coe.int/european-convention-on-human-rights. Directive 2011/93/EU of the European Parliament and of the Council of December 13, 2011, on combating the sexual abuse and sexual exploitation of children and child pornography, and replacing Council Framework Decision 2004/68/JHA, 2011 O.J. (L 335), 1. Directive 2012/29/EU of the European Parliament and of the Council of October 25, 2012, establishing minimum standards on the rights, support and protection of victims of crime, and replacing Council Framework Decision 2001/220/JHA, 2012 O.J. (L 315), 57.

5. Raphaele Parizot, "The Rights of Alleged Victims in Penal Procedures in France," in Scicluna and Wijlens, *Rights of Alleged Victims in Penal Proceedings*, 220.

6. Mary Graw Leary, "A Crime Victim Rights Framework in the USA," in Scicluna and Wijlens, *Rights of Alleged Victims in Penal Proceedings*, 130–45.

7. Charles J. Scicluna, "The Rights of Victims in Canonical Penal Processes," *Periodica* 109, nos. 3–4 (2020): 493–503.

8. Yeshica Calderon, "The Participation of the Victim of Sexual Abuse in Canonical Penal Proceedings," *Studia Canonica* 57 (2023): 676.

9. The victim assistance coordinator provides outreach, accountability, and transparency for victims of clergy sexual abuse. Cf. Archdiocese of Regina, https://archregina.sk.ca/grouppage/core-working-group-mandate/.

10. Calderon, "The Participation of the Victim of Sexual Abuse in Canonical Penal Proceedings," 672–73.

11. USCCB, "Victim Assistance"; https://www.usccb.org/offices/child-and-youth-protection/victim-assistance.

12. Mark Bartchak, "The Position of Alleged Victims in the Canonical Penal Process," in Scicluna and Wijlens, *Rights of Alleged Victims in Penal Proceedings*, 289.

13. Bartchak, "The Position of Alleged Victims," in Scicluna and Wijlens, *Rights of Alleged Victims in Penal Proceedings*, 291.

14. Bartchak, "The Position of Alleged Victims," in Scicluna and Wijlens, *Rights of Alleged Victims in Penal Proceedings*, 298.

15. CIC 83, c. 1311 §2.

16. CIC 83, c. 1430. A promoter of justice is to be appointed in the diocese for penal cases, and for contentious cases in which the public good may be at stake. The promoter is bound by office to safeguard the public good.

17. CIC 83, c. 1721 §1. If the Ordinary decrees that a penal judicial process is to be initiated, he is to pass the acts of the investigation to the promoter of justice, who is to present to the judge a petition of accusation in accordance with Canons 1502 and 1504. §2. Before a higher tribunal, the promoter of justice constituted for that tribunal adopts the role of plaintiff.

18. G. Montini, "The Rights of Alleged Victims in Canonical Penal Procedures Current Penal Procedural Canon Law," in Scicluna and Wijlens, *Rights of Alleged Victims in Penal Proceedings*, 22.

19. CIC 83, cc. 1723, 1481.

20. Bartchak, "The Position of Alleged Victims in the Canonical Penal Process," 305.

21. Gianpaolo Montini states: "The abbreviation SN refers to the apostolic letter *Sollicitudinem Nostram*, motu proprio dated January 6, 1950 from Pius XII for the Eastern (Catholic) Churches: it is the procedural law of the Eastern (Catholic) Churches that remained in force until 30.09.1991. The promulgated text (in Latin) is in: *AAS*. No. 1, 5–120; an English translation is in Paul Pallath, ed., *Code of Eastern Canon Law: English Translation of the Four Apostolic Letters Issued Motu Proprio by Pope Pius XII* (Kottayam: Oriental Institute of Religious Studies India, 2021). Although the procedural rules of the aforementioned motu proprio SN are not formally in force today, they can still be considered binding due to the fact that they emerge as logical deductions from the setting of the current canons 1729–1731, canons that fully transpose, albeit in abbreviated form (as in the style of the current Code), the setting of the aforementioned motu proprio." In G. Montini, "The Rights of Alleged Victims in Canonical Penal Procedures Current Penal Procedural Canon Law," 27.

22. "The injured party, who has been admitted to the exercise of a contentious action, has the right to propose exceptions and proofs [...], as a true party in the case, but with due regard for canon 376, §3" (c. 553, § 1 SN), i.e., in the case of late intervention, which therefore obviously takes place according to the Acts. Cf. also c. 557 SN. In Montini, "The Rights of Alleged Victims in

Canonical Penal Procedures Current Penal Procedural Canon Law," 27.

23. *AAS* 1950, no. 1, 5–120; an English translation is in Pallath, ed., *Code of Eastern Canon Law*; quoted in A. McGrath, OFM, "With Dignity and Respect: How Victims May Participate in Canonical Proceedings," in Scicluna and Wijlens, *Rights of Alleged Victims in Penal Proceedings*, 318.

24. Montini, "The Rights of Alleged Victims in Canonical Penal Procedures Current Penal Procedural Canon Law," 27.

25. McGrath, "With Dignity and Respect," 318.

26. Montini, "The Rights of Alleged Victims in Canonical Penal Procedures Current Penal Procedural Canon Law," 28.

27. Montini, "The Rights of Alleged Victims in Canonical Penal Procedures Current Penal Procedural Canon Law," 30.

28. Cf. SSAT, Congressional Decree in a Disciplinaris, October 29, 2015, prot. no. 48706/14 VT, in *Ius Canonicum* 1 (2018): 328–31, translated into Spanish and commented on by Francisca Pérez-Madrid, *La vigilancia de la recta administración de justicia por el Tribunal de la Signatura Apostólica. Comentario a algunos decretos recientes en materia disciplinar*, in *Ius Canonicum* 1 (2018): 321–54; in Scicluna and Wijlens, *Rights of Alleged Victims in Penal Proceedings,* 30.

29. CIC 83, c. 128. Whoever unlawfully causes harm to another by a juridical act, or indeed by any other act which is malicious or culpable, is obliged to repair the damage done.

30. Montini, "The Rights of Alleged Victims in Canonical Penal Procedures Current Penal Procedural Canon Law," 32.

31. CIC 83, c. 547, §1 SN. "Praeter reum citanda semper est pars cui ex delicto laesio iuridica est illata, quaeque ius habet exercendi actionem civilem."

32. Montini, "The Rights of Alleged Victims in Canonical Penal Procedures Current Penal Procedural Canon Law," 29.

33. Gianpaolo Montini, *Exegetical Commentary on the Code of Canon Law*, vol. 5 (Montreal: Wilson & Lafleur 2004), 2036–48.

34. SSAT (Supremum Signaturae Apostolicae Tribunal), "Congressional Decree in a Disciplinaris," quoted in Montini, "The Rights of Alleged Victims in Canonical Penal Procedures Current Penal Procedural Canon Law," 26. "Exstinctio iudicii poenalis minime secumfert et etiam iudicio de damnis finis imponatur. Exercitium actionis contentiosae ad damna reparanda ab actore pendet, non ab Ordinario. id quoque valet, si pars laesa actionem contentiosam ad damna reparanda in ipso poenali iudicio exerceat."

35. Montini, "The Rights of Alleged Victims in Canonical Penal Procedures Current Penal Procedural Canon Law," 30.

36. Montini, "The Rights of Alleged Victims in Canonical Penal Procedures Current Penal Procedural Canon Law," 31.

37. "New Zealand's List of Shame: Grace Millane and the Other Tourists Killed Here," *New Zealand Herald*, December 9, 2018, https://www.nzherald.co.nz/nz/new-zealands-list-of-shame-grace-millane-and-the-other-tourists-killed-here/GFKHZJLANF7DSYTRZ2W3ZMFB7E/.

38. See VELM 5 §1.

39. Montini, "The Rights of Alleged Victims in Canonical Penal Procedures Current Penal Procedural Canon Law," 23.

40. "Omnino certum manet utramque actionem, seu poenalem et contentiosam ad damna reparanda, quae in eodem delicto fundatur, etiam separatim exerceri posse" (SSAT [Supremum Signaturae Apostolicae

Tribunal], vote annexed to letter October 7, 1989, prot. no. 19126/87 CP) in Montini, "The Rights of Alleged Victims in Canonical Penal Procedures Current Penal Procedural Canon Law," 23.

41. Montini, "The Rights of Alleged Victims in Canonical Penal Procedures Current Penal Procedural Canon Law," 35n44.

42. Carlo Gullo, *Exegetical Commentary*, vol. 4/I (Montreal: Wilson & Lafleur, 2004), 968–70.

43. See https://victimsinfo.govt.nz/assets/adult-jurisdiction-victim-impact-statement.pdf.

44. See c. 1339.

45. S. Kilgallon, "Paedophile priest died—but church didn't tell survivors," May 11, 2024; https://www.stuff.co.nz/nz-news/350271520/paedophile-priest-died-church-didnt-tell-survivors#:~:text=Father%20Magnus%20'Max'%20Murray%20died,least%20once%20during%20those%20months.

46. Calderon, "The Participation of the Victim of Sexual Abuse in Canonical Penal Proceedings," 672.

47. Pontifical Council for Legislative Texts, Instruction *Dignitas Connubii* (Rome: Libreria Editrice Vaticana, 2005).

CHAPTER 5

1. See https://www.abuseincare.org.nz/.

2. See https://www.childabuseroyalcommission.gov.au/.

3. Michael Joyce, CM, "Societies of Apostolic Life," in D. Miller and E. Jaramillo, eds., *Procedural Handbook for Institutes of Consecrated Life and Societies of Apostolic Life* (Washington, DC: Canon Law Society of America, 2021), 268; CIC 83, c. 731 §1. Societies of apostolic life approximate to institutes of consecrated life. Their members, without taking religious vows, pursue the apostolic purpose proper to each society. Living a fraternal life in common in their own special manner, they strive for the perfection of charity through the observance of the constitutions. English translation from Gerard Sheehy et al., eds., *The Canon Law: Letter and Spirit* (Collegeville, MN: The Liturgical Press, 1995). CIC 83, c. 1192 §1. A vow is public if it is received in the name of the Church by a lawful Superior; otherwise, it is private.

4. CIC 83, c. 710.

5. An example would be the Schoenstatt Sisters of Mary in Sydney. Secular institutes were first recognized in 1947 and do not exist in New Zealand.

6. CIC 83, c. 294.

7. CIC 83, c. 298 §1. In the church there are associations that are distinct from institutes of consecrated life and societies of apostolic life. In these associations, Christ's faithful, whether clerics or laity, or clerics and laity together, strive with a common effort to foster a more perfect life, or to promote public worship or Christian teaching. They may also devote themselves to other works of the apostolate, such as initiatives for evangelization, works of piety or charity, and those which animate the temporal order with the Christian spirit. Cf. Sharon Holland, IHM, "Secular Institutes," in *Procedural Handbook for Institutes of Consecrated Life and Societies of Apostolic Life*, 257–66.

8. CIC 83, c. 1192 §1. A vow is public if it is received in the name of the Church by a lawful Superior; otherwise, it is private. §2 It is solemn if it is recognized by the Church as such; otherwise, it is simple. §3 It is personal if it promises an action by the person making the vow; real, if it promises something; mixed, if it has both a personal and a real aspect.

9. CIC 83, cc. 579, 589, 594.

10. CIC 83, cc. 589, 593. Elizabeth McDonough, OP, "Relationship between Bishops and Religious: Mutual Rights and Duties," *Bulletin on Issues of Religious Law* 5, no. 2, October 1989, A Joint Project of Canon Law Society of America, Conference of Major Superiors of Men, Leadership Conference of Women Religious, National Conference of Vicars of Religious. Most religious institutes in New Zealand and Australia are pontifical.

11. McDonough, "Relationship between Bishops and Religious: Mutual Rights and Duties;" 3; CIC 83, c. 588 §3, 676.

12. McDonough, "Relationship between Bishops and Religious: Mutual Rights and Duties," 3; CIC 83, c. 588 §2.

13. CIC 83, c. 667 §3.

14. CIC 83, c. 615.

15. Catholic Health Association, United States, Ministerial Juridic Persons (chausa .org); John of God Health Care is an MPJP.

16. Pope Leo XIII, constitution, *Romanos Pontifices*, May 8, 1881: *Leonis Xlll Pontificis Maximi Acta* (Rome: Ex Typographia Vaticana, 1897), 2:235.

17. A solemn vow is an absolute, public vow taken by a religious in the Roman Catholic Church under which ownership of property by the individual is prohibited and marriage is invalid under canon law.

18. John Huels, "The Demise of Religious Exemption," *The Jurist* 54 (1994): 42.

19. Canons 1917 CIC 198; 134 1983 Code.

20. English trans. *The 1917 Pio-Benedictine Code of Canon Law*, trans. Edward N. Peters (San Francisco: Ignatius Press, 2001); hereafter the translation of the canons of the 1917 Code will be from this source.

21. Canons 1917 CIC 196–210.

22. Also included were abbots and prelates nullius, vicars general, vicars apostolic, and prefects apostolic.

23. Canons 1917 CIC 612; 1261; 874; 603 §1; 533 §1, no. 1.

24. The translations of Vatican documents in this volume are taken from Norman Tanner, *Decrees of the Ecumenical Councils* (London: Sheed and Ward Ltd, 1990).

25. Matthew Kozlowski, *A Canonical Analysis of the Authority Exercised by the Diocesan Bishop and the Religious Superior over the Religious Pastor qua Pastor* (Washington, DC: Catholic University of America, 2016), 54.

26. This new approach to exemption (which considerably lessens its importance as a determinant in diocesan-religious relations) can be seen in c. 586, which calls on local ordinaries to both respect and safeguard the internal autonomy (including discipline and charism) of all religious institutes—whether diocesan or pontifical.

27. Sacred Congregation for Religious and Societies of Apostolic Life and Congregation for Bishops (SCRIS & CB), "Directives for mutual relations between Bishops and Religious in the Church," *Mutuae Relationes*, May 14, 1978, https://www.vatican.va/roman_curia/congregations/ccscrlife/documents/rc_con_ccscrlife_doc_14051978_mutuae-relationes_en.html.

28. English translation from SS. CC. Rel. et S. I. et Episc., *Mutual Relations between Religious and Bishops*, May 14, 1978: *CLD* 9: 304–5.

29. SCRIS & CB, *Mutuae Relationes* 57a; https://www.vatican.va/roman_curia/congregations/ccscrlife/documents/rc_con_ccscrlife_doc_14051978_mutuae-relationes_en.html.

30. Paul VI, *motu proprio*, *Ecclesiae Sanctae,* I. 29 §1. "Vigilance" comes from the Latin "*vigilare*" meaning to watch over

and to ensure that ecclesiastical discipline is observed. Cf. John Faris, *A Practical Commentary to the Code of Canons of the Eastern Churches* (Montreal: Wilson & Lafleur, 2019), 275.

31. The *New Catholic Encyclopedia* defines "scandal" thus: "According to St. Thomas (II-II:43:1) scandal is a word or action evil in itself, which occasions another's spiritual ruin. It is a word or action, that is either an external act—for an internal act can have no influence on the conduct of another—or the omission of an external act, because to omit what one should do is equivalent to doing what is forbidden; it must be evil in itself, or in appearance." See https://www.newadvent.org/cathen/13506d.htm.

32. See also *CCC* 2285: "Scandal takes on a particular gravity by reason of the authority of those who cause it or the weakness of those who are scandalized. It prompted our Lord to utter this curse: 'Whoever causes one of these little ones who believe in me to sin, it would be better for him to have a great millstone fastened round his neck and to be drowned in the depth of the sea.' Scandal is grave when given by those who by nature or office are obliged to teach and educate others. Jesus reproaches the scribes and Pharisees on this account: he likens them to wolves in sheep's clothing."

33. In canon law administrators have the primary role in an organization. Cf. c. 1284 §3. It is earnestly recommended that administrators draw up each year a budget of income and expenditure. However, it is left to particular law to make this an obligation and to determine more precisely how it is to be presented.

34. "Vigilance," or oversight, is akin to the New Zealand Qualifications Authority (NZQA) exercising oversight of Tertiary institutions to ensure compliance with regulations and visiting and issuing an EER report every 3 or 4 years. NZQA does not own any institute and is not responsible for the actions of an institute or its officials.

35. Robert Kaslyn, "The Faculties of Priest Members of Religious Institutes and Societies of Apostolic Life," *The Jurist* 69 (2009): 173.

36. Benjamin Earl, OP, "*Opera Propria*: Property or Patrimony? Consequences for Mutual Relations between Bishops and Religious," *The Canon Law Society of Great Britain and Ireland Newsletter* 200 (November 2021): 33–53; SCRIS & CB, *Mutuae Relationes*, 57a.

37. CIC 83, c. 673.

38. CIC 83, c. 523. Without prejudice to canon 682 §1, appointment to the office of parish priest belongs to the diocesan Bishop, who is free to confer it on whomsoever he wishes, unless someone else has a right of presentation or election. CIC 83, c. 682 §1. If an ecclesiastical office in a diocese is to be conferred upon a member of a religious institute, the religious is appointed by the bishop on presentation by, or at least with the consent of, the competent Superior. §2. The religious can be removed from the office at the discretion of the authority who made the appointment, with prior notice given to the religious Superior; or by the religious Superior, with prior notice being given to the appointing authority. Neither requires the other's consent.

39. Earl, "*Opera Propria*: Property or Patrimony?," 33–53.

40. Paul VI, Second Vatican Ecumenical Council, Decree on the Church's Missionary Activity *Ad Gentes*, 1: *AAS* 58 (1966): 676.

41. James H. Provost, "Canonical Reflections on Selected Issues in Diocesan Governance," in *The Ministry of Governance*, ed.

James K. Mallett (Washington, DC: CLSA, 1986), 218.

42. CIC 83, c. 131.

43. CIC 83, c. 135 §1. The power of governance is divided into legislative, executive, and judicial power.

44. CIC 83, c. 673.

45. Kozlowski, *A Canonical Analysis of the Authority Exercised by the Diocesan Bishop and the Religious Superior Over the Religious Pastor qua Pastor*, 4–5.

46. Richard Hill. "The Apostolate of Institutes," in *A Handbook on Canons 573–746*, ed. Jordan Hite et al. (Collegeville, MN: Liturgical Press, 1985), 217.

47. CIC 83, c. 683 §1. Either personally, or through a delegate, the diocesan Bishop can visit churches or oratories to which Christ's faithful have habitual access, schools other than those open only to the institute's own members and other works of religion or charity entrusted to religious, whether these be spiritual or temporal. He can do this at the time of the pastoral visitation, or in a case of necessity.

48. CIC 83, c. 806 §1. The diocesan Bishop has the right to watch over and inspect the Catholic schools situated in his territory, even those established or directed by members of religious institutes. He has also the right to issue directives concerning the general regulation of catholic schools; these directives apply also to schools conducted by members of a religious institute, although they retain their autonomy in the internal management of their schools.

49. A crime is a grave or mortal sin classified as a crime in canon law.

50. CIC 83, c. 1772; David Cito, in Ángel Marzoa, Jorge Miras, and Rafael Rodríguez-Ocaña, eds., *Exegetical Commentary on the Code of Canon Law* 3, no. 1 (Chicago: Midwest Theological Forum, 2004), 239.

51. Jordan Hite, TOR, "Mutual Rights and Obligations of Bishops and Major Superiors regarding Public Ministry," *Bulletin on Issues of Religious Law* 14 (Spring 1997): 4.

52. CIC 83, c. 970. The faculty to hear confessions is not to be given except to priests whose suitability has been established, either by examination or by some other means.

53. Brendan Daly, "Canon 1336: What Processes Must the Diocesan Bishop Follow to Remove the Faculties of a Priest?" in *Roman Replies and CLSA Advisory Opinions 2017* (Washington, DC: Canon Law Society of America, 2017), 87–95.

54. CIC 83, c. 681 §2.

55. Since 1980, there is meant to be an agreement between diocesan bishops for a priest of one diocese carrying out a ministry or an apostolate in another diocese. Cf. Sacred Congregation for Clergy, "Directive Norms for Cooperation among Local Churches and for a Better Distribution of the Clergy," March 25, 1980, *CLD* 9: 760–787.

56. See https://www.childabuseroyalcommission.gov.au/sites/default/files/CTJH.280.01003.0001_R.pdf.

57. See https://www.britannica.com/topic/Roman-Catholicism/Suppression-of-the-Jesuits.

58. CIC 83, c. 732 applies this norm to societies of apostolic life.

59. Kozlowski, *A Canonical Analysis of the Authority Exercised by the Diocesan Bishop and the Religious Superior Over the Religious Pastor qua Pastor*, 40–41.

60. *AAS* 93 (2001): 737–39.

61. CIC 83, c. 695 §1. A member must be dismissed for the offences mentioned in Can. 1395, 1397, and 1398, unless, for the offences mentioned in Can. 1395 §§2–3, the Superior judges that dismissal is not absolutely necessary, and that sufficient provision has been made in some other way for the amendment

of the member, the restoration of justice and the reparation of scandal.

62. Congregation for the Doctrine of the Faith, *"Sacramentorum Sanctitatis Tutela*: Revised Norms on Dealing with Clerical Sex Abuse of Minors and Other Grave Offenses," *Origins* 40 (2010–2011), 146–51.

63. For example, in Melbourne, Australia, this would be through the Professional Standards Unit. See https://melbournecatholic.org/safeguarding/reporting-abuse-and-safety-related-misconduct.

64. CIC 83, c. 22. Civil laws to which the law of the Church yields are to be observed in canon law with the same effects, insofar as they are not contrary to divine law and unless canon law provides otherwise. Translation of canons of the 1983 Code by the Canon Law Society of America, https://www.vatican.va/archive/cod-iuris-canonici/cic_index_en.html, hereafter the translation of the canons of the 1917 Code will be from this source.

65. Formerly canon 1389. The 1917 Code, canon 2404, states: "Abuse of ecclesiastical power, in the prudent judgment of the Legitimate Superior, shall be punished according to the gravity of the fault, with due regard for the prescriptions of those canons that establish certain penalties for various abuses."

66. CIC 83, c. 134 §1. In law the term Ordinary means, apart from the Roman Pontiff, diocesan Bishops and all who, even for a time only, are set over a particular Church or a community equivalent to it in accordance with Canon 368, and those who in these have general ordinary executive power, that is, Vicars general and episcopal Vicars; likewise, for their own members, it means the major superiors of clerical religious institutes of pontifical right and of clerical societies of apostolic life of pontifical right, who have at least ordinary executive power. §2. The term local Ordinary means all those enumerated in §1, except Superiors of religious institutes and of societies of apostolic life. §3. Whatever in the canons, in the context of executive power, is attributed to the diocesan Bishop, is understood to belong only to the diocesan Bishop and to those others in Canon 381 §2 who are equivalent to him, to the exclusion of the Vicar general and the episcopal Vicar except by special mandate.

67. Pope Francis, apostolic constitution *Pascite Gregem Dei* (Tend My Flock), May 23, 2021, which reforms Book VI of the *Code of Canon Law*.

68. See Carol Glatz, "Days of Covering Up Abuse Allegations Are Over, Says Vatican Adviser," *The Boston Pilot*, May 9, 2019, https://www.thebostonpilot.com/article.php?ID=185023.

69. See Glatz, "Days of Covering Up Abuse Allegations Are Over."

70. See Andrea Tornielli, "New Norms for the Whole Church Against Those Who Abuse or Cover Up," *Vatican News*, May 9, 2019, https://www.vaticannews.va/en/pope/news/2019-05/pope-francis-motu-proprio-sex-abuse-clergy-religious-church.html.

71. See Glatz, "Days of Covering Up Abuse Allegations Are Over."

72. See Glatz, "Days of Covering Up Abuse Allegations Are Over."

73. CIC 83, c. 19.

74. CIC 83, c. 1350.

75. G. Michiels, OFM, *De Delictis et Poenis: Commentarius Libri V Codicis Iuris Canonici*, Editio altera, vol. 1 (Rome: Desclee, 1961), 68–71.

76. *Continence* means the nonuse of the sexual faculties.

77. Congregation for the Clergy, Letter, *Origins* 39 (2008–2009): 82.

78. Congregation for the Clergy, Letter, *Origins* 39 (2008–2009): 83.

79. Cf. VELM 5, note 85.

80. *CCC* §1548. In the ecclesial service of the ordained minister, it is Christ himself who is present to his Church as Head of his Body, Shepherd of his flock, high priest of the redemptive sacrifice, Teacher of Truth. This is what the Church means by saying that the priest, by virtue of the sacrament of Holy Orders, acts *in persona Christi Capitis. CCC* §1552. The ministerial priesthood has the task not only of representing Christ—Head of the Church—before the assembly of the faithful, but also of acting in the name of the whole Church when presenting to God the prayer of the Church, and above all when offering the Eucharistic sacrifice. Cf. *LD* 10; *SC* 33; *PO* 2, 6.

81. CIC 83, cc. 265; 281.

82. CIC 83, c. 523. Without prejudice to Canon 682 §1 appointment to the office of parish priest belongs to the diocesan Bishop, who is free to confer it on whomsoever he wishes, unless someone else has a right of presentation or election.

83. *CCC* §914. The state of life which is constituted by the profession of the evangelical counsels, while not entering into the hierarchical structure of the Church, belongs undeniably to her life and holiness. *CCC* §915. Christ proposes the evangelical counsels, in their great variety, to every disciple. The perfection of charity, to which all the faithful are called, entails for those who freely follow the call to consecrated life the obligation of practicing chastity in celibacy for the sake of the Kingdom, poverty and obedience. It is the profession of these counsels, within a permanent state of life recognized by the Church, that characterizes the life consecrated to God.

84. CIC 83, c. 805. In his own diocese, the local Ordinary has the right to appoint or to approve teachers of religion and, if religious or moral considerations require it, the right to remove them or to demand that they be removed.

85. CIC 83, c. 19. If on a particular matter there is not an express provision of either universal or particular law, nor a custom, then, provided it is not a penal matter, the question is to be decided by taking into account laws enacted in similar matters, the general principles of law observed with canonical equity, the jurisprudence and practice of the Roman Curia, and the common and constant opinion of learned authors.

86. Ministry of Education, New Zealand, *Supporting All Schools to Succeed: Reform of the Tomorrow's Schools System*, November 2019, https://conversation-live-storagesta-assetstorages3bucket-jsvm6zoesodc.s3.ap-southeast-2.amazonaws.com/public/TSR/November-2019/TSR-Government-Response-WEB.pdf.

87. See Elizabeth McDonough, OP, in "Relationship between Bishops and Religious: Mutual Rights and Duties," 4–5. See also Brendan Daly, "The Authority and Obligations of a Diocesan Bishop/Local Ordinary and a Religious Institute in his Diocese," *The Canonist* 13, no. 1 (2022): 74–75, https://acrobat.adobe.com/id/urn:aaid:sc:VA6C2:768b7252-b8a4-4f36-ae8f-2308e82fce91.

88. CIC 83, c. 678 §3. In directing the apostolic works of religious, diocesan Bishops must proceed by way of mutual consultation.

89. CIC 83, cc. 609 §1 and 611 no 2.

90. CIC 83, c. 612.

91. CIC 83, c. 616 §1; Earl, "*Opera Propria*: Property or Patrimony?," 51–52.

CHAPTER 6

1. Former canon 1362; c. 1362 §1. Prescription extinguishes a criminal action after three years unless it concerns: 1/ delicts

reserved to the Congregation for the Doctrine of the Faith; 2/ an action arising from the delicts mentioned in canons 1394, 1395, 1397, and 1398, which have a prescription of five years; 3/ delicts which are not punished in the common law if particular law has established another period for prescription. §2. Prescription runs from the day on which the delict was committed or, if the delict is continuous or habitual, from the day on which it ceased.

2. Pope John Paul II, *motu proprio, Sacramentorum Sanctitatis Tutela* (SST), April 30, 2001; *AAS* 93 (2001): 737–39.

3. SST, §1 Whenever the Ordinary or Hierarch receives a report of a more grave delict, which has at least the semblance of truth, and after having completed the preliminary investigation according to the norm of can. 1717 CIC and can. 1468 CCEO, he is to communicate the matter to the Congregation for the Doctrine of the Faith which, unless it calls the case to itself due to particular circumstances, will direct the Ordinary or Hierarch how to proceed further.

4. The Royal Commission into Institutional Responses to Child Sexual Abuse, *Final Report*, 2017, https://www.childabuseroyalcommission.gov.au/sites/default/files/final_report_-_volume_16_religious_institutions_book_1.pdf (RCIRCSA, *Final Report*).

5. *Vademecum* 1.

6. See Pope Benedict XVI, Letter to the Church in Ireland, March 19, 2010, https://www.vatican.va/content/benedict-xvi/en/letters/2010/documents/hf_ben-xvi_let_20100319_church-ireland.html.

7. DLT, *Penal Sanctions User Guide*, https://www.delegumtextibus.va/content/dam/testilegislativi/TESTI%20NORMATIVI/Testi%20Norm%20CIC/Libro%20VI/LibroVIsussidio/Penal%20sanctions%20User%20guide.pdf.

8. CIC 83. c. 134 §1. In law the term *Ordinary* means, apart from the Roman Pontiff, diocesan Bishops and all who, even for a time only, are set over a particular Church or a community equivalent to it in accordance with Can. 368, and those who in these have general ordinary executive power, that is, Vicars general and episcopal Vicars; likewise, for their own members, it means the major Superiors of clerical religious institutes of pontifical right and of clerical societies of apostolic life of pontifical right, who have at least ordinary executive power. §2. The term local Ordinary means all those enumerated in §1, except Superiors of religious institutes and of societies of apostolic life. §3. Whatever in the canons, in the context of executive power, is attributed to the diocesan Bishop, is understood to belong only to the diocesan Bishop and to those others in Canon 381 §2 who are equivalent to him, to the exclusion of the Vicar general and the episcopal Vicar except by special mandate.

9. Junno Esteves, "Do Not Hide Reality of Abuse, Pope Tells Religious Orders," *National Catholic Reporter*, July 14, 2022; https://www.ncronline.org/news/do-not-hide-reality-abuse-pope-tells-religious-orders.

10. Esteves, "Do Not Hide Reality of Abuse."

11. Clericalism means an attitude toward clergy/religious characterized by excessive deference and an assumption of their moral superiority. In a culture of clericalism, clerics are put on a pedestal and have a sense of entitlement to special treatment and a privileged position.

12. The term *metropolitan* goes back to the early days of the Church when a Roman organizational model was borrowed by the Church. The word *metropolitan* comes from the Greek words for "mother city." The orig-

inal metropolitan diocese normally had other smaller dioceses divided off from it, so it was in a sense the mother diocese.

13. Pontifical Commission for the Protection of Minors, *Universal Guidelines Framework*, March 2024, 4.3.3; https://acrobat.adobe.com/id/urn:aaid:sc:AP:1ed671aa-794e-468b-b48e-3ddcbd32c38a?comment_id=a54f1bf5-2d22-49a5-bc78-04f75524ecce&showComments=true.

14. *Vademecum* 19. "Even in these cases, however, it is advisable that the Ordinary or Hierarch communicate to the DDF the *notitia de delicto* and the decision made to forego the preliminary investigation due to the manifest lack of the semblance of truth."

15. Pope John Paul II, *motu proprio*, *Sacramentorum Sanctitatis Tutela* (SST) April 30, 2001; *AAS* 93, (2001): 737–39.

16. VELM 6. "The procedural norms referred to in this title concern the conduct referred to in article 1, carried out by: a) Cardinals, Patriarchs, Bishops and Legates of the Roman Pontiff; b) clerics who are, or who have been, the pastoral heads of a particular Church or of an entity assimilated to it, Latin or Oriental, including the Personal Ordinariates, for the acts committed durante munere; c) clerics who are or who have been in the past leaders of a Personal Prelature, for the acts committed durante munere; d) those who are, or who have been, supreme moderators of Institutes of Consecrated Life or of Societies of Apostolic Life of Pontifical right, as well as of monasteries sui iuris, with respect to the acts committed durante munere."

17. Dicastery for the Doctrine of the Faith, *Vademecum*, June 5, 2022, 50 states: "Whenever civil judicial authorities issue a legitimate executive order requiring the surrender of documents regarding cases, or order the judicial seizure of such documents, the Ordinary or Hierarch must cooperate with the civil authorities, always respecting any possible agreements, where they exist. If the legitimacy of such a request or seizure is in doubt, the Ordinary or Hierarch can consult legal experts about available means of recourse. In any case, it is advisable to inform the Papal Representative immediately."

18. CIC 83, c. 22. Civil laws to which the law of the Church yields are to be observed in canon law with the same effects, insofar as they are not contrary to divine law and unless canon law provides otherwise.

19. Cf. Margaret Sharbel Poll, *A Reparation of Harm: A Canonical Analysis of Canon 128 with Reference to Its Common Law Parallels* (Ottawa: Saint Paul University, 2002).

20. Myriam Wijlens, *New Commentary on the Code of Canon Law* (Washington, DC: Canon Law Society of America, 2000), 183.

21. "Bishop Arrieta: How Book VI of Canon Law Has Changed," Vatican News, June 1, 2021, https://www.vaticannews.va/en/vatican-city/news/2021-06/book-vi-vatican-penal-code-apostolic-constitution.html.

22. "Bishop Arrieta: How Book VI of Canon Law Has Changed."

23. The Pontifical Commission for the Protection of Minors', UGF: "Vulnerable Adult."

24. Canon 128. Whoever unlawfully causes harm to another by a juridical act, or indeed by any other act which is malicious or culpable, is obliged to repair the damage done.

CHAPTER 7

1. See CIC 83, cc. 1398, 1395, 1378; VELM; SST.

2. Pope Francis. Letter to the People of God, August 20, 2018, https://www.vatican.va/content/francesco/en/letters/2018/documents/papa-francesco_20180820_lettera-popolo-didio.html.

3. Secretariat of State, Instruction "On the Confidentiality of Legal Proceedings," December 6, 2019, https://www.vatican.va/roman_curia/secretariat_state/2019/documents/rc-seg-st-20191206_rescriptum_en.html.

4. Secretariat of State, "On the Confidentiality of Legal Proceedings," no. 4.

5. See CIC 83, c. 1717 §1; canon 1468 §1 CCEO; SST 10; VELM 3.

6. That is, reported him to the authorities.

7. Congregation for Catholic Education, "Guidelines for the Use of Psychology in the Admission and Formation of Candidates for the Priesthood," *Origins* 38, no. 23 (2008): 360; cc. 984, 240.

8. Canon 1371 §6. A person who neglects to report an offence, when required to do so by a canonical law, is to be punished according to the provision of can. 1336 §§2–4, with the addition of other penalties according to the gravity of the offence, https://www.vatican.va/archive/cod-iuris-canonici/eng/documents/cic_lib6-cann1364-1399_en.html#OFFENCES_AGAINST_CHURCH_AUTHORITIES__.

CHAPTER 8

1. Father Frank Morrisey, OMI, states: "The general legislation of the Church does not provide for circular letters as an authentic source of law. Nevertheless, we find this form used more often in recent years to outline procedures and to indicate new obligations....At times, though, a circular letter will accompany a set of norms on a given subject. An example of this can be found in the letter and norms regarding the procedures to be observed in petitioning the Holy See for a dispensation from priestly obligations. In these and in other similar instances it is quite clear that the norms constitute the legislative portion of the communication; the circular letter explains the intention, spirit, and purpose of the rules." See "Papal and Curial Pronouncements: Their Canonical Significance in Light of the 1983 Code of Canon Law," *The Jurist* 50 (1990): 118.

2. Congregation for the Doctrine of the Faith, *Circular Letter to Help Episcopal Conferences Prepare Guidelines for the Treatment of Cases of Sexual Abuse Against Minors by Clerics*, May 3, 2011.

3. See Carol Glatz, "Days of Covering Up Abuse Allegations Are Over, Says Vatican Adviser," *The Boston Pilot*, May 9, 2019, https://www.thebostonpilot.com/article.php?ID=185023.

4. See Glatz, "Days of Covering Up Abuse Allegations Are Over."

5. See Canon 22. Civil laws, to which the law of the Church yields, are to be observed in canon law with the same effects, insofar as they are not contrary to divine law and unless canon law provides otherwise.

6. Jason Horowitz, "Pope Issues First Rules for Catholic Church Worldwide to Report Sex Abuse," *New York Times*, May 9, 2019, https://www.nytimes.com/2019/05/09/world/europe/pope-francis-abuse-catholic-church.html.

7. Chris McGreal, "Somalian Rape Victim, 13, Stoned to Death," *The Guardian*, November 2, 2008, https://www.theguardian.com/world/2008/nov/03/somalia-rape-amnesty.

8. For example, the Italian privacy law allows a family to decide whether they will report a crime to the police and outsiders

do not have the right to take the case to the police. See "How Italian Data Protection Law Differs from the GDPR," https://www.activemind.legal/law/it-data-protection/.

9. *Vademecum* 50. "Whenever civil judicial authorities issue a legitimate executive order requiring the surrender of documents regarding cases, or order the judicial seizure of such documents, the Ordinary or Hierarch must cooperate with the civil authorities."

10. In the 1917 Code, canon 2404: "Abuse of ecclesiastical power, in the prudent judgment of the Legitimate Superior, shall be punished according to the gravity of the fault, with due regard for the prescriptions of those canons that establish certain penalties for various abuses."

11. The pontifical secret is the highest level of confidentiality in the Church and is one of the most misunderstood concepts in church legislation. The word *secret* has the connotation of "cover-up" and keeping incidents "hidden." It needs to be remembered that the word *secretary* comes from the Latin word *secretum* meaning secret. Secretaries handle the highly confidential information of their employers.

12. Apostolic Penitentiary, "Note of the Apostolic Penitentiary on the Importance of the Internal Forum and the Inviolability of the Sacramental Seal," July 1, 2019, http://press.vatican.va/content/salastampa/it/bollettino/pubblico/2019/07/01/0565/01171.html.

13. See Holy See. *Letter.* N. 484.110, February 26, 2020. "Observations of the Holy See With reference to the Response of the Australian Catholic Bishops' Conference to the Recommendations of the Royal Commission," https://www.catholic.org.au/images/Observations_of_the_Holy_See_to_the_Recommendations_of_the_Royal_Commission.pdf.

14. CIC 83, c. 978 §1. In hearing confessions, the priest is to remember that he is equally a judge and a physician and has been established by God as a minister of divine justice and mercy, so that he has regard for the divine honor and the salvation of souls. §2. In administering the sacrament, the confessor as a minister of the Church is to adhere faithfully to the doctrine of the magisterium and the norms issued by competent authority. CIC 83, c. 980. If the confessor has no doubt about the disposition of the penitent, and the penitent seeks absolution, absolution is to be neither refused nor deferred.

15. Apostolic Penitentiary, "Note of the Apostolic Penitentiary on the Importance of the Internal Forum and the Inviolability of the Sacramental Seal": "In the presence of sins that involve criminal offenses, it is never permissible, as a condition for absolution, to place on the penitent the obligation to turn himself in to civil justice, by virtue of the natural principle, incorporated in every system, according to which '*nemo tenetur se detegere*.'"

16. See Linus Neli, *Delicta Graviora* (Bengaluru, India: ATC Publishers, 2018), 41; Gianpaolo Montini, "La tutela penale del sacramento della penitenza. I delitti nella celebrazione del sacramento (Cann. 1378; 1387; 1388)," in Aa.Vv., *Le sanzioni nella Chiesa. XXIII incontro di studio Abbazia di Maguzzano—Lonato (Brescia) 1-luglio–5 luglio 1996* (Milan: Gruppo Italiano Docenti di Diritto Canónico, 1997), 213–35, here at 226–27.

CHAPTER 9

1. Daniel Kroger, "Scandal," in *Encyclopedia of Catholicism*, ed. Richard McBrien (San Francisco: HarperCollins, 1995), 1165.

2. Joseph Fitzmyer, *First Corinthians: A New Translation with Introduction and Commentary* (New Haven: Yale University Press, 2008), 346.

3. Cf. Rudolf Schnackenburg. *The Moral Teaching of the New Testament* (London: Burns & Oates, 1975), 295.

4. Joseph Fitzmyer. *Romans: A New Translation with Introduction and Commentary* (New York: Doubleday, 1992), 695.

5. Thomas Aquinas, *Summa Theologiae,* II-II, q. 43, a. 1: "dictum vel factum minus rectum praebens occasionem ruinae."

6. "Notion of Scandal," in *New Catholic Encyclopedia*, https://www.newadvent.org/cathen/13506d.htm.

7. Raoul Naz, *Dictionnaire de droit canonique* (Paris: Letouzey et Ane, 1935), 7:877.

8. St. Thomas Aquinas, STh I-II, 71, 6.

9. 1917 CIC, c. 2195, §1. See *The 1917 Pio-Benedictine Code of Canon Law*, trans. Edward Peters (San Francisco: Ignatius Press, 2001). Hereinafter all translations of the 1917 Code are from this source.

10. Susan Mulheron, "Canonical Considerations in Response to Scandal in the Church," in *CLSA Proceedings* (Washington, DC: Canon Law Society of America, 2018), 297–319.

11. William Addis and Thomas Arnold, revised by P. Hallett, *A Catholic Dictionary* (London: Routledge & Kegan Paul, 1951), 727.

12. St. Alphonsus Liguori, *Theologia moralis*, 9th ed. (Bassano: Venetiis Apud Remondini, 1785), Lib II, Tract. III, Cap. II. Dub. V. Art. 1.

13. Juan-Carlos Iscara, "A Moral Primer on Scandals," 2010, http://www.angelusonline.org/index.php/index.php?section=articles&subsection=show_article&article_id=4185.

14. Mulheron, "Canonical Considerations in Response to Scandal in the Church," 302–3.

15. Mulheron, "Canonical Considerations in Response to Scandal in the Church," 297–319.

16. Pope Francis, apostolic constitution *Pascite Gregem Dei* (Tend My Flock), May 23, 2021, which reforms Book VI of the *Code of Canon Law.*

17. Raoul Naz, *Dictionnaire de droit canonique*, 7:877.

18. See T. Lincoln Bouscaren and Adam C. Ellis, *Canon Law: A Text and Commentary* (Milwaukee: Bruce Publishing, 1957), 849.

19. Charles Augustine, *A Commentary on the New Code of Canon Law*, vol. 8 (St. Louis: B. Herder Book Co., 1922), 87.

20. Canon 140. Where there is danger of scandal, especially in public theaters, clerics should avoid shows, dances, and spectacles.

21. Canon 138. Clerics shall entirely abstain from all those things that are indecent to their state; they shall not engage in indecorous arts; they shall abstain from gambling games with risks of money; they shall not carry arms, except when there is just cause for fearing; hunting should not be indulged, and [then] never with clamor; taverns and similar places should never be entered without necessity or another just cause approved by the local Ordinary.

22. Synod of Bishops 1967, "Preface to the Latin Edition," *Code of Canon Law Latin-English Edition* (Washington, DC: Canon Law Society of America, 1983), xx.

23. Canon 1394 §1. Without prejudice to the prescript of canon 194, §1, n. 3, a cleric who attempts marriage, even if only civilly, incurs a *latae sententiae* suspension. If he does not repent after being warned and continues to give scandal, he can be punished

gradually by privations or even by dismissal from the clerical state.

24. Pontifical Council for the Interpretation of Legislative Texts, Declaration, "The Exercise of Holy Order by Priests who Attempted Marriage," in William Woestman, OMI, *Ecclesiastical Sanctions and the Penal Process* (Ottawa: Saint Paul University: 2000), 277–78; *Communicationes* 29 (1997): 17–18.

25. Synod of Bishops 1967, "Preface to the Latin Edition," xxi.

26. Synod of Bishops 1967, "Preface to the Latin Edition," xxii.

27. John Lynch, J. Coriden, T. Green, and D. Heintschel, eds., *The Code of Canon Law: A Text and Commentary* (New York: Paulist Press. 1985), 222. The Viganò case illustrates scandal caused by heresy, schism, and apostasy (c. 1364 §2). Clergy are to make reparation for scandal in canon 1341.

28. Synod of Bishops 1967, "Preface to the Latin Edition," xxii.

29. See cc. 277 §1, 326 §1, 696 §1, 703, 1132, 1184, 1311, 1318, 1324, 1328, 1335, 1339, 1341, 1344, 1347, 1349, 1352, 1357, 1361, 1364, 1378, 1394, 1395, and 1399.

30. See cc. 1318, 1328, 1339, 1341, 1344, 1347, 1352, 1357, 1361, 1364, 1394, 1395, 1399.

31. Changed canons in Book VI mentioning scandal include cc. 1311, 1324, 1335, 1349. Note that canon 1378 is now the former canon 1389.

32. Pope John Paul II, *Code of Canons of the Eastern Churches Latin-English*, ed. and trans. Canon Law Society of America (Washington, DC: Canon Law Society of America, 1990).

33. Fred Easton, J. Faris, and J. Abbass, eds., *A Practical Commentary to the Code of Canons of the Eastern Churches* (Montreal: Wilson and Lafleur, 2019), 2518.

34. John A. Alesandro, et al. *Jurisprudence: A Collection of U.S. Tribunal Decisions* (Washington, DC: Canon Law Society of America, 2002), 457. Cf. A. Brown sentence, January 5, 2000, 457.

35. John Beal, James Coriden, Thomas Green, and Sharon Holland, *New Commentary on the Code of Canon Law* (Mahwah, NJ: Paulist Press, 2000), 873.

36. J. Arias in E. Caparros, M. Thériault, and J. Thorn, eds., *Code of Canon Law Annotated*, 2nd ed. (Montreal: Wilson & LaFleur, 2004), 1029, 884.

37. "Church Denies Gotti a Funeral Mass," CBS News, June 15, 2002, https://www.cbsnews.com/news/church-denies-gotti-a-funeral-mass/.

38. Canon 1347 §2. The offender is said to have purged the contempt if he or she has truly repented of the offence and has made suitable reparation for the scandal and harm, or at least seriously promised to make it.

39. Canon 128. Whoever unlawfully causes harm to another by a juridical act, or indeed by any other act which is malicious or culpable, is obliged to repair the damage done.

40. Mario Francesco Card. Pompedda, Apostolic Signatura, June 22, 2002. William Daniel, *Ministerium Iustitiae* (Montreal: Gratianus, 2011), 312; "cum scandalo": *requiritur ut plerique, qui personam eiusque munus activitatemque noscunt, impressionem negativam patiantur, idest ad male quodammodo inducantur.*

41. See Raymond Burke, Canon 915: "The discipline regarding the denial of Holy Communion to those obstinately persevering in manifest grave sin," https://www.ewtn.com/catholicism/library/discipline-regarding-the-denial-of-holy-communion-to-those-obstinately-persevering-in-manifest-grave-sin-1230. The article is also in *Periodica de re canonica* 96 (2007): 3–58.

42. Peter Lah, "The Scandal of Secrecy," *Gregorianum* 2 (2020): 418.

43. Mulheron, "Canonical Considerations in Response to Scandal in the Church," 305.

CHAPTER 10

1. Pontifical Commission for the Protection of Minors, *Universal Guidelines Framework*, March 2024; https://acrobat.adobe.com/id/urn:aaid:sc:AP:1ed671aa-794e-468b-b48e-3ddcbd32c38a?comment_id=a54f1bf5-2d22-49a5-bc78-04f75524ecce&showComments=true.

2. Royal Commission of Inquiry into Abuse in Care, *Whanaketia: Through Pain and Trauma, from Darkness to Light, Whakairihia ki te tihi o Maungārongo*, 204; https://www.abuseincare.org.nz/reports/whanaketia/part-4/chapter-2-2/.

3. Samuel Fernández, "Victims Are Not Guilty! Spiritual Abuse and Ecclesiastical Responsibility," *Religions* 13, no. 5 (2022): 1, https://doi.org/10.3390/rel13050427. "Spiritual abuse in the Catholic context is the misuse of spiritual authority that controls the victim to the point that the abuser, taking the place of God, obstructs or nullifies the victim's spiritual freedom. This type of abuse is perpetrated by an individual or a system supported by the Church as trustworthy. Hence, it always has an ecclesial dimension. This kind of abuse can harm the person at the spiritual, psychological, and physical levels."

4. Lisa Oakley and Justin Humphrey, *Escaping the Maze of Spiritual Abuse: Creating Healthy Christian Cultures* (London: SPCK, 2019), 151.

5. Pam Walsh, "Seminar on Trauma," Christchurch: Tribunal of the Catholic Church, March 23, 2024.

6. Walsh, "Seminar on Trauma."

7. "Kerala Nun Rape Case: Bishop Franco Mulakkal Raped the Victim in the Same Room 13 Times Between 2014 and 2016," in Mirrornownews.com, September 22, 2018, https://www.timesnownews.com/mirror-now/in-focus/article/kerala-nun-rape-case-jalandharbishop-franco-mulakkal-raped-victim-same-room-13-times-remand-report/288455; full details and a thorough analysis of the case are in Rocio Figueroa, Aton Hungyo, and David Tombs, "'If People in the Church Knew': Purity, Stigma and Victim-Blaming." *The Canonist* 14, no. 2 (2023): 280–91.

8. Catholic News Service, "Indian priest, witness against bishop accused of rape, found dead," in Global Sisters Report, October 22, 2018, https://www.globalsistersreport.org/news/equality/indian-priest-witness-against-bishop-accused-rape-found-dead-55533.

9. Nidhi Suresh, "Power, Lust and the Church: Mulakkal Verdict Brings Focus Back on Sex Abuse in Convents Despite Checks," Newslaundry.com, January 19, 2022; https://www.newslaundry.com/2022/01/19/power-lust-and-church-mulakkal-verdict-brings-focus-back-on-sex-abuse-in-convents-despite-checks.

10. Suresh, "Power, Lust and the Church."

11. Suresh, "Power, Lust and the Church."

12. Diana Montagna, "'Descent into Hell': An Alleged Rupnik Victim Speaks Out," *The Pillar*, December 19, 2022, https://www.pillarcatholic.com/p/descent-into-hell-an-alleged-rupnik-victim-speaks-out.

13. Salvatore Cernuzio, "Doctrine of Faith Reviews Rupnik Case Documentation As Investigation Continues," Vatican News, February 21, 2024, https://www.vaticannews.va/en/vatican-city/news/2024-02/dicastery-doctrine-faith-marko-rupnik-investigation-update.html.

14. Archbishop Denis Hart, quoted in Stephen E. de Weger and Jodi Death. "Clergy Sexual Misconduct against Adults in the Roman Catholic Church: The Misuse of Professional and Spiritual Power in the Sexual Abuse of Adults," *Journal for the Academic Study of Religion,* 130.

15. Michael Morrah, "Vatican Orders Investigation into Christchurch Catholic Group Over Allegations of Abuse, Unauthorised Exorcisms," Newshub, November 14, 2023; https://www.newshub.co.nz/home/new-zealand/2023/11/vatican-orders-investigation-into-christchurch-catholic-group-over-allegations-of-abuse-unauthorised-exorcisms.html.

16. Rachel Maher, "Catholic Church Accused of Performing Unlicensed Exorcisms," *New Zealand Herald*, July 26, 2023; https://www.nzherald.co.nz/nz/catholic-church-accused-of-performing-unlicensed-exorcisms/HS2LQHBQA5GZPHMVT22JI3XPTQ/.

17. Congregation for Divine Worship and the Discipline of the Sacraments, *De Exorcismis et Supplicationibus Quibusdam, editio typica* (Vatican City: Libreria Editrice Vaticana, 2021).

18. See https://www.usccb.org/prayer-and-worship/sacraments-and-sacramentals/sacramentals-blessings/exorcism.

19. Juan Arrieta, *Code of Canon Law Annotated*, 4th ed. (Montreal: Wilson & Lafleur, 2004), 1096.

20. See c. 977. The absolution of an accomplice in a sin against the sixth commandment of the Decalogue is invalid except in danger of death.

21. See Substantive Norms, Art. 4 §1. The more grave delicts against the sanctity of the Sacrament of Penance reserved to the judgment of the Congregation for the Doctrine of the Faith are: 1/ the absolution of an accomplice in a sin against the sixth commandment of the Decalogue, mentioned in can. 1384 CIC and in can. 1457 CCEO; 4/ the solicitation to a sin against the sixth commandment of the Decalogue in the act, on the occasion, or under the pretext of confession, as mentioned in can. 1385 CIC and in can. 1458 CCEO, if it is directed to sinning with the confessor himself. See https://www.vatican.va/roman_curia/congregations/cfaith/documents/rc_con_cfaith_doc_20211011_norme-delittiriservati-cfaith_en.html.

22. Dicastery of Legislative Texts, *Penal Sanctions in the Church*, 128, https://www.delegumtextibus.va/content/dam/testilegislativi/TESTI%20NORMATIVI/Testi%20Norm%20CIC/Libro%20VI/LibroVIsussidio/Penal%20sanctions%20User%20guide.pdf.

23. Dicastery of Legislative Texts, *Penal Sanctions in the Church*, 129.

24. Council of Trent, session 24, Decretum de Reformatione, canon 3, in N. Tanner, ed., *Decrees of the Ecumenical Councils*, vol. 2 (Washington, DC: Sheed and Ward, 1990), 761–63.

25. Charles Augustine, *A Commentary on the New Code of Canon Law*, vol. 8 (St. Louis: Herder, 1919), 506.

26. R. P. Beste, OSB, *Introductio in Codicem* (Collegeville: St. John's Abbey, 1946), 995.

27. *CCC* §1548. In the ecclesial service of the ordained minister, it is Christ himself who is present to his Church as Head of his Body, Shepherd of his flock, high priest of the redemptive sacrifice, Teacher of Truth. This is what the Church means by saying that the priest, by virtue of the sacrament of Holy Orders, acts in persona *Christi Capitis. CCC* §1552. The ministerial priesthood has the task not only of representing Christ—

Head of the Church—before the assembly of the faithful, but also of acting in the name of the whole Church when presenting to God the prayer of the Church, and above all when offering the Eucharistic sacrifice. Cf. LG 10; SC 33; PO 2, 6; Canons 265, 281.

28. See *User Guide* 136. *Illegitimate exercise of the sacred ministry* (c. 1389). The last canon of the section on delicts against the sacraments contains a provision of a general nature which includes any other conduct not explicitly mentioned in the previous canons of the entire title III (cf. nn. 116–135) which in any case represents an illegitimate exercise of a priestly function or other sacred ministry. This is therefore a broad category, open to very different delicts, which include violations of the preceptive liturgical provisions on the manner and conditions of celebrating the sacraments, the use of formulas other than those permitted in the liturgy, etc. See *User Guide* 151. *Public sin against the sixth commandment* (c. 1395 §2) defines as a delict the sin against the sixth commandment of the Decalogue committed publicly by a cleric, secular or religious. In this way, autonomy has been granted, as a separate offence.

29. See c. 1361 §4. Remission must not be granted until, in the prudent judgement of the Ordinary, the offender has repaired any harm caused. The offender may be urged to make such reparation or restitution by one of the penalties mentioned in c. 1336 §§2–4; the same applies also when the offender is granted remission of a censure under c. 1358 §1.

30. See Arrieta, *Code of Canon Law Annotated.*

31. Congregation for the Doctrine of the Faith, "Sacramentorum Sanctitatis Tutela, *Revised Norms*," https://www.vatican.va/resources/resources_introd-storica_en.html.

32. Pope Francis, *motu proprio, Come una Madre Amorevole*, "As a Loving Mother," June 4, 2016, https://www.vatican.va/content/francesco/en/motu_proprio/documents/papa-francesco-motu-proprio_20160604_come-una-madre-amorevole.html.

33. Myriam Wijlens, "From Darkness into Light: Canonical Consideration for Church Leaders on Spiritual Abuse," in S. M. Attard and J. A. Berry, eds., *Fidelis et Verax: Essays in Honour of His Grace Mgr Charles J. Scicluna on the Tenth Anniversary of His Episcopal Ordination* (Malta: Kite Group, 2022), 461.

34. Junno Esteves, "Purging Silence: Vatican Expands Abuse Prevention to Lay Movements," Cruxnow, June 25, 2019, https://cruxnow.com/vatican/2019/06/25/purging-silence-vatican-expands-abuse-prevention-to-lay-movements/.

35. See c. 679. When a most grave cause demands it, a diocesan bishop can prohibit a member of a religious institute from residing in the diocese if his or her major superior, after having been informed, has neglected to make provision; moreover, the matter is to be referred immediately to the Holy See.

36. See Wijlens, "From Darkness into Light," 462.

37. Pope Francis, *motu proprio, De Concordia inter Codices*, May 31, 2016, *AAS* 108 (2016): 696.

38. Pope Francis, *motu proprio, Authenticum Charismatis*, amending c. 579 of the *Codex Iuris Canonici*, https://www.vatican.va/content/francesco/de/motu_proprio/documents/papa-francesco-motu-proprio-20201101_authenticumcharismatis.html.

39. Pope Francis. *Praedicate Evangelium*, March 19, 2022. https://press.vatican.va/content/salastampa/it/bollettino/pubblico/2022/03/19/0189/00404.html. This document

reflects changes made to the apostolic constitution *Pastor Bonus* (PB). In this document, the Congregation for Institutes of Consecrated Life was changed to the Dicastery for Institutes of Consecrated Life and Societies of Apostolic Life.

40. Wijlens, "From Darkness into Light," 466.

41. Wijlens, "From Darkness into Light," 467.

42. See cc. 300, 312.

43. See c. 299.

44. See cc. 396 §1, 397 §1.

45. See c. 397 §2.

46. See c. 683 §2.

47. Wijlens, "From Darkness into Light," 481.

CHAPTER 11

1. See c. 17. Ecclesiastical laws are to be understood according to the proper meaning of the words considered in their text and context. If the meaning remains doubtful or obscure, there must be recourse to parallel places, if there be any, to the purpose and circumstances of the law, and to the mind of the legislator. See John Beal, "The 1962 Instruction *Crimen Sollicitationis:* Caught Red-Handed or Handed a Red Herring?," *Studia Canonica* 41 (2007): 201.

2. Popes granted dispensations from priestly celibacy after 1749, when Pope Benedict XIV reserved to himself the right to grant these dispensations.

3. In 1967, the Synod of Bishops enunciated ten principles for the revision of the Code of Canon Law. Principle 2 stated that the Code would incorporate all such norms as are necessary for making clear the provisions of the internal forum in so far as the salvation of souls demands. Principle 9 stated that it is generally agreed that penal laws be *ferendae sententiae*, inflicted only *in foro externo,* and remitted likewise only *in foro externo.* As for penal laws *latae sententiae*, while the abolition of all of these has been proposed by not a few canonists, we suggest that they be reduced to the smallest possible number and concern only the gravest of crimes. See Pontifical Commission for the Revision of the Code of Canon Law, "Principia Quae Codicis Iuris Canonici Recognitionem Dirigant," *Communicationes* I (1969): 82.

4. See Norms *Regulae servandae,* in Edward M. Lohse, "The Origin and Nature of the Suspension *Ad Cautelam* of Article 4 of the 1980 *Normae Procedurales* for Dispensations from Celibacy," *Periodica* 95 (2006): 71; cf. *Canon Law Digest* 1, 812–33.

5. See Edward M. Lohse, "Schema on Priests Who Had Left Ministry," *De Sacerdotibus Lapsis*, June 16, 1962, 69.

6. During the debate on the life and ministry of priests, the General Secretary of the Council read a letter from Pope Paul VI recommending that the issue of priestly celibacy not be addressed by the Council. The Council Fathers applauded this move. Pope Paul VI stated on October 11, 1965: "It is not suitable to have a public debate on this subject which requires not only to preserve this ancient, holy and providential law of priestly celibacy as far as we can, but to reinforce the observance of it by reminding the priests of the Roman Church of the causes and reasons which, particularly today, make one consider this law of celibacy very suitable because through it priests can devote all their love solely to Christ and give themselves completely to the service of souls." Cf. *Canon Law Digest* 6, 231–32.

7. Sacred Congregation of the Holy Office, circular letter, *Litterae Circulares et Normae ad Causas Parandas de Sacra Ordinatione Eiusdemque Oneribus*, February 2,

1964, in X. Ochoa, *Leges Ecclesiasticae post Codicem Iuris Canonici Editae*, III, *Leges Annis* 1959–1968 *Editae* (Rome: Commentarium pro Religiosis, 1972), no. 3162, coll. 4463, quoted in Lohse, "Schema on Priests Who Had Left Ministry," 76.

8. Pope Paul VI, *motu proprio*, *De Episcoporum Muneribus*, June 15, 1966, *AAS* 58 (1966): 470.

9. Pope Paul VI, encyclical letter, *Sacerdotalis Caelibatus*, June 24, 1967, *AAS* 59 (1967): 657–97.

10. Sacred Congregation for the Doctrine of the Faith, "Reduction to the Lay State: Procedural Norms," *AAS* 63 (1971): 303–8; cf. *Canon Law Digest* 7, 110–17. The norms were accompanied by a "Circular Letter to Ordinaries," *AAS* 63 (1971): 309. An official interpretation of the norms was given by the Sacred Congregation for the Doctrine of the Faith, "Reduction to the Lay State: Procedural Norms Interpretation," see *Canon Law Digest* 7, 121–24.

11. See 1917 Code c. 214 §1. A cleric who, coerced by grave fear, receives sacred ordination, and does not later, once the fear has passed, ratify that ordination at least tacitly by the exercise of orders, [and] wanting by such an act to subject himself to clerical obligations, is returned to the lay state by sentence of a judge, upon legitimate proof of coercion and lack of ratification, [by which sentence] all obligations of celibacy and canonical hours cease. §2: The coercion and lack of ratification must be proved according to the norm of canons 1993–1998. English translation *The 1917 Pio-Benedictine Code of Canon Law*, trans. Edward N. Peters (San Francisco: Ignatius Press, 2001); hereafter the translation of the canons of the 19I7 Code will be from this source. Holy Office, Declaration, *Declaratio Quoad Interpretationem Quarundam Dispositionum, Quae Normis, Die XlII Ianuarii 1971 Editis, Statuae Sunt*, June 26, 1972, *AAS* 64 (1972): 641–43. The 1970 norms for dispensations were clarified by the Holy Office in 1971.

12. See Sacred Congregation for the Doctrine of the Faith, response, June 26, 1978, *Canon Law Digest* 9, 1001–2.

13. Official of the Congregation for the Clergy, Press Conference, in Anthony P. Kowalski, *Married Catholic Priests, Their History, Their Journeys, Their Reflections* (New York: Crossroad, 2005), www.jknirp.com/kowal.htm.

14. Gian Paolo Salvini, SJ, "Priests Who 'Desert,' Priests Who 'Come Back,'" April 21, 2007, http://chiesa.espresso.repubblica.it/articolo/169450?eng=y. Of these priests, 11,213 returned to active ministry.

15. Pope John Paul II, "Letter to Priests," April 8, 1979, Holy Thursday, http://w2.vatican.va/content/john-paul-ii/en/letters/1979/documents/hf_jp-ii_let_19790409_sacerdoti-giovedi-santo.html.

16. Pope John Paul II, "Letter to Priests."

17. Sacred Congregation for the Doctrine of the Faith, *Letter to All Local Ordinaries and General Moderators of Clerical Religious Communities Regarding the Dispensation of Priests from Celibacy*, October 14, 1980; Decree, *Normae Procedurales, AAS* 72 (1980): 1132–37, http://www.vatican.va/roman_curia/congregations/cfaith/documents/rc_con_cfaith_doc_19801014_dispensatione-a-coelibatu_en.html; see *Canon Law Digest* 9, 92–99. Sacred Congregation for the Doctrine of the Faith, circular letter, *Per Litteras*, 1132–35, in Lohse, "The Origin and Nature of the Suspension *ad cautelam* of article 4 of the 1980 *Normae Procedurales* for Dispensations from Celibacy," *Periodica* 95 (2006): 85.

18. Lohse, "The Origin and Nature of the Suspension," 87.

19. Laurie Goldstein and David H. Halbfinger, "Church Office Failed to Act on Abuse Scandal," *New York Times*, July 2, 2010.

20. They were, in fact, five priests from the United States of America.

21. Congregation for Divine Worship and the Discipline of the Sacraments, "Letter to the Presidents of the Conferences of Bishops and to the Superiors General," Protocol No. 1080/05, July 13, 2005; See William H. Woestman, *The Sacrament of Orders and the Clerical State* (Ottawa: St Paul University, 2006), 456.

22. Congregation for the Clergy, "To the Eminent and Most Excellent Ordinaries at Their Sees," Prot. No. 2009/0556, April 18, 2009; Congregation for the Clergy, "Quicker Administrative Procedure for Laicising some Priests," *Origins* 39 (2009): 81–86, http://originsplus.catholicnews.com/databases/origins/39/06/3906.pdf.

23. Cardinal Dias, "Special Faculties to the Congregation for the Evangelization of Peoples," Prot. No. 0579/09, March 31, 2009, *Studies in Church Law* 5 (2009): 69–78.

24. See Brendan Daly, *Canon Law in Action* (Sydney: Saint Paul Publications, 2015), 202–16; "Sexual Abuse and Canon Law," *Compass* 43, no. 3 (2009): 33–40.

25. Nicholas P. Cafardi, "The Scandal of Secrecy," *Commonweal*, July 25, 2010, https://www.commonwealmagazine.org/scandal-secrecy.

26. Pope Benedict XVI, *Substantive Norms on Graviora Delicata*, May 21, 2010, http://www.vatican.va/resources/resources_norme_en.html. Pope Benedict XVI reaffirmed this in 2010, explaining that "the norms issued in 1922 were an update, in light of the Code of Canon Law of 1917, of the apostolic constitution *Sacramentorum Poenitentiae* promulgated by Pope Benedict XIV in 1741."

27. Cafardi, "The Scandal of Secrecy."

28. Pope John Paul II, apostolic exhortation, *Pastores Dabo Vobis*, March 25, 1992, *AAS* 84 (1992): 658–804; English translation in *Origins*, 21 (1992–1993): 717, 719–59. This apostolic exhortation on the formation of priests was entitled *Pastores Dabo Vobis* (I will give you Shepherds); the Dogmatic Constitution of the Church of Vatican II was named *Lumen Gentium* (The Light of the Nations).

29. Sacred Congregation of the Holy Office, Instruction, "On the Manner of Proceeding in Cases involving the Crime of Solicitation," *Crimen Sollicitationis*, http://www.vatican.va/resources/resources_crimen-Sollicitationis-1962_en.html. The term *crimen pessimum* ["the foulest crime"] is here understood to mean any external obscene act, gravely sinful, perpetrated or attempted by a cleric in any way whatsoever with a person of his own sex. n. 72: Everything laid down up to this point concerning the crime of solicitation is also valid, with the change only of those things which the nature of the matter necessarily requires, for the *crimen pessimum*, should some cleric (God forbid) happen to be accused of it before the local Ordinary, except that the obligation of denunciation [imposed] *by the positive law of the Church* [does not apply] unless perhaps it was joined with the crime of solicitation in sacramental confession. In determining penalties against delinquents of this type, in addition to what has been stated above, Canon 2359 §2 is also to be taken into consideration. n. 73: Equated with the *crimen pessimum,* with regard to penal effects, is any external obscene act, gravely sinful, perpetrated or attempted by a cleric in any way with pre-adolescent children (*impuberes*)

of either sex or with brute animals (*bestialitas*). n. 74: Against clerics guilty of these crimes, if they are exempt religious—and unless the crime of solicitation takes place at the same time—Religious Superiors also can proceed, according to the sacred canons and their proper constitutions, either administratively or judicially. However, they must always communicate a sentence rendered, or an administrative decision in those cases which are more grave, to the Supreme Congregation of the Holy Office. The Superiors of a non-exempt religious can proceed only administratively. In the case where the guilty party has been expelled from religious life, the expulsion has no effect until it has been approved by the Holy Office. http://www.vatican.va/resources/resources_crimen-Sollicitationis-1962_en.html.

30. Cafardi, "The Scandal of Secrecy."

31. "The 1962 instruction has become known in the press as *Crimen Sollicitationis,* where it has had a life of its own. In 2003, plaintiffs' attorneys Daniel J. Shea and Carmen Durso sent a copy of this newly uncovered 'secret' Vatican document to the U.S. Attorney in Boston, alleging that *Crimen* provided proof that the Vatican had orchestrated a worldwide cover-up of clergy sexual abuse of children. Shea stated that *Crimen* was 'not just a smoking gun but a nuclear bombshell.' The story made headlines around the world"; in Cafardi, "The Scandal of Secrecy."

32. Cafardi, "The Scandal of Secrecy."

33. "The Didache," 6, translation in Nicholas Cafardi, *Before Dallas* (New York: Paulist Press, 2008), 1.

34. Polycarp "Letter to the Philippians," quoted in Charles Scicluna, "Sexual Abuse of Children and Young People by Catholic Priests and Religious: Description of the Problem from a Church Perspective," in *Sexual Abuse in the Catholic Church: Scientific and Legal Perspectives*, ed. R. Hanson, F. Pfafflin, and M. Lutz (Vatican City: Libreria Editrice Vaticana, 2004), 14.

35. Athenagoras of Athens, "A Plea for Christians," chapter 34, "The Vast Differences in Morals between Christians and Their Accusers," trans. B. Pratten, http://www.earlychristianwritings.com/athenagoras.html: "For those who have set up a market for fornication and established infamous resorts for the young for every kind of vile pleasure...who do not abstain even from males, males with males committing shocking abominations, outraging all the noblest and comeliest bodies in all sorts of ways, so dishonouring the fair workmanship of God."

36. Cafardi, *Before Dallas*, 2.

37. See Council of Neocaesarea, Canon I in *The Nicene and Post-Nicene Fathers* Second Series, vol. 14, *The Seven Ecumenical Councils* (Grand Rapids: Eerdmans, 1983), 79.

38. Pope Benedict XV, *motu proprio, Cum Iuris Canonici, AAS* 9 (1917): 484 in Francis Morrisey, OMI, "Papal and Curial Pronouncements: Their Canonical Significance in Light of the 1983 Code of Canon Law," *The Jurist* 50 (1990): 115–16; cf. *Canon Law Digest* 1, 56.

39. Morrisey, "Papal and Curial Pronouncements," 116.

40. All translations of canons of the 1983 Code of Canon Law are from Canon Law Society of America at https://www.vatican.va/archive/cod-iuris-canonici/cic_index_en.html.

41. Canon 34 §2: The ordinances of instructions do not derogate from laws. If these ordinances cannot be reconciled with the prescripts of laws, they lack all force. §3: Instructions cease to have force not only by explicit or implicit revocation of the competent authority who issued them or of the

superior of that but also by the cessation of the law for whose clarification or execution they were given. Michael Moodie stated: "An instruction is a handbook or guideline for those whose responsibilities involve the application of the law in concrete circumstances… [they] are not merely suggestions; they oblige those who are responsible for the application of the law." Michael Moodie in John Beal, James Coriden, and Thomas Green, eds., *New Commentary on the Code of Canon Law* (Mahwah, NJ: Paulist Press, 2000), 100.

42. Sacred Congregation of the Holy Office, Instruction, "On the Manner of Proceeding in Cases Involving the Crime of Solicitation," *Crimen Sollicitationis*.

43. Pope John Paul II, *motu proprio*, *Sacramentorum Sanctitatis Tutela*, 2001.

44. John Huels, in Moodie et al., *New Commentary on the Code of Canon Law*, 57 n. 37.

45. Canon 1362 §1. Prescription extinguishes a criminal action after three years unless it concerns: 1/ delicts reserved to the Congregation for the Doctrine of the Faith; 2/ an action arising from the delicts mentioned in canons 1394, 1395, 1397, and 1398, which have a prescription of five years; 3/ delicts which are not punished in the common law if particular law has established another period for prescription. §2. Prescription runs from the day on which the delict was committed or, if the delict is continuous or habitual, from the day on which it ceased.

46. See Juan Arrieta, "Cardinal Ratzinger and the Revision of the Canonical Penal Law System: A Crucial Role," http://www.vatican.va/resources/resources_arrieta-20101202_en.html.

47. Arrieta, "Cardinal Ratzinger and the Revision of the Canonical Penal Law System."

48. Cf. *Communicationes* XIV (1982), 85. Hence for precisely this reason, not even the new "Norms for Dispensation from Priestly Celibacy" of October 14, 1980, *AAS* 72 (1980): 1136–37 made reference to this procedure, which the previous Norms of 1971 [*AAS* 63 (1971): 303–8)] by contrast had allowed.

49. Canon 6 §1. When this Code takes force, the following are abrogated: 1/ the Code of Canon Law promulgated in 1917; 2/ other universal or particular laws contrary to the prescripts of this Code unless other provision is expressly made for particular laws; 3/ any universal or particular penal laws whatsoever issued by the Apostolic See unless they are contained in this Code; 4/ other universal disciplinary laws regarding matter which this Code completely reorders. §2. Insofar as they repeat the former law, the canons of this Code must be assessed also in accord with canonical tradition.

50. Pope John Paul II, apostolic constitution on the Roman Curia *Pastor Bonus*, June 28, 1988, *AAS* 80 (1988): 841–924.

51. Pope Paul VI, apostolic constitution *Regimini Ecclesiae Universae*, August 15, 1967, http://w2.vatican.va/content/paul-vi/la/apost_constitutions/documents/hf_p-vi_apc_19670815_regimini-ecclesiae-universae.html.

52. Canon Law Society of America Newsletter, quoted in Tom Doyle, "The 1922 Instruction and the 1962 Instruction *Crimen Sollicitationis*," promulgated by the Vatican, October 3, 2008. See Australian Royal Commission papers and quoted by Daly in *The Canonist* 7, no. 1 (2016): 22.

53. http:///www.childabuseroyalcommission.gov.au/exhibits/bb3eaadf-9283-41ef-9694-e560738d186a/case-study-14,-June-2014,-sydney.

54. Tom Kington, "Vatican Leaks: No Respite for Pope Benedict As More Documents Published," *The Guardian*, June 3, 2012, http://www.theguardian.com/world/2012/jun/03/vatican-leaks-pope-benedict-documents.

55. Pope Francis, "Christmas Greeting to Curia Officials," *Origins* 44 (2015): 507. http://originsplus.catholicnews.com/databases/origins/44/31/4431.pdf.

56. See Congregation for the Doctrine of the Faith, The Norms of the Motu Proprio, *Sacramentorum Sanctitatis Tutela* (2001), "Historical Introduction," https://www.vatican.va/resources/resources_introd-storica_en.html.

57. Letter sent to all Bishops and other Ordinaries and Hierarchs of the Catholic Church explaining New Norms for Church Handling of Certain Grave Offenses *(graviora delicta)*, *AAS* 93 (2001): 737–39.

58. *Interview of Msgr. Charles Scicluna conducted by Gianni Cardinale on the Strictness of the Church in Cases of Paedophilia*, March 13, 2012, http://www.vatican.va/resources/resources_mons-scicluna-2010_en.html.

59. Kieran Tapsell, "Address of Rev. Professor Ian Waters, The Pumphouse Hotel, Melbourne, October 2014," in Kieran Tapsell, *Potiphar's Wife: The Vatican's Secret and Child Sexual Abuse* (Adelaide: ATF Press, 2014), 6.

60. Quoted by Tom Doyle, "The 1922 Instruction and the 1962 Instruction *Crimen Sollicitationis*, promulgated by the Vatican," October 3, 2008. See Australian Royal Commission papers and quoted by Daly in *The Canonist* 7, no.1 (2016): 22.

61. "Francis Cardinal George, Archbishop of Chicago, testified in 2008 that the document was known to him as a seminarian and that it was studied as part of a course on moral theology: Q. Did you know that the Office of the Holy See through the Congregation for the Doctrine of the Faith had implemented a protocol, and an instruction to all the superiors across the world regarding solicitation in the confessional? A. What was the year of that protocol, please? Q. The year the protocol was issued was 1962. A. Oh. Okay. Then yes. Q. My question goes to 2002, and did you know that such a protocol had been issued and disseminated by the Office of the Holy See to the superiors? A. Yes. I was a seminarian in 1962 and in moral theology class that was the document that was given us when we discussed the sacrament of Penance." (Deposition in Doe et al vs. Archdiocese of Chicago, Jan. 30, 2008, 24–25).

62. Congregation for the Doctrine of the Faith, *Historical Introduction*, http://www.vatican.va/resources/resources_introd-storica_en.html.

63. See Professor Ian Waters, "The Role of Church Law in Child Abuse Issue: Help or Hindrance?," YouTube, October 29, 2014, https://www.youtube.com/watch?v=7_jaQKTe4VY.

64. Professor Gerardo Nunez, "La Competencia penal de la Congregación para la Doctrina de La Fe, Comentario al motu proprio, *Sacramentorum Sanctitatis Tutela*," *Ius Canonicum* 43, no. 85 (2003): 387, in Tapsell, *Potiphar's Wife*.

65. Ian Waters, "The Role of Church Law in the Child Abuse Issue: Help or Hindrance?" YouTube, October 29, 2014, https://www.youtube.com/watch?v=7_jaQKTe4VY.

66. Secretariat of State, Instruction, *Secreta Continere*, February 4, 1974, *AAS* 66 (1974): 89–92; *Canon Law Digest* 8, 207–10.

67. Beal, "The 1962 Instruction *Crimen Sollicitationis*," 231.

68. Secretariat of State, 89–92; *Canon Law Digest* 8, 209.

69. Pope John Paul II, *motu proprio, Sacramentorum Sanctitatis Tutela, AAS* 93 (2001): 737–39.

70. Pope Benedict XVI revised the *2001 motu proprio* in 2010 giving a victim twenty years after reaching the age of eighteen to complain, and Article 30 of the revised norms provides that: § 1. Cases of this nature are subject to the pontifical secret. §2. Whoever has violated the secret, whether deliberately (*ex dolo*) or through grave negligence, and has caused some harm to the accused or to the witnesses, is to be punished with an appropriate penalty by the higher *turnus* at the insistence of the injured party or even *ex officio.* Footnote 41 then refers to Art. 1 §4 of *Secreta Continere.* The 2010 revision extended the pontifical secret to cover cases involving clergy sexual abuse of intellectually disabled adults and the possession of child pornography. Those who are bound by the pontifical secret are obliged to keep it "forever."

71. Aurelius Yangas, "De Crimine Pessimo et de Compentia S. Officii Relate ad Illud," in *Revista española de derecho canónico* 1 (1946): 433–37, quoted in Beal, "The 1962 Instruction *Crimen Sollicitationis*," 207.

72. Cardinal Castrillón Hoyos, Letter to Irish Bishops January 31, 1997, quoted in Tapsell, *Potiphar's Wife.*

73. Cardinal Castrillón Hoyos, Letter to Bishop Pierre Pican: "Vous avez bien agi et je me réjouis d'avoir un confrère dans l'épiscopat qui aux yeux de l'histoire et de tous les autres évêques du monde aura préféré la prison plutôt que de dénoncer son fils-prêtre." The priest was later sentenced to eighteen years in jail for the rape of the boy and the sexual assault of ten other boys.

74. CDF, *Letter to assist Bishops Conferences*, May 3, 2011, http://www.vatican.va/roman_curia/congregations/cfaith/documents/rc_con_cfaith_doc_20110503_abuso-minori_en.html.

75. Gordon Read, "Further Developments Concerning *Graviora Delicta* Cases," in *The Canon Law Society of Great Britain and Ireland Newsletter* 183, September 2015, 42–46.

76. "Proposals accepted by Pope Francis Regarding Allegations of Abuse of Office by a Bishop When Connected to the Abuse of Minors," in Sharon Euart, RSM, ed., *Roman Replies and CLSA Advisory Opinions 2015* (Washington, DC: Canon Law Society of America, 2015), 66.

77. Canon 401 §2. A diocesan bishop who has become less able to fulfil his office because of ill health or some other grave cause is earnestly requested to present his resignation from office.

78. Article 6 includes cardinals, patriarchs, bishops and legates of the Roman Pontiff; and clerics who are, or who have been, the pastoral heads of a particular Church or of an entity assimilated to it, Latin or Oriental, including the Personal Ordinariates, leaders of a Personal Prelature, Supreme Moderators of Institutes of Consecrated Life or of Societies of Apostolic Life of Pontifical Right, as well as of monasteries *sui iuris* for acts committed *durante munere*; and lay faithful who are or who were Moderators of international associations of the faithful for acts committed *durante munere.*

79. Pope John Paul II, "Address to the Cardinals of the United States," *Origins* 31 (2002): 759.

CHAPTER 12

1. See "Excerpts from the Grand Jury Report on Child Sex Abuse in 6 Pennsylvania Roman Catholic Dioceses," LancasterOnline, August 19, 2018, https://lancasteronline.com/news/local/excerpts-from-the-grand-jury-report-on-child-sex-abuse/article_372db51a-a253-11e8-87fb-1fefdd01c495.html.

2. See Karen J. Terry et al., "The Causes and Context of Sexual Abuse of Minors by Catholic Priests in the United States, 1950–2010," May 2011, https://www.usccb.org/sites/default/files/issues-and-action/child-and-youth-protection/upload/The-Causes-and-Context-of-Sexual-Abuse-of-Minors-by-Catholic-Priests-in-the-United-States-1950-2010.pdf.

3. The weighted proportion of alleged perpetrators in specific Catholic Church authorities included: the St. John of God Brothers (40.4 per cent); the Christian Brothers (22.0 percent); the Benedictine Community of New Norcia (21.5 per cent); the Salesians of Don Bosco (20.9 per cent); the Marist Brothers (20.4 per cent); the Diocese of Sale in Victoria (15.1 per cent); the De La Salle Brothers (13.8 per cent); and the Archdiocese of Adelaide in South Australia (2.4 per cent). See https://www.childabuseroyalcommission.gov.au/religious-institutions.

4. Congregation for Divine Worship and the Discipline of the Sacraments, "Scrutinies Regarding the Suitability of Candidates for Orders," in Canon Law Society of Australia and New Zealand, *Newsletter*, no. 2, 2006, 7–13.

5. John Paul II, Address to the Cardinals of the United States, April 23, 2002, *Origins* 31 (2001–2002): 759.

6. Congregation for Catholic Education, Instruction, "Concerning the Criteria for Discernment of Vocations with Persons of Homosexual Tendencies in View of Their Admission to the Seminary and Holy Orders," August 31, 2005, http://www.vatican.va/roman_curia/congregations/ccatheduc/documents/rc_con_ccatheduc_doc_20051104_istruzione_en.html.

7. Congregation for Catholic Education, Instruction, "Concerning the Criteria for Discernment of Vocations," 8.

8. CDWDS, "Scrutinies Regarding the Suitability of Candidates for Orders," 8.

9. Congregation for the Doctrine of the Faith, Circular Letter to Presidents of Episcopal Conferences, June 19, 1995, III (d), https://www.vatican.va/roman_curia/congregations/cfaith/documents/rc_con_cfaith_doc_20030724_pane-senza-glutine_en.html.

10. Congregation for Catholic Education, Instruction, "Concerning the Criteria for Discernment of Vocations," See "2. Homosexuality and the Ordained Ministry."

11. R. J. Geisinger, SJ, "Orders," in J.P. Beal, J. Coriden, and T.J. Green, *New Commentary on the Code of Canon Law* (Mahwah, NJ: Paulist Press, 2000), 1231.

12. See Canons 213, 843.

13. F.M. Cappello, *Tractatus Canonico-Moralis de Sacramentis*, vol. 2 (Rome: 1935), 416. "Irregularitas est impedimentum perpetuum, iure ecclesiastico propter reverentiam divini ministerii constitutum, prohibens primario suceptionem ordinis et secundario exercitium ordinum susceptorum." Translation, Ronny Jenkins, "Clerical Sexual Abuse as an Irregularity," *Periodica* 94 (2005): 286.

14. J.M. Gonzalez Del Valle, in A. Marzoa, J. Miras, and R. Rodrigues-Ocana, *Exegetical Commentary on the Code of Canon Law* 4, no. 1 (Montreal: Wilson & Lafleur, 2004/Pamplona, 1996), 987.

15. Ronny Jenkins, "Clerical Sexual Abuse as an Irregularity," *Periodica* 94 (2005): 281.

16. Woestman, *The Sacrament of Orders and the Clerical State: A Commentary on the Code of Canon Law*, 3rd ed. (Faculty of Canon Law, Saint Paul University, 2006), 61–62.

17. See Canon 18. "Laws which establish a penalty, restrict the free exercise of rights, or contain an exception from the law are subject to strict interpretation." *The Code of Canon Law*, English translation in *The Canon Law Letter and Spirit*, prepared by The Canon Law Society of Great Britain and Ireland, Australia, E. J. Dwyer, 1995; all 1983 Code translations from this source.

18. Canon 14. "Laws, even invalidating and disqualifying ones, do not oblige when there is a doubt about the law. When there is a doubt about a fact, however, ordinaries can dispense from laws provided that, if it concerns a reserved dispensation, the authority to whom it is reserved usually grants it."

19. Amy Strickland, "Canons 1041, no. 4; 1047 §2, no. 2; 1049, 1329 §2; and 1398: Candidate for Permanent Diaconate and Abortion," in *Roman Replies and CLSA Advisory Opinions 2012* (Washington, DC: Canon Law Society of America, 2012), 93.

20. Canon 1044 §1. "The following are irregular for the exercise of orders received: …No. 3 a person who has committed a delict mentioned in canon 1041, nos. 3, 4, 5, 6."

21. See Canon 18.

22. Canon 2195 §1. See Edward Peters, trans., *The 1917 Pio-Benedictine Code of Canon Law* (San Francisco: Ignatius Press, 2001); hereafter the translation of the canons of the 1917 Code will be from this source.

23. See Canon 1323.

24. See Canon 1323.

25. Woestman, *The Sacrament of Orders and the Clerical State*, 62.

26. Woestman, *The Sacrament of Orders and the Clerical State*, 81.

27. Canon 1049 §3. A general dispensation from irregularities and impediments to receive orders is valid for all the orders.

28. Apostolic Penitentiary, Canon 1041, no. 4. "Dispensation from Irregularity for Reception of Orders for Assistance in Procurement of an Abortion," in *Roman Replies and CLSA Advisory Opinions 2012* (Washington, DC: Canon Law Society of America, 2012), 35–36. The dispensation notes that "the policy of the Penitentiary is not to grant the dispensation until the person has been approved for Orders, namely 6 months before ordination."

29. Pope Francis, apostolic constitution, *Praedicate Evangelium*, March 19, 2022, https://www.vatican.va/content/francesco/en/apost_constitutions/documents/20220319-costituzione-ap-praedicate-evangelium.html.

30. Canon 1048. In more urgent occult cases, if the ordinary or, when it concerns the irregularities mentioned in Canon 1041, numbers 3 and 4, the Penitentiary cannot be approached and if there is imminent danger of grave harm or infamy, a person impeded by an irregularity from exercising an order can exercise it, but without prejudice to the obligation which remains of making recourse as soon as possible to the ordinary or the Penitentiary, omitting the name and through a confessor. The confessor could write to the Cardinal in Charge of the Sacred Penitentiary and explain the circumstances of Father "X." The Cardinal would then reply addressing the case.

31. Canon 1049 §1. Petitions to obtain a dispensation from irregularities or impediments must indicate all the irregularities and

impediments. Nevertheless, a general dispensation is valid even for those omitted in good faith, except for the irregularities mentioned in Canon 1041, n. 4, and for others brought to the judicial forum, but not for those omitted in bad faith. §2. If it is a question of the irregularity from voluntary homicide or a procured abortion, the number of the delicts also must be mentioned for the validity of the dispensation. §3. A general dispensation from irregularities and impediments to receive orders is valid for all the orders.

32. W. Woestman, "Too Good to Be True: A Current Interpretation of Canons 1041, no. 1 and 1044 §2, no. 2," *Monitor Ecclesiasticus* 120 (1995): 619–29. John Beal, "A Response to Professor Woestman on the Interpretation of Canons 1041, no. 1 and 1044 §2, no. 2," *Monitor Ecclesiasticus* 121 (1996): 431–63.

33. Ronny Jenkins, "On the Suitability of Establishing Clerical Sexual Abuse of Minors (canon 1395 §2) as Irregularity ex Delicto to the Reception and Exercise of Orders," *Periodica* 94 (2005): 316.

34. Woestman, "Too Good to Be True," and J.P. Beal, "Too Good to Be True? A Response to Professor Woestman."

35. R. E. Jenkins, "Clerical Sexual Abuse as an Irregularity," *Periodica* 94 (2005): 275–340.

36. John Renken, "The Delicts of Sexual Abuse in Book VI," *Studia Canonica* 56 (2022): 114.

37. John Paul II, Address to the Cardinals of the United States, April 23, 2002, *Origins* 31 (2001–2002): 759.

38. CIC 83, c. 1388 §2. A person who comes forward for sacred orders bound by some censure or irregularity which he voluntarily conceals is *ipso facto* suspended from the order received, apart from what is established in canon 1044, §2, n. 1.

39. See CIC 83, c. 1388 §2.

GLOSSARY

Absolution of an accomplice: a priest invalidly attempting to grant absolution to an accomplice in any mortal or venial sin against the sixth commandment except when the accomplice is in danger of death. It does not matter whether the accomplice is a man or a woman, or what age the person is. The absolution incurs an excommunication reserved to the Apostolic See.

Accused: the person against whom a complaint of sexual abuse is made.

Acta: the collection of documents and testimonies detailing an allegation of sexual abuse that furnish the basis for conducting the process that will address such a delict.

Actio criminalis: an action presented before a Church tribunal against a person accused of committing a canonical delict. It can be barred by prescription.

Administrative leave / Prohibition to exercise sacred ministry: a term used for the temporary removal of a cleric from his assignment during an investigation of sexual abuse, which does not imply guilt in any way.

Administrative penal process: an extrajudicial procedure for determining the truth of an allegation. The bishop or the delegate is assisted by two assessors or advisors who examine the evidence and listen to the defense of the accused. He gives his decision on the matter through a decree.

Advocate: the person who represents the interests of the accused or the victim in a penal action.

Allegation: a complaint, still to be verified, claiming or asserting that someone has abused a child or an adult.

Apostolic visitation: an extraordinary occurrence when the Holy See visits an ecclesiastical authority for the purpose of evaluating the appropriate operation of certain institutions, for example, seminaries, religious institutes, and dioceses.

Assessors: those who act as consulters to the bishop or his delegate in conducting an administrative penal process.

Canon law: the term used to describe the laws of the Roman Catholic Church. The primary source of the norms of law is contained in the *Code of Canon Law* promulgated in 1983 and the *Code of Canons* *of the Eastern Churches* promulgated in 1990. Supplementary law is contained in other legal documents.

Church authority: a bishop, a leader of a religious institute, and the senior administrative authority of an autonomous lay organization, and their authorized delegates, responsible for the Church body to which the accused person is or was connected at the time of the alleged abuse.

Civil authorities: the local law enforcement agency, whether it be the police department, the sheriff's department, the state police post, or an area child protection agency. It is distinguished from religious authority.

Cleric: those ordained in sacred ministry in the Church, divided into deacons, priests, and bishops.

Clericalism: an attitude toward clergy/religious characterized by excessive deference and an assumption of their moral superiority. In a culture of clericalism, clerics are put on a pedestal and have a sense of entitlement to special treatment and a privileged position.

Complainant: the person who has alleged abuse against Church personnel. In most but not all cases the complainant will also be the person against whom it is alleged that the abuse was directed.

Delict: a crime in canon law which is an external and morally imputable violation of a law to which a canonical penalty is attached.

Dicastery: the business of the Holy See is conducted through various offices or dicasteries (formerly congregations). The Dicastery for the Doctrine of the Faith, which has as its duty the promotion and safeguarding of the doctrine of faith and morals in the Catholic world, is competent for addressing the delict of sexual abuse of minors. The Dicastery advises a diocesan bishop or religious ordinary on the process to be undertaken in a particular case and authorizes the corrective measures that need to be taken.

Delegate: the person who investigates a complaint of abuse.

Delict: a crime in canon law, an external violation of a law or precept, gravely imputable by reason of malice or negligence.

Diocese: a particular church entrusted to the responsibility of a bishop usually established by territory within the Catholic Church.

Diocesan Review Board: a panel of people that functions as a confidential consultative body to the bishop/eparch. The board is to offer advice to the bishop/eparch in his assessment of allegations of sexual abuse of minors and in his determination of a cleric's suitability for ministry.

Dismissal from the clerical state: a penalty imposed on a cleric for a particularly grievous delict. It can be imposed in a judicial proceeding or, in an especially grievous case of the sexual abuse of minors, *ex officio* by a direct action of the Holy Father. Sacred ordination to the priesthood never becomes invalid. The penalty of dismissal, however, means that the one ordained loses the juridic condition of a cleric and his rights as a cleric. He can no longer perform ministerial functions except in danger of death.

Dispensation from the obligations of priesthood: sacred orders, once received validly, never become invalid. A priest or deacon, however, who recognizes his inability to continue to function as a cleric, can request from the Holy Father a dispensation from the juridic obligations connected with priesthood, including that of celibacy. The grace of such a dispensation is granted only for the gravest causes. He can no longer present himself as a priest or perform ministerial functions except in danger of death.

Eparchy: a diocese in the Eastern Catholic Churches under the responsibility of an Eparch.

Ephebophile: term used to describe a person who desires to have sexual contact with postpubescent children between the ages of fourteen and seventeen.

Excommunication: a medicinal penalty prohibiting a person from celebrating or receiving sacraments, participating in liturgical celebrations, and exercising any governing power or office.

Expiatory penalty: to deter offenders, to restore right order and to repair the harm caused to the community. The imposition of this penalty does not require a warning and includes penalties of dismissal from the clerical state and removal from an office.

External forum: is the place in which publicly verifiable information is available. For example, common administrative acts such as appointments and dispensations are to be in writing when they concern the external forum.

Extrajudicial process: the extrajudicial penal process, sometimes called an *administrative process*, is a type of penal process that abbreviates the formalities called for in the judicial process, for the sake of expediting the course of justice without eliminating the procedural guarantees demanded by a fair trial.

Faculty: Church authorization, given by the law itself or by a local Ordinary, to perform certain official Church acts such as preaching or hearing confessions.

Grooming: a pattern of behavior aimed at engaging a child as a precursor to sexual abuse. It includes establishing a "special" friendship/relationship with the child. It can include the conditioning of parents and other adults to think that the relationship with the child is "normal" and positive.

Holy See: term used in referring to the central government of the Catholic Church under the authority of the Bishop of Rome, also known as the Holy Father, or the Pope, who resides in Vatican City State.

Impediment: a quality that prevents reception of a sacrament while the quality exists. The most common temporary impediments are for marriage and Holy Orders.

Imputability: the degree of a person's moral responsibility for an action.

Instance: a term used in the procedural law of the Church to indicate a particular level of judicial action (for example, First or Second Instance), and the possibility of further appeal to a higher tribunal.

Internal forum: is divided into either the sacramental internal forum or the extra-sacramental internal forum. It is sacramental when it is exercised within the sacrament of Penance. Within the sacramental internal forum there is the added safeguard of the seal of confession. It is nonsacramental when it is exercised outside the sacrament of Penance in spiritual direction, private counseling, or dealing with automatic or *latae sententiae* penalties.

Irregularity: a perpetual impediment prohibiting primarily the reception of order, and secondarily the exercise of orders received

Judge: the person in canon law charged with the responsibility of conducting a canonical trial whereby a decision is given in which a controversial matter is to be determined or a penalty is to be imposed.

Medicinal penalty: is aimed at reforming the offender by such penalties such as suspension and excommunication. Unless suspension or excommunication are automatic penalties imposed by the law itself, the offender must be warned first and told that if he carries out this action then he will be suspended or excommunicated (c. 1347).

Minor: a person under the age of eighteen.

Moral certainty: is the standard of proof in Church cases according to canon 1608. Moral certitude and beyond a reasonable doubt have common roots and are similar in standards to each other.

Notary: in a canonical proceeding the person who authenticates the *Acta* of the case.

Occult: something which is known by only a small, select group of people and is not publicly known.

Ordinary: one who possesses ordinary power of governance, meaning apart from the Roman Pontiff, diocesan bishops, and all who, even for a time only, are set over a particular Church or a community equivalent to it in accordance with canon 368, and those who in these have general ordinary executive power, that is, vicars general and episcopal vicars; likewise, for their own members, it means the major superiors of clerical religious institutes of pontifical right and of clerical societies of apostolic life of pontifical right, who have at least ordinary executive power.

Paedophile/Pedophile: term used to describe a person who desires to have sexual contact with prepubescent children between the ages of birth and thirteen.

Paramountcy principle: in all decision-making processes in an investigation of child sexual abuse, the welfare of the child must be the dominant concern.

Particular law: legislation for a diocese or a group such as a religious institute.

Penal trial: the judicial canonical process within which the truth of an allegation is determined, and a penalty is imposed, if the accused is found to have responsibility for the delict.

Personal prelature: a group in the Church for a particular mission led by a leader called a prelate.

Pontifical secret: the highest level of confidentiality in the Church.

Precept: a personal law in a decree requiring someone to do or not to do an action after there is evidence of misconduct. Precepts specify the individual, the situations, and the circumstances encompassed by the law. The penal precept binds immediately and should have a determined penalty.

Preliminary investigation: the initial inquiry by which a diocesan bishop or Ordinary, usually through a delegate, determines whether an allegation of a delict such as sexual abuse of a minor has a semblance of truth.

Prescription: in penal law the canonical provision for time limits within which a criminal action can be brought to justice.

Procurator: a person authorized to act on behalf of their client.

Promoter of justice: the person appointed in each diocese and in the higher tribunals of the Church whose responsibility is to provide for the public good. In penal proceedings he/she brings the accusation on behalf of the Church and prosecutes it before the tribunal.

Religious: a member of an institute of consecrated life or a society of apostolic life.

Religious institute: an institute of consecrated life approved by Church authority.

Removal of faculties: the faculties of a cleric can be removed administratively through no fault of the priest—for example, he has developed dementia. The faculties can also be removed as a penalty after a penal process.

Res iudicata: the conclusion of a canonical trial when the decision is no longer subject to appeal and the decision of the judges can be executed.

Safe environment: term used to refer to a wide assortment of practices that contribute to preventing child abuse of any kind.

Safety plan: a formal, written supervision program for a cleric who, it has been established, has sexually abused someone.

Seal of confession: the serious obligation of confidentiality imposed on a confessor in the sacrament of Penance not to reveal the sins confessed to anyone, under pain of excommunication.

Sexual abuse of a minor: contact or interaction between a minor and an adult when the minor is being used for sexual stimulation of the adult. This occurs when an adult engages a minor in any sexual activity, including direct sexual contact as well as sexual noncontact, such as frottage, exhibitionism, and the distribution, collecting, and/or intentional viewing of child pornography.

Solicitation: a delict involving the suggestion or invitation of a priest in the sacrament of Penance to a penitent to commit a sin against the sixth commandment, even with the priest himself.

Suspension: is a medicinal censure by which a cleric is forbidden fully or partially to exercise the power of order, the power of governance or of office (c. 1333 §1), or of all of those simultaneously (c. 1334 §2).

Trauma-informed: founded on the principles of safety, trustworthiness, choice, collaboration, and empowerment, trauma-informed services do not harm, retraumatize, or blame victims for their efforts to manage their traumatic reactions.

Trial: a canonical trial for the accused cleric that can be conducted by a diocesan or interdiocesan tribunal. These are Church trials, as opposed to civil trials that may carry jail terms or other penalties.

Victim/survivor: a person who has abuse of any kind in their background and has or is working to overcome the negative effects of that abuse.

Victim assistance coordinator: a person to help victims/survivors make a formal complaint of abuse to a diocese or eparchy. The victim assistance coordinator can arrange a personal meeting with the bishop and provides support for the needs of the individual and families.

Victim-centered approach: engaging with victims in a way that prioritizes listening, avoids retraumatization, and systematically focuses on their safety, rights, well-being, expressed needs, and choices.

Votum: an authoritative opinion; in forwarding a case to the Dicastery for the Doctrine of the Faith, a bishop or religious superior offers his authoritative opinion on the matter addressed in the specific case.

Vulnerable adult: any person aged eighteen years or older who is at increased risk of experiencing abuse, such as people: who are elderly; who have a disability; who suffer from mental illness; who have diminished capacity; who have cognitive impairment; who have suffered previous abuse; who are experiencing transient risks; who in receiving ministry are subject to a power imbalance; who identify as First Nations and/or Indigenous; who are from a culturally and linguistically diverse background; who are of diverse sexuality; who have any other impairment or adversity that makes it difficult for them to protect themselves from abuse.

SOURCES

Dicastery for the Doctrine of the Faith, "Glossary," https://www.vatican.va/resources/resources_CDF-glossary_en.html.

Implementation Advisory Group and the Governance Review Project Team, *The Light of the Southern Cross*, May 1, 2020, chrome-extension://efaidnbmnnnibpcajpcglclefindmkaj/https://drive.usercontent.google.com/download?id=1TXZd4SP-EBk4VtH9JyB9PMSmjY9Mfj7E&authuser=0&acrobatPromotionSource=GoogleDriveNativeViewNDV.

Pontifical Commission for the Protection of Minors, *Universal Guidelines Framework*, March 2024, https://www.tutelaminorum.org/universal-guidelines-framework/.

United States Conference of Catholic Bishops, Office of Child and Youth Protection, "Glossary," https://www.usccb.org/offices/child-and-youth-protection/glossary.

SELECTED BIBLIOGRAPHY

VATICAN DOCUMENTS

Apostolic Penitentiary. "Note of the Apostolic Penitentiary on the Importance of the Internal Forum and the Inviolability of the Sacramental Seal." June 29, 2019. https://www.vatican.va/roman_curia/tribunals/apost_penit/documents/rc_trib_appen_pro_20190629_forointerno_en.html.

Code of Canon Law 1983. Vatican City: Libreria Editrice Vaticana, 1983. https://www.vatican.va/archive/cod-iuris-canonici/cic_index_en.html.

Congregation for Clergy. *Circular Letter*, April 18, 2009, Prot. No. 2009/0556. In Renken. *The Penal Law of the Roman Catholic Church*, 491–99.

Congregation for the Doctrine of the Faith. "*Vademecum*: On Certain Points of Procedure in Treating Cases of Sexual Abuse of Minors Committed by Clerics." July 16, 2020. http://www.vatican.va/roman_curia/congregations/cfaith/documents/rc_con_cfaith_doc_20200716_vademecum-casi-abuso_en.html.

———. "*Sacramentorum Sanctitatis Tutela*: Revised Norms on Dealing with Clerical Sex Abuse of Minors and Other Grave Offenses." *Origins* 40 (2010): 146–51. See also https://www.vatican.va/resources/resources_introd-storica_en.html.

Congregation for the Evangelization of Peoples. Private letter concerning dismissal from the clerical state ex officio et in pœnam, June 3, 1997, Prot. No. 2154/97. In William H. Woestman, OMI. *The Sacrament of Orders and the Clerical State*, 3rd ed. Ottawa: Saint Paul University, 2006.

Dicastery for the Doctrine of the Faith. "Glossary." https://www.vatican.va/resources/resources_CDF-glossary_en.html.

Francis, Pope. "Address of His Holiness Pope Francis Commemorating the 50th Anniversary of the Institution of the Synod of Bishops." October 17, 2015.

———. Apostolic Exhortation, *Evangelii Gaudium*. November 24, 2013. http://www.vatican.va/content/francesco/en/apost_exhortations/documents/papa-francesco_esortazione-ap_20131124_evangelii-gaudium.html.

———. Apostolic Exhortation, *Gaudete et Exsultate*. March 19, 2018.

———. Apostolic Letter issued *motu proprio*, *Come una Madre Amorevole* (As a Loving Mother). June 4, 2016.

———. Apostolic Letter issued *motu proprio*, *Vos Estis Lux Mundi*. May 7, 2019.

———. "Christmas Greetings to the Roman Curia, Address by His Holiness Pope Francis." December 21, 2019.

———. Encyclical Letter, *Laudato Si'*. May 24, 2015.

———. "Letter of His Holiness Pope Francis to the People of God." August 20, 2018.

———. Rescript, "Some Amendments to the Normae de Gravioribus Delictis." December 3, 2019.

Implementation Advisory Group and the Governance Review Project Team, *The Light of the Southern Cross*, May 1, 2020. https://drive.google.com/file/d/1TXZd4SP-EBk4VtH9JyB9PMSmjY9Mfj7E/view.

International Theological Commission. "Synodality in the Life and Mission of the Church." 2018. http://www.vatican.va/roman_curia/congregations/cfaith/cti_documents/rc_cti_20180302_sinodalita_en.html.

John Paul II, Pope. "Address to the Cardinals of the United States," *Origins* 31 (2001–2002): 759.

———. Apostolic Letter issued *motu proprio*, *Sacramentorum Sanctitatis Tutela*, 2001.

———. "Discourse to the Tribunal of the Holy Roman Rota." In *Teachings of John Paul II*, II/1 (1979), 411–12.

———. *Dominum et Vivificantem*. On the Holy Spirit in the Life of the Church and the World. May 19, 1986.

———. Post-synodal Apostolic Exhortation, *Pastores Dabo Vobis*. March 15, 1992.

———. Post-synodal Apostolic Exhortation, *Pastores Gregis*. October 16, 2003.

John XXIII, Pope. Instruction, *Crimen Sollicitationis*, 1962. http://www.vatican.va/resources/resources_crimen-Sollicitationis-1962_en.html.

Paul VI, Pope. Apostolic Letter issued *motu proprio*, *Ecclesiae Sanctae*. August 6, 1966. http://www.vatican.va/content/paul-vi/en/motu_proprio/documents/hf_p-vi_motu-proprio_19660806_ecclesiae-sanctae.html.

Pontifical Commission for the Protection of Minors, Universal Guidelines Framework, March 2024. https://www.tutelaminorum.org/universal-guidelines-framework/.

BOOKS

Abbo, J. A., and Hannan, J. *The Sacred Canons: A Concise Presentation of the Current Disciplinary Norms of the Church*. 2nd ed. 2 vols. St. Louis: B. Herder Book Co., 1960.

Akpoghiran, Peter. *The Catholic Formulary*. 6 vols. New Orleans: Guadalupe Book Publishers, 2014.

Armstrong, Christopher. *A Critical Appraisal of Latae Sententiae Penalties in the 1983 Code of Canon Law*. Canon Law Studies 548. Washington, DC: Catholic University of America, 1996.

Bartchak, Mark. *Responsibility for Providing Spiritual Formation in Diocesan Seminaries According to the 1983 Code of Canon Law, with Special Reference to the United States*. Washington, DC: Catholic University of America, 1992.

Beal, John P., James A. Coriden, and Thomas J. Green, eds. *New Commentary on the Code of Canon Law*. Mahwah, NJ: Paulist, 2000.

Black, Henry. *Black's Law Dictionary*. St. Paul, MN: West Publishing Co., 1983.

Bouscaren, T. Lincoln, and Adam C. Ellis. *Canon Law: A Text and Commentary*. Milwaukee: Bruce, 1957.

Cafardi, Nicholas. *Before Dallas*. Mahwah, NJ: Paulist Press, 2008.

Calvo, Randolf, and Nevin Klinger, eds. *Clergy Procedural Handbook.* Washington, DC: Canon Law Society of America, 1992.

Caparros, Ernest, ed. *Exegetical Commentary on the Code of Canon Law.* 8 vols. Montreal: Wilson and Lafleur, 2004.

Caparros, Ernest, Michel Thériault, and Jean Thorn, eds. *Code of Canon Law Annotated.* 2nd ed. Montreal: Wilson and Lafleur, 2004.

Cappello, Felix. *Summa Iuris Canonici.* 5 vols. Rome: Apud Aedes Universitatis Gregorianae, 1951.

———. *Tractatus Canonico-Moralis De Sacramentis.* 2 vols. Taurini-Romae: Marietti, 1947.

Carr, John. *The Suspension of a Cleric by the Administrative Procedure According to the 1983 Code of Canon Law.* Ottawa: Saint Paul University, 1989.

Catechism of the Catholic Church: Revised in Accordance with the Official Latin Text. Vatican City: Libreria Editrice Vaticana, 1997.

Catholic Church England and Wales. "Catholic Safeguarding Advisory Service (CSAS) Procedures Manual." http://www.csasprocedures.uk.net.

Cholij, Roman. *Clerical Celibacy in East and West.* Herefordshire, UK: Fowler Wright Books, 1989.

Codex Iuris Canonici (1917). Rome: Typis Polyglottis Vaticanis, 1917. Translated by Edward Peters and published as *The 1917 or Pio-Benedictine Code of Canon Law.* San Francisco: Ignatius, 2001.

Cogan, Pat, ed. *Sacerdotes Iuris.* Ottawa: Saint Paul University, 2005.

Condon, Edward. *Heresy by Association: The Canonical Prohibition of Freemasonry in History and in the Current Law.* Washington, DC: Catholic University of America, 2015.

Coriden, J. A., T. J. Green, and D. E. Heintschel, eds. *The Code of Canon Law: A Text and Commentary.* Mahwah, NJ: Paulist, 1985.

Coronata, M. Conte a. *Institutiones Iuris Canonici.* 5 vols. Rome: Domus Editorialis Marietti, 1944.

Cuschieri, A. *The Sacrament of Reconciliation: A Theological and Canonical Treatise.* Lanham, MD: University Press of America, 1992.

Daly, Brendan. *Canon Law in Action.* Sydney: Saint Paul Publications, 2015.

Daniel, William, trans. *Ministerium Iustitiae: Jurisprudence of the Supreme Tribunal of the Apostolic Signatura.* Montreal: Wilson & Lafleur, 2011.

De Paolis, V, and D. Cito, *Le sanzione Nella Chiesa. Commento al Codice di Diritto Canonico Libro VI.* Vatican City: Urbaniana University Press, 2001.

Diermeier, Joseph. "Loss of the Clerical State: Specific Focus on Dismissal from the Clerical State." JCL thesis, The Catholic University of America, 2010.

Doktorczyk, Stephen. *Persistent Disobedience to Church Authority: History, Analysis and Application of Canon 1371 no. 2.* Rome: Editrice Pontifica Universita Gregoriana, 2016.

Dublin Archdiocese Commission of Investigation. "2009 Commission of Investigation Report into the Catholic Archdiocese of Dublin" (Murphy Report). Accessed February 13, 2020. http://www.justice.ie/en/JELR/Pages/Dublin_Archdiocese_Commission_of_Investigation.

Dugan, Patricia, ed. *The Penal Process and the Protection of Rights in Canon Law: Proceedings of a Conference Held at the Pontifical University of the Holy Cross.*

Rome, March 25–26, 2004. Montreal: Wilson and Lafleur, 2005.

Dugan, P., P. Gargaro, P., and V. Vondenberger. *Canon Law 101, Penal Law, Priest Problems and Legal Issues*. Philadelphia: Canon Law Books, 2017.

Fagothey, Austin. *Right and Reason: Ethics in Theory and Practice*. Saint Louis: C. V. Mosby, 1967.

Gillon, Chris, and Damian Grace. *Reckoning: The Catholic Church and Child Sexual Abuse*. Adelaide: ATF Press, 2014.

Glynn, John. *The Promotor of Justice: His Rights and Duties*. Canon Law Studies 101. Washington, DC: Catholic University of America, 1936.

Gray, Jason. *The Evolution of the Promoter of the Faith in Causes of Beatification and Canonization: A Study of the Law of 1917 and 1983*. Rome: Lateran University, 2015. http://www.jgray.org/docs/Promotor_Fidei_lulu.pdf.

Grocholewski, Z, and V. Carcel Orti, eds. *Dilexit Iustitiam*. Vatican City: Libreria Editrice Vaticana, 1984.

Hannan, P. *The Canonical Concept of "Congrua Sustentatio" for the Secular Clergy*. Canon Law Studies 302. Washington, DC: Catholic University of America, 1950.

Hanson, R., F. Pfafflin, and M. Lutz, eds. *Sexual Abuse in the Catholic Church: Scientific and Legal Perspectives*. Vatican City: Libreria Editrice Vaticana, 2004.

Hite, J, et al., eds. *Readings, Cases, Materials in Canon Law*. Collegeville, MN: Liturgical Press, 1986.

Huels, J. *The Pastoral Companion: A Canon Law Handbook for Catholic Ministry*. Illinois: Franciscan, 1995.

Huser, R. J. *The Crime of Abortion in Canon Law*. Washington, DC: Catholic University of America, 1942.

International Commission on English in the Liturgy. *The Rites of the Catholic Church*. 2 vols. Collegeville, MN: Liturgical Press, 1990.

Kennedy, Robert. *State Protection of Confessional Secrecy in the United States of America*. Rome: Pontificia Universitas Lateranensis, 1975.

Kurtscheid, Bertrand. *A History of the Seal of Confession*. Translated by F. Marks. London: Herder, 1927.

Limbourn, Brian. *The Sacrament of Reconciliation and General Absolution*. Ottawa: Saint Paul University, 2002.

Ludicke, Kalus, and Ronny Jenkins. *Dignitas Connubii: Norms and Commentary*. Washington, DC: Catholic University of America, 2006.

Martini, Carlo. *Prêtres, quelques années après: Méditations sur le ministère presbytéral*. Translated from Italian into French by Francois Vial. Paris, Cerf, 1992.

McBride, James. *Incardination and Excardination of Seculars: An Historical Synopsis and Commentary*. Canon Law Studies 145. Washington, DC: Catholic University of America, 1941.

Miller, Donna, and Eileen Jaramillo, eds. *Procedural Handbook for Institutes of Consecrated Life and Societies of Apostolic Life*. Washington, DC: Canon Law Society of America, 2021.

Min, Nereus Tun. "The Diocesan Bishop's Concern for Clerical Celibacy in the Light of Canon 277 §3: Bishops of Myanmar and Priestly Celibacy." Doctoral thesis. Pontificia Università Urbaniana, 2001.

Morrissey, Robert. *Abortion and the Excommunication of Canon 1398 in the 1983 Code of Canon Law*. Washington, DC: Catholic University of America, 1992.

Murphy, Richard, *The Canonico-Juridical Status of a Communist*. Washington, DC: Catholic University of America, 1959.

National Conference of Catholic Bishops (United States of America). *Norms for Priestly Formation*. 2 vols. Washington, DC: National Conference of Catholic Bishops, 1992.

Neli, Linus. *Delicta Graviora: "More Grave Delicts" in the Catholic Church*. Bengaluru, India: ATC Publishers, 2018.

New Zealand Catholic Bishops' Conference. *Programme for Priestly Formation*. Wellington: New Zealand Catholic Bishops' Conference, 2004.

Noldin, H., and A. Schmitt. *Summa Theologiae Moralis*. Oeniponte: Typis et Sumptibus Feliciani Rauch, 1955.

Olattupuram, Thomas. *The Vow of Poverty in Religious Life: Canon 600*. Rome: Pontificia Università Lateranense, 2006.

O'Neill, Kevin, and Peter Black. *Life, Death, and Catholic Medical Choices*, Missouri: Ligouri, 2011.

Palmer, Paul. *Sacraments and Forgiveness: History and Doctrinal Development of Penance, Extreme Unction and Indulgences*. 2 vols. London: Darton, Longman and Todd, 1960.

Papale, C. "Il Delitto contro il sacramento della penitenza riservati alla congregazione per la Dottrina della fide." *Quaderni Ius Missionale* 7 (2016).

———. *Il Delitto contro il sacramento dell'eucaristia riservati alla congregazione per la dottrina della fede*. Vatican City: Urbaniana University Press, 2017.

———. *Il processo penale canonico: commento al Codice di Dirritto Canonico, Libro VII*. 2nd ed. Vatican City: Urbaniana University Press, 2012.

Peters, Edward, ed. *Incrementa in Progressu 1983 Codicis Iuris Canonici*. Montreal: Wilson and Lafleur, 2005.

Pontificia Commissio Codici Iuris Canonici Recognoscendo. *Relatio Complectens Synthesim Animadversionum Ab Em. Mis. Atque Exc. Mis. Patribus Commissionis Ad Ultimum Schema Codici Iuris Canonici Exhibitarum, Cum Responsionibus a Secretaria et Consultoribus Datis*. Vatican City: Typis Polyglottis Vaticanis, 1981.

Price, David. "Penal Law Revisited for the '90s." In *Proceedings of the Twenty-Eighth Annual Conference*, 60–77. Adelaide: Canon Law Society of Australia and New Zealand, 1994.

Ratzinger, Joseph. *Salt of the Earth: The Church at the End of the Millennium*. Translated by Adrian Walker. San Francisco: Ignatius, 1997.

Renken, John, *The Penal Law of the Roman Catholic Church: Commentary on Canons 1311–1399 and 1717–1731 and Other Sources of Penal Law*. Ottawa: Saint Paul University, 2015.

Roberti, Cardinal Francesco, and Pietro Palazzini, eds. Translated by Henry Yannone. *Dictionary of Moral Theology*. Westminster, PA: Newman Press, 1962.

Rossetti, Stephen. *A Tragic Grace: The Catholic Church and Child Sexual Abuse*. Collegeville, MN: Liturgical Press, 1996.

Schneider, Francis J. *Obedience to the Diocesan Bishop by the Diocesan Priest in the 1983 Code of Canon Law*. Canon Law Studies 533. Washington, DC: Catholic University of America, 1990.

Schwartz, John. *The Obligation of Accepting Ecclesiastical Appointments (Canon 128)*. Canon Law Studies 6. Washington, DC: Catholic University of America, 1948.

Secretariat for Priestly Life and Ministry. *Priests for a New Millennium*. Washington,

DC: United States Conference of Catholic Bishops, 2000.

Sheehan, Joseph. *The Obligations of Respect and Obedience of Clerics Toward Their Ordinary (Canon 127)*. Canon Law Studies 344. Washington, DC: Catholic University of America, 1954.

Sheehy, G, et al., eds. *The Canon Law: Letter and Spirit*. Collegeville, MN: The Liturgical Press, 1995.

Stickler, Alphons. *The Case for Clerical Celibacy: Its Historical Development and Theological Foundations*. Translated by Brian Ferme. San Francisco: Ignatius, 1995.

Tanner, Norman P., ed. *Decrees of the Ecumenical Councils*. 2 vols. Washington, DC: Sheed and Ward, 1990.

Thompson, A. Keith. *Religious Confession Privilege and the Common Law*. Leiden: Martinus Nijhoff, 2011.

Tillard, Jean-Marie. *Dilemmas of Modern Religious Life*. Wilmington, NC: Michael Glazier, 1984.

United States Conference of Catholic Bishops. "Essential Norms for Diocesan/Eparchial Policies Dealing with Allegations of Sexual Abuse of Minors by Priests or Deacons." *Origins* 32, no. 25 (2002): 415ff. http://www.usccb.org/issues-and-action/child-and-youth-protection/upload/Charter-for-the-Protection-of-Children-and-Young-People-revised-2011.pdf.

United States Conference of Catholic Bishops: Office of Child and Youth Protection: "Glossary." https://www.usccb.org/offices/child-and-youth-protection/glossary.

Vogels, Heinz. *Celibacy: Gift or Law? A Critical Investigation*. London: Burns and Oates, 1992.

Vondenberger, Victoria, RSM. "The Promoter of Justice." In *Canon Law 101: Penal Law, Priest Problems and Legal Issues*, ed. P. Dugan, P. Gargaro, and V. Vondenberger. Philadelphia: Canon Law Books, 2017.

Wernz, Francisco, and Pietro Vidal. *Ius Canonicum*. 7 vols. Rome: Apud Aedes Universitatis Gregorianiae, 1943.

Wijlens, Myriam. *Sharing the Eucharist: A Theological Evaluation of the Post Conciliar Legislation*. New York: University Press of America, 2000.

Woestman, William H. *Ecclesiastical Sanctions and the Penal Process*. Ottawa: Saint Paul University, 2000.

———. *Sacraments: Initiation, Penance, Anointing of the Sick*. Ottawa: Saint Paul University, 1992.

———. *The Sacrament of Orders and the Clerical State*. 3rd ed. Ottawa: Saint Paul University, 2006.

Zubacz, Gregory. *The Seal of Confession and Canadian Law*. Montreal: Wilson and Lafleur, 2009.

ARTICLES

Alesandro, John. "A Study of Canon Law: Dismissal from the Clerical State in Cases of Sexual Misconduct." *The Catholic Lawyer* 36, no. 3 (2017): 257–300.

Arrieta, Juan. "Cardinal Ratzinger and the Revision of the Canonical Penal System: A Crucial Role." http://www.vatican.va/resources/resources_arrieta-20101202_en.html.

Austin, Rodger. "Submission on Canon Law to the Royal Commission into Institutional Responses to Child Sexual Abuse in Australia." *The Canonist* 8, no. 2 (2017): 276–328.

Beal, John. "Administrative Leave: Canon 1722 Revisited." *Studia Canonica* 27 (1993): 293–320.

———. "Too Good to Be True? A Response to Professor Woestman on the Interpretation of Canons 1041, 1° and 1044 §2, 2°." *Monitor Ecclesiasticus* 121 (1996): 431–63.

Brewer, Dexter. "The Right of a Penitent to Release the Confessor from the Seal: Considerations in Canon Law and American Law." *The Jurist* 54 (1994).

Brundage, Thomas. "The Promotor [*sic*] of Justice in the 1983 Code of Canon Law." Washington, DC: Catholic University of America, 2005.

Catholic Church England and Wales. "Catholic Safeguarding Advisory Service (CSAS): Procedures Manual." http://www.csasprocedures.uk.net.

Ghirlanda, Gianfranco. "The Significance of the Apostolic Constitution Anglicanorum Coetibus." http://www.catholicculture.org/culture/library/view.cfm?recnum=9178.

Green, Thomas. "Penal Law: A Review of Selected Themes." *The Jurist* 50 (1990).

Huels, John. "Denial of a Sacrament Without Due Process." In CLSA Advisory Opinions 1984–1993, 236–38. Washington, DC: Canon Law Society of America, 1995.

International Theological Commission. Report, "Penance and Reconciliation." *Origins* 13 (1984): 513–24.

Jehaut, Rikardus. "Loss of the Clerical State by a Rescript of Dispensation: Procedural Norms and Responsibilities of the Diocesan Bishop." *The Canonist* 9, no. 2 (2018): 177–203.

Jenkins, R. E. "Clerical Sexual Abuse as an Irregularity." *Periodica* 94 (2005): 275–340.

Kozlowski, John, OP. "Understanding the *Ius Vigens* of the Mandatory Dismissal Process." *The Jurist* 75 (2015): 387–427.

Lohse, Edwards. "The Origin and Nature of the Suspension *Ad Cautelam* of Article 4 of the 1980 Normae Procedurales for Dispensations from Celibacy." *Periodica* 95 (2006).

Mascord, Brian. "When in Rome: A Letter from Bishop Brian as He Prepares for Ad Limina Visit." *Catholic Education Diocese of Wollongong News*. June 10, 2019. https://www.dow.catholic.edu.au. Accessed February 13, 2020.

Mbandji, Valère Nkouaya. "La prescription canonique et les délits commis par les clercs." Paper to the Canadian Canon Law Society 52nd Annual Convention 2017.

Mendonça, Augustine. "The Bishop as the Mirror of Justice and Equity in the Particular Church: Some Practical Reflections on Episcopal Ministry." *Canonical Studies* (2002): 28.

Morrisey, Francis. "Denial of a Sacrament without Due Process." CLSA Advisory Opinions 1984–1993, 240–41. Washington, DC: Canon Law Society of America, 1995.

———. "Violations of Canon 277 (with an Adult): Appropriate and Just Responses." *The Canonist* 1, no. 2 (2010): 55–67.

National Review Board for the Protection of Children and Young People 2004. "A Report on the Crisis in the Catholic Church in the United States." Accessed February 13, 2020. http://www.usccb.org/issues-and-action/child-and-youth-protection/upload/National-Review-Board-Report-2004.pdf.

Provost, James. "Offences against the Sixth Commandment: Toward a Canonical Analysis of Canon 1395." *The Jurist* 55 (1995): 632–63.

———. "Some Canonical Considerations on Closing Parishes." *The Jurist* 53 (1993): 362–70.

Rainer, Eligius. *Suspension of Clerics: An Historical Synopsis and Commentary*. Canon Law Studies 111. Washington, DC: The Catholic University of America, 1937.

Reynolds, J. 2019, "Pope Francis Makes It Mandatory for Clergy to Report Sex Abuse." BBC News. May 9, 2019. Accessed February 13, 2020. https://www.bbc.com.

"Royal Commission into Institutional Responses to Child Sexual Abuse 2017." Final Report, volume 16, Religious Institutions: Book 2. Accessed February 13, 2020. https://www.childabuseroyalcommission.gov.au/sites/default/files/final_report_-_volume_16_religious_institutions_book_2.pdf.

"Royal Commission into Misconduct in the Banking, Superannuation and Financial Services Industry 2019." Final Report, volume 1. Accessed February 13, 2020. https://www.royalcommission.gov.au/sites/default/files/2019-02/fsrc-volume-1-final-report.pdf.

Rzeznik, Thomas. "The Church in the Changing City: Parochial Restructuring in the Archdiocese of Philadelphia in Historical Perspective." *U.S. Catholic Historian* 24, no. 4 (2009): 73–90.

Sacred Congregation for the Clergy. "Private Letter on 'Pastoral Councils.'" Omnes Christifideles, January 25, 1973. Also published as "Patterns in Local Pastoral Councils." *Origins* 3, no. 12 (1973): 186–90. Accessed February 13, 2020. https://www.pastoralcouncils.com/bibliography/vatican-documents/postconciliar/circular/.

Scicluna, Charles. "Days of Covering Up Are Over." https://www.catholicnews.com/services/englishnews/2019/days-of-covering-up-abuse-allegations-are-over-says-vatican-adviser.cfm.

———. "Promoter of Justice at the Congregation for the Doctrine of the Faith: The Procedure and Praxis of the Congregation for the Doctrine of the Faith Regarding Graviora Delicta." http://www.vatican.va/resources/resources_mons-scicluna-graviora-delicta_en.html. Accessed September 15, 2011.

———. "Response to and Prevention of Clerical Sexual Misconduct: Current Praxis." *Origins* 43 (2013–2014): 357–64.

Sherr, R. "A Canon, a Choirboy, and Homosexuality in Late Sixteenth-Century Italy: A Case Study." *Journal of Homosexuality* 21, no. 3 (1991): 1–22.

Truth, Justice and Healing Council. "Where from and Where to—The Truth Justice and Healing Council, the Royal Commission and the Catholic Church in Australia." Final Report, volume 1. Accessed February 13, 2020. http://www.tjhcouncil.org.au/.

United States Conference of Catholic Bishops. "Charter for the Protection of Children and Young People." June 2011. http://www.usccb.org/issues-and-action/child-and-youth-protection/upload/Charter-for-the-Protection-of-Children-and-Young-People-revised-2011.

Vaillaint, G. "Restructuring Parishes a Move from Necessity to Audacity." *La Croix International*. August 9, 2018. Accessed February 13, 2020. https://international.la-croix.com.

Waters, I. "The Australian Bishops and Canon Law." In *Health and Integrity in Church and Ministry Conference Papers*, edited by S. Crittenden, 103. Sydney: Franciscan Friars, 2019.

Winfield, N. "Analysis: Pope's Sex Abuse Summit: What It Did and Didn't Do." AP News, February 26, 2019. Accessed February 13, 2020. https://apnews.com.

Woestman, William. "Too Good to Be True: A Current Interpretation of Canons 1041, 1° and 1044 §2, 2°." *Monitor Ecclesiasticus* 120 (1995): 619–29.

INDEX

abortion, 149–50, 153
abuse, sexual: changes to penal law, 77–79, 125–26, 140, 155–56; crime, 2, 68, 76, 91, 94, 140; failure to act/report, 69, 74–75, 76–77, 82–83, 84–85, 87, 97–98, 105–6, 124, 126–27; irregularity, 152; laws, 76–79; mandatory reporting, 79–82, 90–94; preventing, 79; and religious, 68, 81, 61–62, 65–66; and religious institutes, 73, 128–29; rights of abusers, 71; scandal, 105–6; schools, 85; and seal of confession, 100–102; secrecy, 141–43; VELM, 67, 77–78, 84–85, 125; vulnerable people, 2–3, 86–87, 127. *See also* reporting; victims
abuse, spiritual, 119–30, 196n3
abuse of authority, 12, 74, 79, 87–88, 123–24, 12
advocate, 20, 47, 48, 50, 52–53, 55
Akpoghiran, Peter, 26–27
allegations of abuse, 1, 5–7
anonymity, 12–13, 93
Apostolic See, 66–67
appeals, 24, 43, 180n146
Arietta, Juan, 16, 33, 86, 122
"As a Loving Mother." See *Come una Madre Amorevole*
assesors, 20
associations of the faithful, 58, 184n7
Athenagoras of Athens, 135
Augustine, 149
Australian Royal Commission into Institutional Responses to Child Sexual Abuse, 57, 146

baptism, 173n40
Barbarin, Philippe, 127
Barthchak, Mark, 48, 49
Beal, John, 131, 143, 154
Benedict XIV, Pope, 141
Benedict XVI, Pope, 28–29, 79, 133, 139, 143, 147, 205n70. *See also* Ratzinger, Joseph
Bertone, Tarcisio, 138
Beste, R. P., 124
Bible, 103–4
bishops: authority, 60, 63–64, 72; complaints about, 82; diocesan, 17, 71–73, 167n60, 169n9; failure to act, 126, 144–45; governance, 64; *Mutuae Relationes*, 61–62; obligations, 71–73; pastor, 167n60, 169n9; and personal prelatures, 58; preliminary investigation, 17; proper works, 62; and religious, 57, 60–62, 64–66, 72, 73, 74; and religious institutes, 130; responsibility, 70, 84–85, 124–25, 130; right to remove abusers, 128; supervision, 72–73; and victims, 124–25; visitation, 130
Burke, Raymond, 117–18

Cafardi, Nicholas, 134, 135
Calderon, Yeshica, 48
celibacy, 132–33
circular letters, 192n1
Cito, David, 64
civil authorities/law, 11, 69–70, 84, 95–102
clericalism, 190n11
clerical religious institutes, 58
Come una Madre Amorevole, 85, 126, 144
competence, 3, 4, 16–17, 39–40
complaints advisory committee, 11
concluding an investigation/procedure, 10–11, 21, 24
confidentiality, 98–99, 193n11
Congregation for Clergy, 133
Congregation for Divine Worship and the Discipline of the Sacraments, 133, 148
Congregation for the Doctrine of the Faith, 82–83, 96, 138–40, 144, 148
Congregation for the Evangelization of Peoples, 133
constraint of silence, 3
continence, 71, 114
cover-ups, 2
credibility, 13, 21
crime: abuse of authority, 12, 74, 87, 116–17; apostasy, heresy, and schism, 115; attempted, 109–10; civil law, 84, 97; cover-up, 2; Dicastery for the Doctrine of the Faith, 18, 22; extraordinary circumstances, 116; failure to act/report, 69, 76, 84, 94; information, 49; irregularities, 151; marriage, clerical, 115–16; 1983 Code, 151; penal processes, 19; preliminary investigation, 36; promoter of justice, 27–28, 39, 41, 42; religious superior, 68; rights of victims, 46; sacrament of Penance, 48; *Sacramentorum Sanctitatis Tutela*, 76; scandal, 104–5; sexual abuse, 2, 67, 76, 91, 94, 140; sin, 105, 151; solicitation, 134–35, 201n29; VELM, 67; vulnerable people, 2–3, 86
Crimen Sollicitationis, 134–35, 139, 141, 143, 145
Curia, 139–40

Death, Jodi, 121
Decalogue, 2
deceased accused, 13
decisions, 21–22, 23–24
decree of adjudication, 21–22, 170n33
defense, 21
delegates, 20–22
del Val, Merry, 134
de Weger, Stephen E., 121
Dicastery for the Doctrine of the Faith (DDF), 10–11, 18, 22, 38, 39, 83
Dicastery of the Apostolic See, 22
Didache, 135
diocesan bishop. *See under* bishop
diocesan institutes, 58, 129
dioceses, 71–72
dismissal from clerical state, 42, 137–38
dispensation, 132–33, 137, 153–54, 207n31
driving, 9–10

Earl, Benjamin, 74
Elvira, Council of, 135
evangelical counsels, 189n83
evidence, 6, 10, 13, 21, 40–41, 42
exempt religious institutes, 59–61
exorcism, 122
extrajudicial processes, 15–16, 20–23

failure to act/report: bishop, 126, 144–45; crime, 69, 76, 84, 94; promoter of justice, 42; reporting, 68–69, 76–77, 84–85, 87, 93; sexual abuse, 69, 74–75, 76–77, 82–83, 84–85, 87, 97–98, 105–6, 124, 126–27
false accusations, 27, 41
Fernandez, Samuel, 119
Fessio, Joseph, 133
forum, external and internal, 106, 107, 108, 128
Fourth Lateran Council, 28

France, 28
Francis, Pope, 19, 47–48, 68, 70, 77, 79, 81, 84, 85, 92, 124, 125, 126, 127, 129, 139–40, 144, 155
Franck, Maria Ines, 46
funerals, 111

Gabriele, Paolo, 139
George, Julie, 120
Glynn, John, 28
Gratian, 27
Gray, Jason, 27, 44
Grocholewski, Z., 41, 42
guilt, 1, 9, 42

Harishankar, S., 121
Hart, Denis, 121
Hill, Richard, 64
Hummes, Cláudio, 133
Humphrey, Justin, 119

imputability, 8
informing the accused, 167n58
Innocent III, Pope, 27–28, 149
Innocent IV, Pope, 28
instructions, status of, 135–37
interviews, 17, 48–49, 53
irregularities, 148–57, 207nn30–31

Jenkins, Ronny, 155
Jesus Christ, 189n80, 197n27
John Jay Study, 146
John Paul I, Pope, 132
John Paul II, Pope, 67, 76, 82, 132–33, 138, 140, 143, 145, 146, 155
John XXIII, Pope, 134
joinder of issue, 40
judges, 39–40, 43, 169n22, 172n33, 175n66, 177nn95–97
Judicial Vicar, 39
Justinian, 28

Kattuthara, Kuriakose, 120
Kozlowski, Matthew, 61, 64, 66

laity, 2, 32, 58
Lara, Castillo, 137–38
latae sententiae penalties. *See* penalties: automatic
Leary, Mary Graw, 47
Lega, Michele, 28
Leo XIII, Pope, 59
"Letter to People of God," 92
libellus, 175n91
Liguori, Alphonsus, 105

Magdeburg, Council of, 28
marriage, 30, 31–32, 33, 34–36, 47, 110–11, 172nn39–40, 173nn42–44, 175n70, 178n116
McCarrick, Theodore, 78, 127
McDonough, Elizabeth, 74
McGrath, Aidan, 51
McKenna, Kevin, 13, 46
metropolitan (term), 190n12
Millane, Grace, 54
Milligan, Philip, 128
ministerial public juridic persons (MPJP), 59
monasteries, 58–59
Montini, Gianpaolo, 49–50, 50–51, 52, 53, 101
Mulakkal, Franco, 120
Mutuae Relationes, 61–62

Naz, Raoul, 106
Neocaesarea, First Council of, 135
1917 Code, 29–32, 106–7, 133–35
1983 Code, 32–42, 107–11, 124–25, 137, 150–51
notary, 4
notitia de delicto, 1, 6, 16, 82
Nunez, Gerardo, 142
nuns, 59

Oakley, Lisa, 119
opening an investigation, 3
Ordinary (term), 188n66, 190n8
Ottaviani, Alfredo, 134

Page, Roch, 131
pastoral care, 9
Pastor Bonus, 138
Paul, apostle, 103–4, 148–49
Paul VI, Pope, 61, 132, 199n6
pedophilia, 133, 135, 137, 138–39, 154
Pell, George, 127
penal processes, 12, 19–20, 49–50, 112–13
penalties: appeal, 43; automatic, 108–9; extrajudicial process, 15–16, 22–23; medicinal, 111–12; 1917 Code, 107; 1983 Code, 107–11; penal process, 19–20; procedures, 111–12; promoter of justice, 27, 42, 43; provisions, 113; remission, 114; reparation of harm, 87
Pennsylvania Grand Jury Report into Child Sexual Abuse in Six Pennsylvania Roman Catholic Dioceses, 146
personal prelatures, 57
petitions, 39–40
Pius IX, Pope, 141
Pius XII, Pope, 51, 134
plaint of nullity, 41, 43, 173nn41–44
Polycarp, 135
Pompedda, Mario Francesco, 117
Pontifical Commission for the Protection of Minors, 4, 144
pontifical institutes, 58
pornography, 2, 77
power imbalance, 74, 120–21
precautionary measures, 7–8
preliminary investigation: anonymous complaints, 12–13; bishop, 17; civil authorities, 11; closing, 10–11; competence, 3; credibility, 13; crime, 36; Dicastery for the Doctrine of the Faith, 10; evidence, 6; exercise of sacred ministry, 7–8; good reputation, 8–9; imputability, 8; interview of victim, 49; *notitia de delicto*, 1; pastoral care, 9–10; penal process, 12; and promoter of justice, 36–38; resolving damages, 49; review, 11–13; rights, 9; sacrament of Penance, 6–7; suitable person, 3–5; VELM, 1–3; whistleblowers, 9
priests leaving ministry, 131–33
privacy, right to, 5
private associations, 110
procedural law, 35
prohibition from exercise of sacred ministry, 7–8, 18
promoter of justice, 173n26–174n32: appeals, 43; appointment, 29, 32; and canonization, 44–45; conflicts of interest, 30, 34; contentious cases, 30–31, 33, 43; criminal action, 30; failure to act, 42; laity, 32; marriage cases, 30, 31–32, 33, 34–36; nullity of orders, 43–44; origins, 27–29; penal process, 36, 38–42, 49–50; preliminary investigations, 36–38; public good, 33; qualifications, 29, 32; regional tribunal, 33–34; role, 26–27, 30, 31, 32, 45; term of office, 29, 33; trials, 30–31
proofs, 3–4, 21, 27
Provida Mater Ecclesiae, 31–32
public good, 33, 49–50, 174n58

questioning, 40, 123

rape, 120–21
Ratzinger, Joseph, 137–38. *See also* Benedict XVI
religious, 57, 60–62, 64–66, 74, 81, 141
religious institutes, 58–61, 65–67, 72, 73, 110, 128–30. *See also specific kinds, e.g.,* diocesan institutes
reply of the accused, 41
reporting: anonymous, 82; civil laws, 97; DDF, 83; failure to, 68–69, 76–77, 84–85, 87, 93; laity, 2; mandatory, 79–82, 88, 90–94, 97, 143–44; spiritual abuse, 129–30; UGF, 88; VELM, 2, 68, 93–94
report of investigation, 10
reputation, 8–9, 28
rights: of abusers, 71; of the accused, 9, 49; in Catholic Church, 47; defending, 168n2; European Union law, 46; to intervention,

52–53; legal aid, 54–55; U.S. law, 46–47; VELM, 48; of victims, 46–56
Roman law, 27
Royal Commission of Inquiry into Abuse in Care in New Zealand, The, 57
Rupnik, Marko, 121

sacrament of Penance, 6–7, 13, 48, 102, 123
Sacramentorum Sanctitatis Tutela, 76, 77, 126, 140
Sacramentum Poenitentiae, 133, 141
Sacred Congregation of Bishops and Regulars, 29
Sacred Congregation for the Propagation of the Faith, 29
scandal, 62, 65, 103–18, 186nn31–32
Schema de Sacerdotibus Lapsis, 131–32
schools, 64, 73–74, 85
Scicluna, Charles, 56, 70, 97, 140–41
seal of confession, 98, 100–102
secrecy, culture of, 141–43, 145, 193n11
Secreta Continere, 142
secular institutes, 57
sentencing, 43
sexual manipulation, 121
sin, 104, 105, 130, 151
Sinature, 117
sisters (religious), 59
societies of apostolic life, 57
solicitation, 27, 76, 123, 134–35, 139, 141, 142
Sollicitudinem Nostram, 51
Sons of the Holy Redeemer, 121–22
Strickland, Amy, 149
suitability for ordination, 146–48. *See also* irregularities
suitable person, 3–5
superior, religious, 68
Synod of Bishops, 107–8

"Tabular Summary for Cases of *Delicta Reservata*," 14
Tapsell, Kieran, 141
Thomas Aquinas, 104, 105
trials: advocate, 50, 52–53; penal, 15, 39–42; preliminary investigation, 5; promoter of justice, 30–31; renunciations, 41–42; victim's rights, 54;

Universal Guidelines Framework (UGF), 82, 88
unlawful sacred ministry, 122–23

Vatican II, 131
Vattoli, Augustine, 121
victim assistance coordinator, 48
victims: advocate for, 47, 48, 55; award for damages, 49; and bishops, 124–25; care for, 46, 55–56, 124–25; children, 4; confidentiality, 98–99; damages, 54; family, 54; impact statement, 55–56; intervention, 52–53; interviews, 17, 48–49, 53; justice, 71; legal aid, 54–55; needs, 50–51; party to process, 53; privacy, 5, 7; processes, 48; protection from accused, 51; PTSD, 48; rights, 46–56; and seal of confession, 100–102; secrecy, 143
Vidal, P. Petri, 28
Vondenberger, Victoria, 40
Vos Estis Lux Mundi (VELM), 1–3, 47–48, 67–69, 77–78, 84–85, 93–94, 96–97, 125, 127, 144–45
vows, 58, 59, 63
vulnerable people, 2–3, 86–87, 127–28

Walshe, Thomas, 121
Wernz, P. Francisco, 28
whistleblowers, 9, 99–100
Wijlens, Myriam, 127
Wilson, Philip, 139
witnesses, 177n109
Woestman, Bill, 26, 154
work, proper/entrusted, 62

Yanguas, Aurelio, 143
"You Are the Light of the World," 84